A Prophetic, Public Church

Witness to Hope Amid the Global Crises of the Twenty-First Century

Mary Doak

LITURGICAL PRESS ACADEMIC

Collegeville, Minnesota
www.litpress.org

Cover design by Monica Bokinskie. Photos courtesy of Getty Images and Wikimedia Commons.

Scripture quotations are from New Revised Standard Version Bible © 1989 National Council of the Churches of Christ in the United States of America. Used by permission. All rights reserved worldwide.

Excerpts from documents of the Second Vatican Council are from *Vatican Council II: Constitutions, Decrees, Declarations; The Basic Sixteen Documents*, edited by Austin Flannery, OP, © 1996. Used with permission of Liturgical Press, Collegeville, Minnesota.

© 2020 by Order of Saint Benedict, Collegeville, Minnesota. All rights reserved. No part of this book may be used or reproduced in any manner whatsoever, except brief quotations in reviews, without written permission of Liturgical Press, Saint John's Abbey, PO Box 7500, Collegeville, MN 56321-7500. Printed in the United States of America.

Library of Congress Cataloging-in-Publication Data

Names: Doak, Mary, 1961– author.
Title: A prophetic, public church : witness to hope amid the global crises of the twenty-first century / Mary Doak.
Description: Collegeville, Minnesota : Liturgical Press Academic, 2020. | Includes bibliographical references. | Summary: "In this book, Mary Doak shows how the church must rectify its own historic failures to embody the unity-in-diversity it proclaims, especially with regard to women and Jews. Only then, and through responding to the demands of the current global crises, can we learn what it means to be the church-that is, to be a prophetic witness and public agent of the harmony that God desires and the world deeply needs"—Provided by publisher.
Identifiers: LCCN 2019045393 (print) | LCCN 2019045394 (ebook) | ISBN 9780814684504 (paperback) | ISBN 9780814684757 (epub) | ISBN 9780814684757 (mobi) | ISBN 9780814684757 (pdf)
Subjects: LCSH: Christianity—Forecasting. | Catholic Church—Forecasting. | Women in Christianity. | Christianity and other religions—Judaism. | Judaism—Relations—Christianity.
Classification: LCC BR145.3 .D63 2020 (print) | LCC BR145.3 (ebook) | DDC 262/.02—dc23
LC record available at https://lccn.loc.gov/2019045393
LC ebook record available at https://lccn.loc.gov/2019045394

"In *A Prophetic, Public Church*, Mark Doak provides an ecclesiology of the church based less on what the church 'is' than what it 'does'—and what it does, or should, is be a prophetic sign and instrument of the ways of being human together that God has always hoped for us. Without shying away from the past failures of the Christian community to be that effective sign, particularly in relation to anti-Semitism and misogyny, Doak provides a theology of hope in the church's potential to transform our public life. In highlighting the potential of the church to challenge injustice in our economic life, our responses to climate change, and our treatment of migrants in our midst, Doak demonstrates her own participation in our church's vocation to be the sacrament of the reign of God in our world."

—Brian Flanagan
Marymount University

"From its very beginnings, Christianity has utilized women and Jews in its texts and teachings to represent the abject 'other' or second-class creatures to be redeemed within salvation history, with devastating effects. Doak challenges Christians to confront their contribution to the justification of abuse of women and Jews in history and current contexts when they retain them as symbols rather than allowing them to represent themselves. Expect to read a book not only about being better churches but also about being better human beings."

—Cristina Lledo Gomez
BBI - The Australian Institute of Theological Education

"Set in the context of our fractured society, Mary Doak analyzes the challenges to the Church's mission of being a sign and instrument of communion. Blind spots which distort Christian faith include its traditional supersessionist anti-Judaism and devaluation of women, as well as today's neoliberal idolatry of the market, degradation of the environment, and hostility towards the millions displaced or forced to migrate. Profoundly researched, she draws on numerous studies and contemporary scholars, some of them controversial. But Doak's approach is always nuanced, wise, and deeply Catholic. This is a major ecclesiological work that should be widely read."

—Thomas P. Rausch, SJ
Emeritus T. Marie Chilton Professor of Catholic Theology
Loyola Marymount University

"In this highly readable book, Mary Doak offers a passionate and engaged discussion of the great issues facing today's church. Drawing on the writings of Vatican II she focuses on the church as a prophetic agent of political, social, and economic change. In what is an ecclesiology of doing rather than being, she offers a hope-filled vision that will provoke and challenge those inside and outside the churches as they seek the transformation of society."

> —Mark D. Chapman
> Professor of the History of Modern Theology
> University of Oxford

"Only a public theologian of Mary Doak's scholarly achievements and a burning sense of justice can produce a book such as this. *A Prophetic, Public Church* examines the most pressing issues of our day, including religious anti-Semitism, misogyny, global economy, climate change, and global migration. Digging deep into the teachings of Vatican II and Pope Francis, it offers a prophetic voice that calls for repentance and transformation both within and without the Church. An unparalleled scholarly *tour de force*, this book is a must-read for all Christians, especially those living in the United States, as they confront the moral challenges of the twenty-first century and seek the prophetic wisdom of the Bible and the Tradition to meet them with justice. I recommend this book with the greatest enthusiasm."

> —Peter C. Phan
> The Ignacio Ellacuria, SJ, Chair of Catholic Social Thought
> Georgetown University

"Mary Doak speaks out of a deep and mature love for the Catholic Church. She calls for all Christians to renew their sense of community and mission to the world by acknowledging in thought and action what it means to follow Jesus in the face of contemporary crises. By focusing on the historical mistreatment of Jews and women, as well as the urgent present matters of global inequality, climate change, and migration, Doak has her finger precisely on the point where many critical lines of the church and the world intersect. In all cases, Doak strives for balanced and inclusive positions without abandoning her passionate, prophetic commitment to Christian faith and the urgent call to justice. I am glad to have this book to which I can refer the many people, young and old, who express to me their struggles over the very issues addressed here."

> —Dennis M. Doyle
> Professor of Religious Studies
> University of Dayton

This book is dedicated in love and hope to my daughter, Sara, whose generation will have no choice but to deal with the ecological, economic, and political challenges of the twenty-first century;

to my husband, Phil, whose commitment to a faith-based response to the climate crisis inspires the church to be what it is called to be;

and to the memory of Gerard Mannion (1970–2019), whose life exemplified the joyful community that is our best hope.
Let Your Perpetual Light Shine upon Him

Contents

Acknowledgments ix

Introduction: A Prophetic yet Public Church xi

Chapter 1: Called to Communion:
 The Vision of the Second Vatican Council 1

Chapter 2: Overcoming Religious Anti-Semitism:
 Communion with the Church's External Other 39

Chapter 3: Overcoming Misogyny:
 Communion with the Church's Internal Other 75

Chapter 4: A Prophetic, Public Church
 in a Global Economy 117

Chapter 5: A Prophetic, Public Church
 in a Climate Crisis 151

Chapter 6: A Prophetic, Public Church
 amid Global Migration 185

Conclusion 221

Index 227

Acknowledgments

This book is the culmination of many years of research and theological conversation, and I am deeply grateful to the many people and institutions who have supported and inspired me throughout this process. Friends and family, and especially my daughter and husband, have graciously tolerated my absence as I focused on this writing. The University of San Diego generously provided a sabbatical leave and Faculty Research Fellowships that made much of the research for this book possible. Hans Christoffersen and the staff of Liturgical Press have been a delight to work with and their careful editing made this book much better than it would have been.

Among the many colleagues who have contributed to, and encouraged, my thinking on the issues of this book, special mention and thanks are due to J. Matthew Ashley, Susie Paulik Babka, Jamall Calloway, Rosemary Carbine, Victor Carmona, Colleen Carpenter, Christopher Carter, Shai Cherry, Bahar Davary, Michael Driscoll, Orlando Espín, Russell Fuller, Daniel Groody, Aaron Gross, Gustavo Gutiérrez, Anita Houck, Jennifer Herdt, Mary Catherine Hilkert, Jennifer Jesse, Paul Kollman, Louis Komjathy, Robert Krieg, Gerard Mannion and the Ecclesiological Investigations network, Timothy Matovina, Gerald McKenny, Peter Mena, Rico Monge, Lance Nelson, Peter Phan, Elena Procario-Foley, Emily Reimer-Barry, Michael Signer, Karen Teel, Karma Leshe Tsomo, and Michele Watkins. They have enriched my life as well as my thought, for which I remain truly grateful.

Introduction

A Prophetic yet Public Church

> The joys and hopes, the grief and anguish of the people of our time, especially of those who are poor or afflicted, are the joys and hopes, the grief and anguish of the followers of Christ as well.
>
> —*Gaudium et Spes* (GS) 1[1]

There is a great need for community today, especially in the United States and, I suspect, in many of the other so-called first-world countries. Harvard sociologist Robert Putnam noted the deterioration of community bonds in American society over twenty years ago, a phenomenon he termed "bowling alone."[2] Individualism's promise of freedom to pursue one's own goals and desires, unhindered by responsibility to others, has not resulted in the self-fulfillment envisioned. Instead, the young are experiencing high rates of anxiety, with depression, addictions, and even suicide becoming widespread. Putnam's further warning that individualism is depleting the social capital of mutual good will is borne out by

---

1. Vatican II, Pastoral Constitution on the Church in the Modern World (*Gaudium et Spes* [GS]) 1. Quotations of documents of the Second Vatican Council are taken from Austin Flannery, ed., *Vatican Council II: Constitutions, Decrees, Declarations; The Basic Sixteen Documents* (Collegeville, MN: Liturgical Press, 2014).

2. Robert D. Putnam, *Bowling Alone: The Collapse and Revival of American Community* (New York: Simon and Schuster, 2000), 15–137.

the current polarization of society.³ Animosity toward those of different race, class, gender, or political persuasion is so common and vicious in the United States that it is reasonable to wonder whether sufficient commitment is left to sustain a shared national life.

At the same time, the world is more interconnected and interdependent than ever before. Videos posted on social media "go viral" and are watched by people on the other side of the planet. More problematically, the capitalist economy has become a truly global system, so that any serious economic disruption in one country will have consequences—perhaps devastating ones—for other nations around the world.

It is an irony of contemporary life that we find ourselves so solitary and lonely while interconnected to an extent unimaginable only decades ago. Is there a better emblem of the modern condition than the ubiquitous sight of people staring at their cell phones, texting and surfing the web while oblivious to those around them? So much of our day is spent interacting with devices that mediate the connections and communications of contemporary life that little time is left to be truly with others, or even with oneself. Perhaps the most apt description of the solitariness of contemporary life is "texting alone."

An ongoing theological tragedy in all of this aloneness is that Christianity, which is fundamentally oriented to healing relationships and building the harmonious communion of God's reign, is widely interpreted through the lens of individualism. Especially in the United States, Christian faith often is reduced to a "me-and-Jesus" relationship, a matter of one's own inner state (or spirituality) that has no relevance to society. Alfred North Whitehead's definition of religion as "what the individual does with [one's] own solitariness"⁴ is generally assumed, and faith commitments are commonly considered a private matter, of no concern to anyone else and certainly not in need of the support of the frequently disparaged "institutionalized religion."

---

3. Putnam, *Bowling*, 287–363.

4. Alfred North Whitehead, *Religion in the Making* (New York: New American Library, 1926), 16.

This state of affairs is disastrous for the church as well as for the world. Even among those who are committed to Christian faith, church membership is often of low—or no—importance. If spirituality can be cultivated on one's own and without the irritation of stuffy ritual, then why bother getting out of bed on Sunday morning? There is no longer enough social prestige attached to being seen at church to make it worthwhile; not surprisingly, membership in nearly all churches in the United States is dropping.[5]

Yet the human race faces crises requiring global cooperation for their solution. Even though nations are riven with conflict and competition, humanity must find a way to work together for the common good of the whole planet. The current global economy is leaving nearly half of the world's population struggling to meet basic needs while burning fossil fuels at a rate that is disrupting the environment and dramatically changing the conditions of life on earth (often in ways that most hurt the poorest).[6] These problems can be resolved only if people around the globe put the interests of the long-term, global common good above their immediate personal benefit, even though a capitalist economy encourages people to seek their own short-term good above all else.

This divided, hurting world is in dire need of forces able to strengthen communities and build coalitions dedicated to solving our common problems and working for the greater good. Even considered solely from a sociological perspective, churches are significant as institutions that reinforce social bonds. Churches such as the Catholic Church—which has extensive organizational structures that establish community, identity, and coordination not only locally but also at national and international levels—are especially significant. Given the global dimensions of the economic and climate challenges we face, churches and other religious groups could play an important role in healing animosity and bridging divisions.

---

5. Pew Research Center, "U.S. Public Becoming Less Religious," October 29, 2015, https://www.pewforum.org/2015/11/03/u-s-public-becoming-less-religious/pf-2015-11-03_rls_ii-84/.

6. World Bank, "Nearly Half the World Lives on Less than $5.50 a Day," press release, October 17, 2018, https://www.worldbank.org/en/news/press-release/2018/10/17/nearly-half-the-world-lives-on-less-than-550-a-day.

Despite the lamentable divisions within Christianity, a consensus on the purpose of the church is emerging that is directly relevant to the current need for relationships and community. Drawing on established Orthodox theology, the Second Vatican Council (1962–1965) developed an understanding of the church's mission that is increasingly accepted by Protestant Christians as well: the church is called to be a sign and instrument of the union of all in God.[7] That is, the church serves the world through its witness to what it means to be a community united in love, while also working to increase that unity of justice, peace, and love throughout society.

These two dimensions, sign and instrument (or prophetic witness and public agent), of the church's mission are properly understood as inseparable. The church cannot be a faithful witness to God's desire for the unity of all while also adopting a sectarian stance that rejects any responsibility for "the joys and hopes, the griefs and anxieties" of the rest of society (GS 1). Nor can the church be a credible agent of greater justice and peace in the world if the church cannot manage to live as a (more or less) just and harmonious community itself. For Catholic Christians, of course, the language of "sign and instrument" is sacramental language referring to the graced experiences through which the healing and transforming presence of God is both signified and communicated. The church is supposed to be a sacrament of the communion of *all* in God.

To fulfill this mission, the church must be prophetic in its opposition to the injustices and corruptions that are the antithesis of the loving community of God's reign. The Hebrew Bible prophets condemned as an outrage to God the injustice and inequality that had become established in their society. Today, the devastation of the natural world, the suffering inflicted on workers and animals, and the inequality that leaves so many at the margins of society demand that the church speak and witness prophetically against these abuses that are too often taken for granted as integral to the global economy.

Yet at the same time, the church's task is not only to denounce but also to be an instrument of transformation. This requires a public church, by which I mean one that engages the current po-

---

7. Vatican II, Dogmatic Constitution on the Church (*Lumen Gentium* [LG]) 1.

litical processes in order to develop policies and structures that decrease suffering, that preserve the earth, and that support human dignity, equality, and inclusion.

In what follows, I will describe the witness of loving ecclesial communion in the church primarily as the church's "prophetic" function, in order to emphasize that the church's alternative way of being as a community should be a sign that reveals and disrupts the distortions of the world. I will discuss the church's work to increase harmony and justice in the broader world as its "public" activity, especially insofar as this work involves ecclesial engagement with others beyond the church and with the current governing structures of society.[8]

Of course, there is no such neat division between prophetic and public, just as there is no clear separation of sign and instrument. The church's witness is a public sign that is visible to the larger society and may in fact do more to transform the world than Christians' efforts to change public policy. Similarly, the church's public work, cooperating with non-Christians to effect change for the good of all, is a prophetic witness against the tribal divisions afflicting humanity. Nevertheless, given the prophetic quality of the church's role as sign and the public character of the church's work as instrument, I find it helpful to accentuate the prophetic dimensions of the witness of loving communion within the church, while stressing the public aspects of ecclesial social and political efforts, especially cooperation with others for more just sociopolitical structures and policies.

It is a fair question whether the church can in fact be both prophetic and public. Is it possible to be involved in political processes without becoming corrupted by the power politics of the current system? Is not such an engaged church already compromised in its witness against the injustices of the status quo?

To be sure, there is a real danger that the church will become so intent on preserving its public role that its prophetic vision will be muted, if not lost altogether. This is a temptation the church has succumbed to time and again. But the alternative temptation to

---

8. My use of the terms *prophetic* and *public* is thus largely consistent with that of Kristin E. Heyer in *Prophetic and Public: Social Witness of U.S. Catholicism* (Washington, DC: Georgetown University Press, 2006).

stand over against the world in self-righteous purity is not acceptable for a church that proclaims a God who refused to abandon the world to its sin but rather became incarnate in this suffering world to share its pain and to transform it from within. I remain convinced, and will argue below, that there is no inherent contradiction between the prophetic and public functions of the church. On the contrary, these tasks are inseparable: the church cannot credibly denounce injustice and division while refusing to cooperate with others to make the world more just. God's grace is intended not for the condemnation of the world but for its salvation.[9]

A Practical/Political Ecclesiology: Prioritizing Mission over Nature

The ecclesiological approach of this project differs considerably from that of most theologies of the church, even though the work here is based on a widely accepted understanding of the mission of the church. This difference arises because ecclesiology frequently centers on the nature of the church, with delineation of the church's proper offices and structures based on the presentation of the church's nature, or what the church *is*.[10] While there is much of

---

9. "Christ . . . came into this world . . . to save and not to judge, to serve and not to be served" (GS 3).

10. Even when the church is primarily defined as mission or as sacrament, the ecclesiology developed tends to focus nevertheless on the nature of the church so commissioned rather than on the commission itself as integral to understanding the church. See, for example, Avery Dulles, *Models of the Church* (Garden City, NY: Doubleday, 1974). In my judgment, the dominance of nature and structure over mission in the history of ecclesiology is also evident in the magisterial works of Roger Haight, *Christian Community in History*, 3 vols. (New York: Continuum, 2004–2008); and Richard P. McBrien, *The Church: The Evolution of Catholicism* (New York: HarperCollins, 2008), though McBrien's approach includes the church's mission as central to ecclesiology. See also Thomas P. Rausch, *Towards a Truly Catholic Church: An Ecclesiology for the Third Millennium* (Collegeville, MN: Liturgical Press, 2005). For emerging ecclesiological emphases privileging mission, in addition to McBrien above, see the essays in Richard R. Gaillardetz and Edward P. Hahnenberg, *A Church with Open Doors: Catholic Ecclesiology for the Third Millennium* (Collegeville, MN: Liturgical Press, 2015). Richard R. Gaillardetz, *Ecclesiology for a Global Church: A People Called and Sent* (Mary-

value in this theological work, I argue here for a different approach, one that begins instead with the mission of the church, with what the church is *for* and is called *to do*. Starting from the church's purpose in history sheds new light on church offices and structures, especially as these serve or impede the church's mission, though that important study will not be undertaken here. Instead, this book will take up the more fundamental project of clarifying that the church's mission is inseparable from the problems of a deeply divided, individualistic, and yet increasingly globally connected world. This point is obscured in theological reflections focusing on the church's supposedly unchanging nature, and so remains only inchoately grasped by much of the church.

Beginning with the church's mission further emphasizes that the church exists to serve the world and is integrally involved in society and even in the world's politics. So-called Catholic social teachings will remain marginalized as the Catholic Church's "best-kept secret" as long as the church is defined in primarily static terms—that is, by what the church is—and apart from the church's mission in and to the world.[11] Societal injustice then appears as a secondary or even a minor concern that does not affect the church in itself. The problem may be less that Catholics are unaware of official Catholic social teachings than that the qualification of these teachings as "social" has rendered them subordinate or marginal to the life of the church. We need to be more consistent and consciously aware that the church is inherently involved in all aspects of society because, as persons-in-community, human beings cannot be redeemed apart from the community relations that are essential to who we are.

The approach to ecclesiology here is practical/political also because it presumes that we cannot know what it means to be a sign and instrument of communion in the broken world of our day without engaging the major obstacles to, and the great opportunities

---

knoll, NY: Orbis, 2008); and Gerard Mannion, *Ecclesiology and Postmodernity: Questions for the Church in Our Time* (Collegeville, MN: Liturgical Press, 2007) are also concerned to incorporate the church's mission more clearly into an ecclesiology focused on the nature and character of the Christian community.

11. Edward P. DeBerri et al., *Catholic Social Teaching: Our Best Kept Secret*, 4th ed. (Maryknoll, NY: Orbis, 2003), 3–5.

for, more just and loving communion. At this moment in history, globalization is the source of unprecedented possibilities and challenges for the harmonious unity of humanity. In this respect, globalization is not only a sociological fact but an ecclesiological demand: Christians can truly know what it means to be church-as-sign-and-instrument-of-communion only by living in witness to and working for greater global harmony today. The current realities of economic inequality, global climate change, and massive human migration are thus properly ecclesiological issues as well as topics for Christian social ethics.

A Note on Terminology

Church is a notoriously ambiguous term, used to refer to specific ecclesial communities as well as to the community of all Jesus' disciples. This ambiguity risks conflating the church as a whole with one particular church, an error I try to avoid below. Even though this project is engaged primarily with the texts and traditions of the Catholic Church to which I belong, the ecclesiological conclusions are intended to apply to all who strive to follow Jesus. The term *church* should be understood here as designating the entire body of Christ's disciples and/or all mainstream churches and ecclesial traditions, unless the context clearly indicates a more narrow meaning. When the Catholic Church or another specific ecclesial body is intended, the particular name will be used rather than the general term *church*, again excepting when the context determines otherwise.

Outline of the Argument

The first major task undertaken in chapter 1 is to provide a nuanced understanding, as developed in the documents of Vatican II and in some later ecclesiologies, of the church's mission to be a sign and instrument of the union of all in God. While this perspective on the church's mission is now commonly found in statements about the church across Christian denominations, including in the work of the Faith and Order Commission of the World Council of Churches, few have developed the meaning of this mission as fully as Vatican II has.[12] Especially important for this project are the emphasis on unity-in-diversity and the theological anthropology of persons-in-community, as these are fundamental to the proper enactment of the church's mission amid the diversity of the contemporary world. Notwithstanding its rootedness in the Catholic tradition, Vatican II provides a solid basis for a consensus Christian understanding of the mission of the church, a clear foundation on which not only Catholics but most Christians can better witness to and work for global communion in our time.

Because the church must be a sign as well as an instrument of unity, chapters 2 and 3 address two of the church's signal failures to maintain unity-in-diversity. Chapter 2 is concerned with the religious anti-Semitism that was present as early as the New Testament period and continues to distort ecclesial self-understanding today, even though the most explicit of these teachings of contempt have been repudiated. The church cannot fully serve God's plan of unity-in-diversity in the contemporary world without overcoming its ongoing failure to make theological room for Judaism (and, by extension, for other religions as well). The second historical failure, discussed in chapter 3, also begins in the New Testament period: the teachings and practices that position women as less than full members of the church. While Christian contempt for Judaism impedes unity with the religious diversity beyond the church, Christian misogyny fails to achieve an internal unity that fully incorporates the diversity of women within the church.

Both religious anti-Semitism and misogyny continue to influence church beliefs and practices, even though few mainstream Christians intentionally embrace either. This is a serious problem: a church that cannot fully embody unity-in-diversity with its primary other outside of the church or with half of those within the church will not be a very compelling or prophetic witness to the world of what true communion might be. Moreover, solutions for the major global challenges to unity-in-diversity today require cooperation across religious differences and, because these global issues affect women

---

12. See, for example, World Council of Churches, *The Church: Towards a Common Vision*, Faith and Order paper no. 214 (Geneva: World Council of Churches Publications, 2013).

in distinct ways, adequate solutions cannot be based on the assumed normativity of men. In other words, the historical failures to affirm Jews and women continue to undermine the church's ability to be a sign or an instrument of unity-in-diversity in the world. Neither anti-Judaism nor misogyny can be set aside as of marginal relevance in any ecclesiology appropriate to the twenty-first century.

Chapters 4–6 discuss the major issues confronting the world today. Chapter 4 focuses on being church in the midst of a global economy that could make it possible for all people to enjoy the world's resources, yet more often disrupts local economies and increases inequality and exclusion. Chapter 5 addresses global climate change, the most pressing problem the world faces today and one that threatens to change irrevocably the conditions of life on this planet. This issue demands that the church develop a concept of unity that recognizes the intrinsic value of creation, and thus, as Pope Francis has argued, is more adequate to the unity envisioned in the Bible as well as to the challenge of ending environmental degradation. Chapter 6 explores the widespread human migration that is destabilizing the communities that lose members while also placing pressures on the established communities that receive the migrants.

These three issues are clearly interrelated aspects of globalization, since it is the global economy's use of natural resources, especially fossil fuels, that is driving climate change, and both economic and climatic shifts are forcing population migrations. Furthermore, each of these affects women distinctly: for example, women overall have access to fewer resources, often feel the impact of global warming more directly in their efforts to secure food, water, and fuel for their families, and are especially vulnerable during migration to being trafficked. When the church ignores the specific conditions of women's lives, it fails to pursue the communion that will unite all of humanity in their diversity. A truly prophetic, public church must be a feminist church actively engaged in overcoming the various and interrelated failures of communion in the world today. A prophetic, public church must also work with people of other faiths and of no faith, and it must do this in a way that relinquishes triumphalism, including the remnants of Christian supersessionism, evincing instead the mutually enriching dialogue and respect that the church seeks to increase in society.

Again, the discussion of each of these issues will begin with the most developed Catholic documents on the topic because, though I will argue that they remain imperfect, they provide nuanced arguments that incorporate much of contemporary theology while nevertheless serving to provide common ground on which Christians should be able to agree. The detailed and developed—and even somewhat conservative—character of official Catholic documents makes them a gift to the whole church, as they reflect deeply and carefully on the meaning of Christian faith in a way that is clarifying yet consensus oriented. While Pope Francis emerges somewhat as the hero of this book for his degree of theological insight into the issues this book addresses, it should be remembered that he builds on a well-established tradition of thought, including the work of Vatican II; of his immediate predecessors, Pope St. John Paul II and Pope Benedict XVI; and of bishops and theologians around the world.

The book's conclusion provides a summary of the need for ecclesial witness to and work toward unity amid these global crises. Poverty, migration, and environmental degradation are by no means new issues for the church, but they are now occurring on a global scale and with an unprecedented impact on human life and on the planet itself. The church must therefore do church differently to fulfill its ecclesial mission to be a sign and instrument of genuine community in the twenty-first century.

Chapter 1

Called to Communion

The Vision of the Second Vatican Council

If one asks an evangelical Christian what the church is for, one is likely to get a clear response, something to the effect of "to save souls by spreading Christian faith." If one had asked a Catholic Christian of the early twentieth century that same question, the answer might have been similar and no less definite: "to provide the sacraments that save our souls." In either case, the respondent would probably have no doubt that the church serves a significant purpose by helping people to escape an afterlife of eternal suffering and achieve instead a heavenly paradise of bliss with God. Odds are that these Christians would not be concerned that their account of the church's purpose bears little relation to Jesus' preaching of a reign of God where God's will is done on earth, as it is in heaven. Nor would they likely note the absence here of the Hebrew Bible's vision of a just harmony in a society that cares for its land and animals.

Catholics and mainstream Protestants today may be more aware of the importance of social justice in the Bible, but they are often less certain about the role of the church. Unwilling to consign non-Christians to hell, many will describe the purpose of the church and its sacraments primarily as a support for one's personal life of faith—with the unstated implication that the church exists for those who need that sort of assistance. The church may be helpful in providing a faith community and rituals that console and encourage Christians, especially in times of crisis. Overall, however, the church itself hardly seems crucial, whether to one's own life or to society.

What is largely missing in these common views of the church is an awareness of the growing ecumenical consensus that the mission of the church is to be a sign and instrument of communion, an agent of desperately needed unification in this globalizing yet also deeply divided age. Instead, the default view in mainstream Western culture is that religion is a private matter. It is not surprising, then, that many people approach church membership as yet another consumer option one chooses, for as long as that membership provides personal benefits that outweigh the costs.[1] The sense of being called to a significant and noble task—to be, as a people, a sacrament of harmonious communion and an instrument of God's love to mend a broken world—may be central to church documents, but this view is foreign to the privatized Christianity assumed by many Christians. It is any wonder that so few idealistic young people are interested in dedicating their lives to the service of the church? Or that Pope Francis is criticized by fellow Catholics for being "too political" in his statements about climate change, vast economic inequality, and the deaths of unwelcomed refugees?

Yet the church as envisioned by the Second Vatican Council (or Vatican II), the most recent gathering of the world's Catholic bishops in solemn council, is a thoroughly public church, concerned not only with individual souls but with the redemption of all dimensions of society. If, as Charles Curran has aptly noted, the church's mission before Vatican II was viewed as a double mission, with the clergy divinizing the world that the laity humanize, Vatican II describes the church as serving the single purpose of increasing the communion of all in God.[2] Laity may have the greater responsibility to develop this communion in the world while the clergy primarily strengthen and nurture communion within the church, yet ultimately

---

1. Vincent J. Miller provides an illuminating account of this phenomenon in his *Consuming Religion: Christian Faith and Practice in a Consumer Culture* (New York: Continuum, 2003).

2. Charles E. Curran, *The Social Mission of the U.S. Catholic Church: A Theological Perspective* (Washington, DC: Georgetown University Press, 2011), esp. 57.

these two dimensions are inseparable, as I will argue below. Because persons are both sacred and social, there are not two separate purposes of the church, and personal salvation cannot be isolated from the redemption of the world.

While this vision of the church's mission to be a sign and instrument of the union of all in God is advanced in the documents of Vatican II, it is by no means solely a Catholic interpretation.³ A similar view of the church's mission is endorsed by the Faith and Order Commission of the 350-member World Council of Churches in its document *The Church: Towards a Common Vision*.⁴ This account of the church is also affirmed in non-Catholic theologies as different as those of the Anglican theologian John Milbank and the formerly Anabaptist theologian Miroslav Volf.⁵ Moreover, the goal of divine-human communion has long been central to the theology of the Orthodox Church, which is a major source for Vatican II's formulation of the church's mission.⁶

Even though most Christians are unaware of this significant—and too little celebrated—ecumenical consensus on the purpose of the church, there can be no doubt that this agreement is possible because the view resonates with a *sensus fidelium*, a sense of the faithful, that is deeper than the privatized accounts of the church that many Christians articulate. The work of Christians through the centuries and around the globe provides ample evidence that they sense a call

---

3. I further explore this common ecclesiology in my article "The Unity and Disunity of Our Hope," in Mark Chapman, ed., *Hope in the Ecumenical Future* (New York: Palgrave MacMillan, 2017).

4. World Council of Churches, *The Church: Towards a Common Vision*, Faith and Order paper no. 214 (Geneva: World Council of Churches Publications, 2013), esp. 15.

5. See especially John Milbank, *Theology and Social Theory: Beyond Secular Reason* (Oxford, UK: Blackwell, 2006), 422–432; and Miroslav Volf, *After Our Likeness: The Church as the Image of the Trinity* (Grand Rapids, MI: William B. Eerdmans, 1998).

6. For a discussion of the influence of Orthodox thought on the Catholic Church's Second Vatican Council, see Marie-Dominique Chenu, "The New Awareness of the Trinitarian Basis of the Church," in *Where Does the Church Stand? Concilium 146*, ed. Giuseppe Alberigo and Gustavo Gutierrez (New York: Seabury, 1981), 14–21.

to act together to seek a more just and loving world for the good of all humanity. The *comunidades de base* (Christian base communities) in Latin America, the Catholic Worker communities in the United States, and the many faith and justice committees in Christian congregations everywhere witness to an abiding commitment to increasing love and harmony on earth as a fundamental dimension of Christian discipleship.

However, there is an important and recurring criticism of this socially engaged church, especially as envisioned in official Catholic teachings: Some contend that such a public church cannot maintain the appropriately critical stance integral to the prophetic alternative so desperately needed. Even among those who affirm that the church's mission includes being an instrument as well as a sign of communion in the world, it is commonly argued that the church is most faithfully an instrument to transform this world through its witness to another way of being community. Those who take this position insist that it is not possible to be what I call here a "public" church, engaged with the political processes of secular society, while also maintaining a prophetic witness against the corrupt and sinful power arrangements of the status quo.[7] From this perspective, any Christian attempt to increase justice in society through participating in its unjust politics obscures the Gospel's condemnation of the world's distance from the reign of God. Instead of tacitly accepting the distortions of worldly politics, the church should "be the church," so that the stark alternative of its countercultural witness will remind the world that there are more fulfilling and joyful ways of being human than the self-seeking power struggles of contemporary secular society.

There can be no doubt that the neglect of the church's witness, of its call to be a sign of communion, is a significant problem. The

---

7. Stanley Hauerwas certainly approaches this position in many of his books and articles, as, for example, in *A Community of Character: Toward a Constructive Christian Social Ethic* (Notre Dame, IN: University of Notre Dame Press, 1981). See also articles in Michael L. Budde and Robert W. Brinlow, eds., *The Church as Counterculture* (Albany, NY: SUNY, 2000); and Kristin Heyer's engagement with Michael Baxter's version of this position in *Prophetic and Public: Social Witness of U.S. Catholicism* (Washington, DC: Georgetown University Press, 2006), esp. 59–117.

politically engaged church has indeed at times focused more on changing laws to make society act differently than on changing itself to be a prophetic witness to an alternative way of life. If Christians cannot themselves behave better, what chance is there that laws will achieve the desired transformation?

Nevertheless, official Catholic teachings, along with the teachings of many other church bodies, insist that the church must be both a prophetic witness of true loving community and a public agent seeking to make sociopolitical structures more just. Of course, the question of whether it is possible to be an actor within, while also being an alternative to, public life is ultimately a practical one. It will be resolved best by examples of the church successfully engaging political processes without compromising its prophetic witness (or, conversely, by the church's failure to do so). Yet I will argue here that the Catholic Church has sound theological reasons to insist that the prophetic and public dimensions of the church cannot be separated any more than can the aspects of a sacrament as sign and instrument. In other words, Catholic ecclesiology, rooted in a sacramental sensibility, cannot coherently eschew either the prophetic task of counterculture witness or the public task of sociopolitical transformation. Sign and instrument, witness and action, are integrally related.

Moreover, ours is a time of growing polarization between groups in society. The witness of an alternative community that retains its distinct identity in and through its commitment to the broader society is a more countercultural witness than is a church that mirrors the withdrawal into identity enclaves so prevalent today. The church will be truly distinct only by refusing to take part in the tribalization currently dividing society by pitting groups against each other.[8]

Our task in this chapter is to explore Vatican II's prophetic and public vision of the church's mission, especially as developed in its two fundamental documents on the church: the Dogmatic Constitution on the Church (*Lumen Gentium*) and the Pastoral Constitution

---

8. Vincent J. Miller develops this point in his "Media Constructions of Space, the Disciplining of Religious Traditions, and the Hidden Threat of the Post-Secular," in William A. Barbieri, *At the Limits of the Secular: Reflections on Faith and Public Life* (Grand Rapids, MI: Eerdmans, 2014), 162–196.

on the Church in the Modern World (*Gaudium et Spes*). These constitutions affirm that diversity is integral to the unity the church strives for, and so they explore what unity-in-diversity means for the life of the church as well as for the church's role in a pluralistic, global reality. The Declaration on Religious Freedom (*Dignitatis Humanae*) and the Declaration on the Relation of the Church to Non-Christian Religions (*Nostra Aetate*) provide additional clarification of how the church can seek the unity of all humanity while honoring the diversity of non-Christian perspectives.[9]

Gaudium et Spes is particularly important here for its emphasis on human beings developing as persons-in-community. Official Catholic teaching rejects both the extreme individualism that neglects responsibilities to the broader society and the extreme communalism that disregards the dignity and rights of the individual. This concept of human personhood, insisting that persons develop fully only in communities that are enriched by the diverse contributions of distinct persons, could be the most significant contribution of Christianity to public life today, particularly where Western possessive individualism is dominant.[10]

Although Vatican II provides a detailed account of the mission of the church in and to the world, these documents do not and cannot constitute the final statement on the church's mission. Such theological finality is never possible in a church that continues to grow in understanding of a mystery that will always surpass human comprehension. Indeed, it is a testimony to the fertility of the council's work that its documents have inspired further ecclesiological insights in the global Catholic Church. While a comprehensive investigation of the wealth of contemporary ecclesiology is far beyond the scope of this chapter, a brief discussion here of major advancements in post–Vatican II ecclesiology will serve to clarify the contributions and the limits of Vatican II's vision of the church, especially with

---

9. Vatican II, Declaration on Religious Freedom (*Dignitatis Humanae* [DH]); and Vatican II, Declaration on the Relation of the Church to Non-Christian Religions (*Nostra Aetate* [NA]).

10. Franklin I. Gamwell, *Politics as a Christian Vocation: Faith and Democracy Today* (Cambridge, UK: Cambridge University Press, 2005), 113–129. I have developed a version of this argument in my *Divine Harmony: Seeking Community in a Broken World* (Mahwah, NJ: Paulist Press, 2017).

regard to the role of the church as a sign and instrument of communion in the world.[11]

Our goal is not to provide a study of Vatican II in itself, about which many excellent works have been written, but rather to investigate what it means to be church in the face of the considerable challenges of the twenty-first century.[12] At its best, the church is far from irrelevant; indeed, I contend that the most critical issues today demand a heroic commitment to unity-in-diversity along the lines envisioned by Vatican II and by other churches and ecclesial organizations. At the same time, contemporary problems, particularly issues of global economic inequality, climate change, and massive population shifts, are of a magnitude that neither church nor world has ever experienced before. These issues require—and inspire—further insight into what it means to be faithful to the church's mission at this historical moment, as will be explored in later chapters.

Engaging Vatican II: A Synchronic Approach

It is difficult to overestimate the significance of Vatican II, the largest ecumenical (or worldwide) council in the history of the Catholic Church. This council has been identified as the beginning of a truly global Catholicism, with 2,800 bishops participating from 116 countries.[13] The deliberations of these bishops in 5 sessions held in Rome between 1962 and 1965 resulted in 16 official documents

---

11. Excellent surveys of contemporary global ecclesiologies can be found in Veli-Matti Kärkkäinen, *An Introduction to Ecclesiology: Ecumenical, Historical, and Global Perspectives* (Downers Grove, IL: Intervarsity Press, 2002); and Paul Avis, ed., *The Oxford Handbook of Ecclesiology* (UK: Oxford University Press, 2018).

12. A few excellent, readable studies of the Second Vatican Council are Giuseppe Alberigo, *A Brief History of Vatican II*, trans. Matthew Sherry (Maryknoll, NY: Orbis, 2006); John W. O'Malley, *What Happened at Vatican II* (Cambridge, MA: Harvard University Press, 2008); and Richard R. Gaillardetz and Catherine E. Clifford, *Keys to the Council: Unlocking the Teaching of Vatican II* (Collegeville, MN: Liturgical Press, 2012). For a more focused conversation, see John J. Markey, *Creating Communion: The Theology of the Constitutions of the Church* (Hyde Park, NY: New City Press, 2003).

13. John O'Malley, "Opening the Church to the World," *New York Times*, October 10, 2012, https://www.nytimes.com/2012/10/11/opinion/vatican-ii-opened-the-church-to-the-world.html; Karl Rahner, "Towards a Fundamental Theological Interpretation of Vatican Council II," *Theological Studies* 40 (1979): 718.

approved by the council with overwhelming majorities. This work led to dramatic changes in the Catholic liturgy as well as in official teachings about Judaism and religious freedom. Catholic teachings on such matters as the authority of Scripture, the role of the laity, and ecumenism were all updated. The impact of Vatican II also extended beyond the boundaries of the Catholic community, as the council declared itself open to new forms of cooperation with non-Catholics within and beyond Christianity. Many non-Catholics welcomed this invitation to more positive relations and common action with the Catholic Church.

One of the central achievements of Vatican II, and the focus of our attention here, is the council's nuanced vision of a public yet thoroughly prophetic mission of the church. It is widely recognized that Vatican II was deeply concerned with questions of the church, and two of its four constitutions (*Lumen Gentium* and *Gaudium et Spes*) were devoted specifically to ecclesiology. Pope St. John XXIII opened the council with an encouragement to define the relationship between church and world in a positive manner, reversing the then common Catholic stance of hostility toward modernity. This pope specifically rejected the negativity of "prophets of gloom," and called the church leaders to recognize that "Divine Providence is leading us to a new order of human relations."[14] It was time to move beyond the ecclesial defensiveness of the past century and, as Pope John is often reported to have proclaimed, to "throw open the windows of the church and let the fresh air of the Spirit blow through."[15]

The council fathers at Vatican II thus undertook the task of *ressourcement*, or returning to Christian sources, especially the Bible and the writings of the early church, in order to achieve an *aggior-*

---

14. John XXIII, "*Humanae Salutis* (Opening Address to the Second Vatican Council), in *The Documents of Vatican II: With Notes and Comments by Catholic, Protestant, and Orthodox Authorities*, ed. Walter M. Abbott (New York: America Press, 1966), 712.

15. This comment, or a similar one, is commonly attributed to Pope John XXIII. It is possible that he never said it, given the variant forms of the quotation and lack of evidence or source, but it certainly expresses how people experienced the hopeful, renewing sense of the council. See, for example, John Gehring, *The Francis Effect* (Lanham, MD: Rowman & Littlefield, 2015), 56.

namento, or updating of the teachings of the church.¹⁶ Of course, like all good theology, councils generally involve some degree of both retrieval and updating, since new understandings and explanations of Christianity must be adequate to the tradition and appropriate to the current situation.¹⁷ Indeed, *aggiornamento* and *ressourcement* are best understood not as separate tasks but as one interrelated task of renewal through attention to the authoritative sources in light of the questions of the day. As John Markey has noted, ecumenical councils provide the Catholic Church with an opportunity to look back—at where the church has been and what it has learned since the last council—in order to move forward.¹⁸

It is undoubtedly a mistake, then, to interpret Vatican II or any Catholic council as a total break with the past. A radically remade church lacking continuity with the tradition of thought and practice from Christianity's beginnings would obviously not be Catholic.

At the same time, it is also a mistake to interpret the council as providing no new teachings but merely repeating—in perhaps updated language—the long-established positions of the church. After all, it is the rare ecumenical council that does not further the church's thought or practice in some way.¹⁹ Informed by the sources, by long-standing traditions of thought and practice, and by advances in theological argument and experiences that shed new light on the meaning of Christian faith, councils strive to come to a deeper understanding of the Christian message in light of the challenges of the time. Councils are often occasions for the development of doctrine, and this one made undeniable advancements

---

16. Richard R. Gaillardetz, *The Church in the Making: Lumen Gentium, Christus Dominus, Orientalium Ecclesiarium* (Mahwah, NJ: Paulist Press, 2006), xvi–xvii.

17. David Tracy famously defended this understanding of the task of theology. See his *Blessed Rage for Order: The New Pluralism in Theology* (New York: Seabury Press, 1975), esp. 22–34.

18. Markey, *Creating Communion*, 13–19.

19. Christopher Bellitto's excellent, brief discussion of the ecumenical councils supports this conclusion. See Christopher M. Bellitto, *The General Councils: A History of the Twenty-One Church Councils from Nicaea to Vatican II* (Mahwah, NJ: Paulist Press, 2002).

in Christian understanding, especially in relation to Judaism and religious freedom.[20]

As mentioned above, this brief chapter will not attempt to do justice either to the important historical event that the council was or to the full range of insights and teachings it developed. Our focus is on the conciliar documents' nuanced account of the public and prophetic mission of the church. A further limitation is that this discussion will consider only the final documents as approved by the council. There are valuable insights to be gained through study of the history of the drafting and redrafting of Vatican II's documents, but this chapter is concerned with the meaning and coherence of the written positions adopted by the council. Hence, priority will be given to what Ormond Rush terms a "synchronic" approach, in which the council's documents are interpreted as whole texts and in relation to each other.[21]

As many have argued, it does little good to promote partisan interpretations that cite passages taken out of their contexts within their particular documents or within the entire set of conciliar documents. To be sure, these documents, like most committee writings (and much nuanced thought!), contain statements that remain in some tension with each other. Nevertheless, they are not incoherent juxtapositions of contradictory positions. Instead, the documents of Vatican II set forth an account of the church's role in the world that is on the whole coherent, persuasive, and inspiring, as I will show here.[22]

Called to Be a Sacrament of Unity

Although *Lumen Gentium* is primarily concerned with the nature and structures of the church, it provides the foundational vision

---

20. Despite the considerable contention over whether Vatican II should be interpreted as a council whose teachings are continuous with the tradition or change the tradition, neither approach is adequate, and it is long past time to cease this misguided debate.

21. Ormond Rush, *Still Interpreting Vatican II: Some Hermeneutical Principles* (New York: Paulist Press, 2004), 7.

22. See Gaillardetz, *Church in the Making*, xvi-xviii, for a perspective that emphasizes the tensions and contradictions within the conciliar documents.

and theological basis for many theological positions that are further elaborated in other conciliar documents, including those on ecumenism, the role of the laity, and religious freedom. Of particular interest for our purposes, *Lumen Gentium* establishes the sacramental and eschatological approach to the church's mission that *Gaudium et Spes*'s lengthy discussion of the church's role in the world further develops.

The first paragraph of *Lumen Gentium* provides a concise yet profound statement of the church's mission, declaring that the church is called to be "a sacrament—a sign and instrument, that is, of communion with God and of the unity of the entire human race" (LG 1). The church is not merely a source of sacramental rituals; it functions itself as a sacrament (a "sign and instrument") of unity. As a gathering into communion, the church mediates the divine grace that increases unity within and beyond the church, especially as the church witnesses to the joy of loving harmony in God.

Catholic theology maintains that the sign quality and the instrumental effectiveness of a sacrament are inseparable, though they may be distinguished. As a sacrament of communion, then, the church must be both a powerful sign and an effective public instrument of the unity of all in God. When the church lives a compelling example of harmonious unity, the church stands as an alternative that contrasts with—and thus makes clearer—the evil of the world's divisions and exclusions. At the same time, this prophetic witness increases the credibility of the church's efforts to extend unity in the world. Moreover, it would seem that experiencing the deep joy of loving communion in the church would inspire the faithful to spread that love as far as possible throughout society and in every dimension of life.

Just as the sign and instrument aspects of the church's mission are inseparable, so also the vertical and horizontal dimensions of the desired communion are indivisible, as Yves Congar emphasized.[23] That is, the vertical communion with God cannot be achieved apart from the horizontal communion with others because to enter into

---

23. See especially the discussion of Congar's contribution on this point in Markey, *Creating Communion*, 46. See also Gaillardetz, *Church in the Making*, 47.

union with God is to be at the same time united to all else in God.[24] It follows that a church that seeks communion with the divine will immerse itself in, rather than turn away from, the struggles of the world that God is redeeming and to which God has sent the church.

Richard McBrien further specifies the church's mission for the sake of God's reign as a fourfold mission involving word or proclamation, worship, witness as a community, and service to transform the world, both directly and through political action.[25] In my judgment, word and worship are integral to both the church's witness and its agency or service in the world, and so are more accurately described as aspects of the twofold mission to be sign and instrument. I am also concerned to interrupt the tendency of Christians to reduce the church's purpose to word and worship, especially in an individualistic interpretation that considers the church as a provider of instruction and a sacramental dispensary. Too often word and worship replace, rather than inform, the church's mission of witness to and service of God's reign. In what follows, then, the focus will be on the church's mission to be a sign and instrument, with the understanding that without word and worship the church can be neither the sign nor the instrument it is called to be.

Eschatological and Trinitarian

While intimately engaged with this world and its history, the church's sacramental mission is nevertheless thoroughly eschatological in its orientation toward the ultimate goal of unity in God. As described in *Lumen Gentium*, God intended even in creation that humanity would one day participate in God's life (LG 2). The church serves this divine plan by working as a sign and instrument of God's grace to increase communion until finally, beyond history, the "human race, the universe itself, . . . will be perfectly established in Christ" (LG 48).

---

24. Pope Benedict XVI has been especially clear in his eucharistic theology that communion with God has this social dimension. See especially his encyclical On Christian Love (*Deus Caritas Est*), 13–14, http://w2.vatican.va/content/benedict-xvi/en/encyclicals/documents/hf_ben-xvi_enc_20051225_deus-caritas-est.html.

25. Richard P. McBrien, *The Church: The Evolution of Catholicism* (New York: HarperCollins, 2008), esp. 3–4.

Christianity thus offers hope to those adrift in the timelessness of the contemporary world. Rejecting the deadening malaise of a time without end and a history without a telos, the church believes that time matters because it has a goal: in and through history God is bringing us to the promised eschatological harmony of the reign of God. This transcendent hope *beyond* history makes possible a hope *for* history and also for history's victims since, as both Johann Baptist Metz and Pope Benedict XVI have pointed out, it is only when there is a goal—and a God—beyond history that there is hope for recompense for the otherwise unremedied injustices of a merciless history.[26]

Because harmony with God and with others will never be fully and completely achieved until the eschaton, there is an "eschatological reserve" here that relativizes temporal projects. The transcendent dimension of Christian hope warns us that political and historical achievements are partial and finite at best, and should not be treated as ultimate or pursued without restraint, as political causes so often—and so dangerously—are. This transcendence further safeguards the church's independence from political authorities, who have no competence in eschatological matters, while reinforcing the proper secularity of governmental affairs within history, as will be discussed below. Still, it is important to recognize that this transcendent, eschatological hope does not devalue this world and what can be achieved in history since, as *Gaudium et Spes* maintains, "the expectation of a new earth must not weaken but rather stimulate our concern for cultivating this one. For here grows the body of a new human family, a body which even now is able to give some kind of foreshadowing of the new age" (GS 39).

This eschatologically oriented mission is also thoroughly Trinitarian, realized in and through the Trinity's redemptive activity. As *Lumen Gentium* reminds us, the Creator's plan to bring humanity into the Trinitarian divine life "has already begun in Christ, is carried

---

26. Johann Baptist Metz, *Faith in History and Society: Toward a Practical Fundamental Theology*, trans. J. Matthew Ashley (New York: Herder and Herder, 2007); Benedict XVI, On Christian Hope (*Spe Salvi*) 42–44. http://w2.vatican.va/content/benedict-xvi/en/encyclicals/documents/hf_ben-xvi_enc_20071130_spe-salvi.html.

forward in the mission of the Holy Spirit and through Him continues in the Church" (LG 48). In sum, God intended to bestow the gift of union with God from the beginning of creation, established this union in history through the redemptive incarnation of the Son, and is bringing it to completion by the power of the Holy Spirit.

Unity-in-Diversity within the Church

Just as the one God is not monolithic but a Trinity of distinct persons in loving communion, so too the unity the church serves is properly understood as a unity-in-diversity. It is a mistake to think that the church should strive to impose a uniformity or sameness, as though unity wipes out differences. To the contrary, diversity is essential to unity. After all, without differences, what is there to unite?

Lumen Gentium's discussion of diversity proceeds first through reflection on the distinct gifts, roles, and ranks that contribute to the unity of the church and the fulfillment of its mission in the world. The dignity of the laity, for example, does not consist in the laity being the same as the clergy but rather is rooted in the predominantly lay vocation to transform the world, while the clerical vocation is primarily centered on building up the church. Both are essential aspects of the church's one mission, and they are equally paths to holiness (LG 31). Furthermore, the church values the distinct gifts that contribute differently to the good of the whole church; the clergy are not to stifle these gifts of the Holy Spirit but rather to identify, foster, and direct them toward the strengthening of the ecclesial body (LG 30).

Diversity is thus fundamental to the life of the church, including diversity in cultures, in languages, and even in ecclesial rites. *Lumen Gentium* celebrates the diversity of traditions within the church and affirms the value of non–Roman Catholic churches with particular liturgies, rules, and governing structures that increase the catholicity of the church (LG 13). *Gaudium et Spes* builds on *Lumen Gentium*'s endorsement of diversity, providing a more developed account of culture as integral to the identity of historically located persons as well as to their comprehension of the gospel message. The variety of cultures is one of the gifts of the world to the church, since it is through culture that Christians understand and probe more deeply the meaning of their faith (GS, esp. 53, 58). Appreciating the diverse cultures within the church, Christians should learn to value cultural diversity in society as well.

Lumen Gentium further elaborates on the unity-in-diversity appropriate to the church through its description of the relationship between pope and bishops as one of communion and collegiality. Bishops are not mere representatives of the pope; they are the ordinary pastors of their dioceses, with their own proper and immediate authority. Together the bishops form a college governing the whole church with the pope (LG 21–23). The church is not then accurately described as a single pyramid with the pope at the top but rather as a church of churches, or "a communion of communions," with multiple levels of community bonds and responsibility.[27] This global communion is represented by the college of bishops united with each other and with the pope, who is a member of the college as well as the head of that body. Indeed, as is suggested by the papal title *pontifex maximus* (great bridge), the papal ministry of guarding the unity of the church requires that the pope not stifle legitimate differences but rather, like a bridge, bring them into unity (LG 13).

Lumen Gentium also clarifies that ecclesial diversity, recognized and protected as essential to the organic unity of the church, includes a legitimate variety of viewpoints and opinions on temporal and spiritual matters. Such disagreement must not be suppressed or silenced. Instead, the church should be a place of dialogue in which differences of opinion are engaged with mutual respect and esteem. The laity have the freedom—indeed, at times the responsibility—to share their views about the good of the church with their pastors, and these concerns are to be received as a contribution rather than rejected as disobedience (LG 37).

As Gaillardetz and Clifford suggest, in this time of public polarization, an ecclesial practice of respectful, even loving, dialogue would be an important witness and a valuable contribution to

---

27. See the arguments in Markey, *Creating Communion*, 142–144; and J.-M. R Tillard, *Church of Churches: The Ecclesiology of Communion* (Collegeville, MN: Liturgical Press, 1992).

society.[28] Imagine what difference it might make if Christians truly approached disagreements—with each other or with non-Christians—as occasions for seeking greater understanding in conversations oriented toward love rather than vilification of the other. This might be the most prophetic, the most countercultural, and quite possibly the most difficult witness the church could provide today.

Of course, there are some differences that cannot be incorporated into the unity of the church but instead divide it. How does the church witness to unity-in-diversity in relation to disagreements on matters deemed essential to the church's life and vision?

This raises the issue of ecumenism, the search for unity among Christians who have separated from each other. Given the mission of the church to witness to and work for greater unity in the world, ecumenism is not merely a social nicety or political strategy but an essential matter of ecclesial mission. When the differences that should enrich the church instead divide the church, the Body of Christ is wounded by a failure of communion that impedes the church's ability to be either a compelling sign or a credible instrument of unity in society. Of course, this separation is an important reminder that the church too remains in need of the salvation that God offers the world through the church. However, and notwithstanding the church's obvious divisions, *Lumen Gentium* affirms that some degree of Christian unity abides because of the common baptism, shared essential beliefs, and the power of the Holy Spirit; all who share baptism and other essential beliefs are still part of the one Body of Christ (LG 15). While continuing to seek a deeper mutual understanding and a more complete union, Christians must persist in fostering the faith and love that unites them as one body, avoiding acrimony or mutual antagonism no matter how fundamental the disagreements between them.[29]

Unity-in-Diversity beyond the Church

As important as the prophetic witness of the church's unity-in-diversity is, the church has an additional responsibility to work for greater unity amid the differences that divide the world beyond the

---

28. Gaillardetz and Clifford, *Keys to the Council*, 100–101.
29. See also the more detailed reflection in Vatican II, The Decree on Ecumenism (*Unitatis Redintegratio*).

church. This involves strengthening human bonds within and across national boundaries, an aspect of the church's mission that *Gaudium et Spes* discusses at length. But this also, then, entails seeking greater unity with those who disagree with Christianity's fundamental religious beliefs. What does unity-in-diversity mean with regard to those who reject Jesus as the Christ, who do not believe in God, or who dismiss religion altogether?

Lumen Gentium again provides brief but significant statements on these issues, which are further developed in *Gaudium et Spes*, *Nostra Aetate*, and *Dignitatis Humanae*. These documents see no difficulty in maintaining the church's uncompromising witness to its beliefs while at the same time nurturing relationships of love and respect with those who disagree. In place of the common (if simplistic) assumption that the only available options are a dogmatic condemnation of others' views or a pluralism that takes no stand, Vatican II challenges all to seek the truth through respectful dialogue with one another.[30] Of course, this requires that we have enough in common to be able to dialogue, which we do because—as the council reminds us,—Christians believe that all of humanity shares a common origin and goal.[31] Such dialogue also presumes that everyone has some truth to contribute, which both *Lumen Gentium* and *Nostra Aetate* explicitly affirm: the goodness and truth that exist in non-Christian religions and among those who have no religion at all must be recognized and protected, even by the church.[32] Moreover—and this is key—unity-in-diversity is based not on intellectual agreement or commonality of opinion but on the dignity of the person and our need for one another.[33] Since the triune God is at work in the world to bring all into communion, the church must engage with all of humanity, cooperating with divine grace wherever it is encountered.

A more detailed account of what this means for the church as instrument of unity-in-diversity in the world is provided by *Gaudium et Spes*, with its focus on the church's relations with the world (*ad extra*). The signal contribution and guiding idea of *Gaudium et Spes* is the human being as person-in-community, a point central to

30. See *inter alia* NA 2; DH 3; GS 28.
31. NA 1; GS 12, 19.
32. LG 16; NA 2.
33. See esp. GS 12, 24; and DH 1, 11.

Catholic social teaching and integral to the principles of sociopolitical development elaborated in the latter half of *Gaudium et Spes* (GS 12). Christian revelation teaches that the person has irreducible dignity and value because he or she is made in the image of God, but also and especially because the person is destined for participation with others in the divine life (GS 19, 24, 32). Created for union with God and in the image of the relational Trinity, humans are inherently sacred and social, intended for interpersonal communion with each other in God. An individualistic ethic is therefore inadequate to the human person, who, while of infinite worth in him- or herself, is fulfilled only in relations to others (GS 24, 25, 30).

Here again we find an insistence on unity-in-diversity rather than uniformity: each person contributes uniquely to the enrichment of the community while at the same time achieving his or her selfhood only in and through a community of distinct persons. Thus, unity is not to be achieved in society (or in the church) by denying the rights and freedoms that accord with the dignity of the person, though the proper exercise of these rights requires that they be consistent with the ultimate good of the community that allows people to flourish.[34]

Christianity should, then, contribute to the public debate an unwavering support for the dignity of all persons as made for God and achieved in communion with others in God. To be sure, both the value of the person and the importance of community are often recognized by non-Christians, whether on the basis of other religious traditions or as discerned through reason and experience. Nevertheless, too often society (and sometimes the church) errs either by denying personal rights for the putative good of the whole or, more commonly in Western cultures, by reinforcing an individualism that neglects responsibility to the community. The witness of an uncompromising endorsement of the inviolable dignity of the person realized in community remains a valuable social corrective.

Secularity without Secularism

Recognition of the secularity of the world is integral to the church's public mission, especially as set forth in *Lumen Gentium*

---

34. GS 26–31; DH 4, 7.

as part of the dignity of the lay vocation and further developed in *Gaudium et Spes* and *Dignitatis Humanae*. These Vatican II documents endorse the legitimate autonomy of the temporal sphere, affirming that society is appropriately secular in the sense that it operates according to its own principles.[35] More simply put, divine revelation is not necessary for people to identify the essential requirements of a just and well-ordered society, because the Creator has made those requirements accessible to human reason. This embrace of reasoning is not a bracketing of Christianity but rather is consistent with Christian beliefs that a good God imbued creation with the principles for its development and gave humanity the reasoning capacity to discover those principles.

This secularity is defended as basic to the dignity of the lay vocation, which involves developing the expertise to direct society and to cultivate the world for the good of all. In this undertaking, the laity do not simply consult revelation or follow the clergy's instructions, because judgement about temporal affairs is proper to the vocational competence of the laity.[36] The church does not claim revealed or privileged knowledge about the specifics of how best to arrange society, organize politics, or structure the economy. Instead, these documents insist, it is the lay vocation to discern through reason and experience which solutions are most likely to increase human dignity in harmonious community, a task that can and must be done in coordination with non-Christians who contribute their own reason and experience to this shared endeavor.

Nevertheless, secularity as so understood does not mean that religion is a private matter irrelevant to politics or the common good of society. Such a privatized view of religion, sometimes called *secularism*, is condemned as a false assumption that "material being does not depend on God and that humanity can use it as if it had no relation to its creator" (GS 36). Secularism, or religious privatization, is unacceptable to the Catholic tradition and evidently contrary to the public and prophetic mission of the church as envisioned by Vatican II, which identifies work to increase unity in the world as integral to the purpose of the church.

---

35. LG 36; GS 36.
36. LG 36; GS 43.

If misinterpreted, this "secularity without secularism" may seem incoherent. On the one hand, the autonomy of society can be (mistakenly) understood as meaning that religion is irrelevant to society, a position that *Gaudium et Spes* clearly refuses with its lengthy discussions of the implications of Christianity for many aspects of social life. On the other hand, the rejection of secularism because the things of the world cannot be used apart from their end in God may be (again, mistakenly) interpreted as denying the proper autonomy of the temporal realm. If the things of the world must be used in accord with their end in God, does it not follow that revelation of that end is essential to the correct governance of the socioeconomic and political order? What then remains of the autonomy of the temporal sphere?

This dilemma disappears, however, if God's plan for the temporal "use of things" is evident in the principles internal to those things themselves, as affirmed by these documents. Christianity helps to clarify those principles insofar as they are related to creation's ultimate meaning and supernatural goal, but the principles for temporal flourishing can be discovered through reason and experience. While Vatican II thus encourages an open dialogue about the needs of society among all positions, including religious ones, this dialogue ultimately depends on appeals to reason and experience to determine what human flourishing means in this life and how the public realm is best organized to foster that flourishing.

To be more specific, *Gaudium et Spes* sets forth an understanding of Christian revelation as teaching the principle of persons-in-community, the belief that persons possess an inviolable dignity in themselves that is nevertheless oriented to and realized in harmony with others in society. Still, and despite the fact that this principle is obscured or neglected in society, one need not appeal to revelation to defend human dignity or to critique extreme individualism as detrimental to persons and to society. The supernatural end of everlasting communion within the divine life reinforces but surpasses the natural end of a good life with personal dignity in a relatively harmonious society. The natural end is discernible by reason; the supernatural end is based on a revelation that illuminates, but remains distinct from, the natural end.

The conciliar support for a secularity without secularism is not, then, inherently incoherent or nonsensical. It rejects the secularism that would privatize religion, barring Christianity and other faith positions from the public dialogue. As *Dignitatis Humanae* maintains, "religious groups [should] not . . . be prevented from freely demonstrating the special value of their teaching for the organization of society" (DH 4). At the same time, political debate is properly limited to the good of society and should not involve using political authority to compel explicitly religious beliefs or practices, which are matters governing authorities lack competence in, just as the clergy lack competence in the best ways to structure political and socioeconomic affairs (DH 3).

The council's affirmation of secularity, which makes possible its full endorsement of religious freedom in *Dignitatis Humanae*, is also fundamental to the church's mission to serve as an instrument of unity-in-diversity in the world. This mission cannot be disengaged from politics, yet there is no single or uniquely Christian politics. Furthermore, since an adequate grasp of the good of society is not dependent on divine revelation, the church can and must seek common ground through dialogue with others outside of the church. Society is appropriately secular because it is a meeting place of all regardless of religious belief; society is inappropriately secular, however, when religious values and perspectives are banned from the public discussion. Thus the church witnesses to a true unity-in-diversity by committing itself to working with all for greater harmony in society and in a world that includes not just Christians but all of humanity and, finally, all of creation.

The Church's Public Mission and the Challenges of the "Modern" World

Determining how the church can best fulfill its mission to work for greater unity-in-diversity requires attention to the context and situation of the world at the time. Although it has been over fifty years since *Gaudium et Spes* was written, the major challenges to the church's mission identified in this document remain significant issues today. Rapid change has continued, and the globalization that was already increasing connections between the world's populations during Vatican II has become a dominant reality. Inequality, oppression, and human division also remain. When we consider the advances in eradicating diseases and extreme poverty alongside the enormous injustice, violence, and suffering that continue, we must conclude that what *Gaudium et Spes* proclaimed in the mid-twentieth century remains true today: the "world . . . is at once powerful and weak, capable of doing what is noble and what is base, disposed to freedom and slavery, progress and decline, amity and hatred" (GS 9).

Somewhat surprisingly, *Gaudium et Spes* has been criticized for an undue optimism about human beings. In fact, as the above quotation suggests, the document takes sin quite seriously as the obstacle to unity and the reality from which we need redemption. Indeed, *Gaudium et Spes* addresses human sinfulness in each of its first four chapters, describing sin as a disruption of our communion with God, with each other, within ourselves, and with the natural world (GS 13, 25, 37, 41). Even though grace is at work in history to bring the world to redemption, *Gaudium et Spes* acknowledges that "human history . . . will be harassed by sin" until the final redemption at the end of history (GS 40).

Notwithstanding this attention to sin, *Gaudium et Spes* has an appropriately positive tone due to its belief in the goodness of creation and the presence of grace redeeming the world. While some have interpreted this positive attitude as evidence that the council was unduly influenced by a modern optimism about progress, I contend instead that the document is simply being faithful to the Catholic tradition: official Catholic teachings have long insisted that the goodness of creation remains despite the effects of original sin. While there is sin in the world, the world is not inherently or totally evil, nor is sinful humanity beyond redemption. To the contrary, God is at work in and through the church as well as beyond the church to save the world, a world that Christ entered "to save and not to judge, to serve and not to be served" (GS 3).

Part Two of *Gaudium et Spes* further specifies the prophetic and public role of the church by outlining Christian contributions on major issues of social concern, including marriage/family, culture, economics, politics, and global peace, all of which continue to be important topics in public theology. As should be expected, the discussion of each dimension of society is informed by the Christian belief that the fulfillment of human life is communion with one another in God. While I cannot here do justice to the nuanced social teachings developed in these chapters of *Gaudium et Spes*, a brief look at some of the key insights in each area will clarify the meaning and significance of the church's sacramental mission to be a sign and instrument of unity in the contemporary world.

No one is likely to be surprised that *Gaudium et Spes* considers marriage to be an important concern of the church. Marriage is at the same time a fundamental social institution and one that appears to be particularly vulnerable in Western society, as divorce rates are high, new forms of marriage are being experimented with, and many are opting out of marriage altogether. The council fathers had good reason to insist that a significant element in the church's witness to persons-in-community is the understanding and practice of marriage as a communion of life between two people who pledge themselves to each other in mutual self-gift (GS 49). This is a major testimony to the goal of persons-in-community, and one that takes place at a most fundamental level of personal commitment.

Important questions remain, of course, about official ecclesial assumptions that heteronormativity is integral to the divine plan. This is a topic on which much further thought and discussion are needed.[37] Nevertheless, the practice of marriage as a commitment of life for the good of the other and of the new family remains a profound witness against the self-centered and recreational approach to sexuality that is so widespread in Western society (GS 47).

At the same time, this vision of marriage as mutual self-gift between two people recognized as having equal dignity also challenges the patriarchal marriage that has dominated much of human history and is still too common today. Women are not property to be traded among men; a true communion of life consistent with the dignity of all human persons requires that adult women make a free choice

---

37. Within the extensive literature on this topic, see especially Margaret A. Farley, *Just Love: A Framework for Christian Sexual Ethics* (New York: Continuum, 2006); Richard R. Gaillardetz, *A Daring Promise: A Spirituality of Christian Marriage* (Liguori, MO: Liguori Publications, 2007); Emily Reimer-Barry, *Catholic Theology of Marriage in the Era of HIV and AIDS: Marriage for Life* (Lanham, MD: Rowman and Littlefield, 2015); and Francis, On Love in the Family (*Amoris Laetitia*), https://w2.vatican.va/content/dam/francesco/pdf/apost_exhortations/documents/papa-francesco_esortazione-ap_20160319_amoris-laetitia_en.pdf.

to enter into a marriage (GS 48–49). This hardly sounds radical, yet in many areas of the world and even in some parts of the United States, girls who have not yet completed their early teens can be pressured into legally valid marriages.[38] Emphasizing the equal personal dignity of wife and husband, and elevating the "unitive" aspect of marriage to the level of a primary purpose of marriage, *Gaudium et Spes* confirms the importance of the communion between the married couple as a sign and instrument of harmony in the world.[39]

Turning next to the topic of culture, *Gaudium et Spes* calls all, including the church, to foster the diversity of cultures as an enrichment of human communion. Culture is here recognized as integral to the historical, social, and spiritual dimensions of the person. No mere means of expression, culture is constitutive of how we understand ourselves, the world, and even the Gospel (GS 53). *Gaudium et Spes* thus warns against the global homogenization—or what we might call the "McDonaldization"—that imposes a uniform culture to the detriment of the rich particularity of cultural diversity (GS 56). It is no easy task to protect the wisdom of local cultures, especially given the power of global capitalism, and alas *Gaudium et Spes* does not tell us precisely how to do this. More intent on providing a vision than a plan of action, this document also fails to clarify what steps the church must take to overcome its own habits of colonization in order to celebrate cultural diversity as a contribution to the church, which, as the story of Pentecost indicates and Vatican II confirms, is not tied to any one culture but is intended to be equally at home in all cultures (GS 58).[40]

---

38. See the stories and legal statutes discussed in Nicholas Kristof, "An American 13-Year-Old, Pregnant and Married to Her Rapist," *New York Times*, June 1, 2018, https://www.nytimes.com/2018/06/01/opinion/sunday/child-marriage-delaware.html.

39. See especially note 168 in Abbott, *Documents*, 254, as well as GS 49–50.

40. Further development in the theology of culture is provided *inter alia* by Orlando O. Espín, *Grace and Humanness: Theological Reflections because of Culture* (Maryknoll, NY: Orbis, 2007); Diego Irarrázaval, *Inculturation: New Dawn of the Church in Latin America* (Maryknoll, NY: Orbis, 2000); and Peter C. Phan, *In Our Own Tongues: Perspectives from Asia on Mission and Inculturation* (Maryknoll, NY: Orbis, 2003). For an example of the theological opposition

In addressing its third major topic of contemporary concern, socioeconomic issues, *Gaudium et Spes* clearly and unapologetically ventures into territory that continues to strike many Christians as beyond the proper concerns of religion. Rather than accepting the modern ideological contention that an unfettered profit motive will automatically provide the best economic outcome, the council fathers emphasize society's responsibility to organize and direct the economy for the good of all. An economy that enriches the few while leaving many in need is an unacceptable injustice and a violation of the communion God intends for humanity (GS 64, 69). Justice demands that action be taken "to put an end as soon as possible to the immense economic inequalities which exist in the world, which increase daily" (GS 66). Moreover, the undue dominance of the profit motive so common in capitalism is consistent with neither the dignity of the person nor the welfare of society. Aware of the tendency for the modern economy to supplant all other values, the council fathers reject the preoccupation with seeking economic benefit to the detriment of other aspects of human development, including spiritual growth (GS 63).

Gaudium et Spes further maintains that, in an economy that fosters true human dignity, labor will take precedence over capital. After all, people matter more than things. Furthermore, work is a right and a responsibility, since it is through work that people develop and express themselves as well as contribute to the good of society (GS 67). Working to increase human well-being is a key aspect of the development of persons-in-community.

In an important note of realism, *Gaudium et Spes* endorses the right of laborers not only to organize but also to strike when necessary to achieve just working conditions (GS 68). The goal of a harmonious community in which differences are resolved through dialogue and for the good of all remains, of course, the ideal. To the extent possible, workers and owners should strive together for outcomes that are fair to all. But the council fathers acknowledge that the ideal of mutual cooperation is not always achievable, and true communion is not built by accepting injustice in the name of harmony. In this imperfect world,

---

to *Gaudium et Spes's* theology of culture, see Tracey Rowland, *Culture and the Thomist Tradition: After Vatican II* (New York: Routledge, 2003).

agonistic activity is sometimes required to interrupt an unjust status quo. The ultimate aim of such struggle, however, must always be to move toward a more perfect mutuality rather than simply to gain power at the expense of the other.[41]

Gaudium et Spes's treatment of the importance of justice in socioeconomic institutions lays the foundation for the document's subsequent discussion of politics and its role in serving the common good. The document continues the Catholic tradition of affirming that political authority is an appropriate and even essential aspect of human society. In contrast to some Christian views of politics as a necessary evil to constrain sinners, this Catholic approach maintains that government is a good that enables the coordination of human activity in community (GS 74). In this Catholic perspective, given the social nature of persons oriented to communion, political authority would have existed even in a world without sin, though of course the human inclination to sin makes political authority all the more necessary.

But *Gaudium et Spes* does more than reiterate established Catholic teachings about political authority. Reflecting further on the dignity of the person and the orientation to community, the council fathers clarify Catholic teaching with regard to personal rights and the importance of citizens' participation in their government. Consistent with the dignity of the person, who has the obligation and so the right to seek the truth freely and through honest dialogue, *Gaudium et Spes* repeats John XXIII's support for freedom of religion and expression, thus clearly ending the teaching that those deemed in error have no right to express that error publicly (GS 73).[42] This right to religious freedom is more thoroughly defended, of course, in *Dignitatis Humanae*, which further emphasizes the importance of

---

41. Further developments in the church's concern for equitable economic development will be discussed in chapter 4 of this work.

42. See also John XXIII, On Establishing Universal Peace in Truth, Justice, Charity, and Liberty (*Pacem in Terris*), 13, 14, http://w2.vatican.va/content/john-xxiii/en/encyclicals/documents/hf_j-xxiii_enc_11041963_pacem.html. See also Richard P. McBrien, *Caesar's Coin: Religion and Politics in America* (New York: Macmillan, 1987); and the succinct discussion of the Catholic debates over religious freedom before Vatican II in Robert McClory, *Faithful Dissenters: Stories of Men and Women Who Loved and Changed the Church* (Maryknoll, NY: Orbis, 2000), 7–24.

an open and free dialogue in the social search for truth, while also clarifying that religious freedom is not an absolute right but one that can and should be limited by the government in accordance with public order and the norms of justice (DH 2, 4, 7).

Gaudium et Spes's unequivocal support for participatory politics is especially notable since official Catholic teaching began to accept democracy only in the twentieth century. While insisting that the church is not tied to any particular political system, *Gaudium et Spes* nevertheless endorses those forms of government in which all citizens are able to participate in establishing their government and in voting for the common good. The document also affirms the church's commitment to participatory community by reminding citizens that they have a "right and duty to promote the common good by casting their votes" (GS 75). The principle of subsidiarity is implicitly affirmed in the caution against higher levels of governmental authority assuming responsibility for matters that can be better handled at local levels and by those most immediately affected (GS 75).

Finally, *Gaudium et Spes* takes up the challenge of global relations and the need for world peace. In a world that is both increasingly interconnected and in possession of devastatingly destructive modern weapons, the universal community that the church witnesses to—and that God intends for humanity—must not be neglected. The church's mission to unite cannot be satisfied by any form of tribal unity, whether that is within the church or within the life of one's nation or state, since the desired eschatological communion encompasses all the peoples of the world (GS 92).

Gaudium et Spes's discussion of international relations includes some somber notes of realism along with its inspiring ideal of global communion. The document acknowledges that, due to the reality of human sin, peace will never be perfectly or finally achieved within history, but must be struggled for in all times and by all peoples (GS 78). Particular attention must be given to remedying injustice and inequality, which are themselves forms of violence as well as provocations to violence (GS 77, 78). Solutions to problems of dire poverty usually require international cooperation because nations are seldom able to resolve these issues alone. Furthermore, *Gaudium et Spes* reminds us, the most well-off nations have greater resources and so also a greater responsibility to assist impoverished peoples

(GS 86). From the Catholic perspective of commitment to global communion, no nation can rightly claim that the suffering of human beings elsewhere is not its concern. Here, then, the same principle of subsidiarity that protects local communities from unnecessary intrusions by centralized authority demands that higher levels, and even international agencies, step in when they are needed (GS 83).

Through its discussion of these five areas of the church's social mission, *Gaudium et Spes* specifies the church's public and prophetic mission in important ways. Christians should not strive only for communities of unity-in-diversity within the church, as important as that is, but must also work to extend that unity in the world in ways that contribute to the flourishing of all humanity. There is much to be done to ensure that marriages are strengthened, cultural diversity is valued, the economy is structured to serve the genuine welfare of all, political systems protect personal freedoms and participatory community, and the international community works together to solve the world's ongoing problems peacefully and with justice. This was the case in 1965, when the world's population was about 3.5 billion; it is even more the case now, as the world's population nears 8 billion.

Global Developments in Post–Vatican II Ecclesiology

An adequate treatment of the advances in ecclesiology in the more than fifty years since the close of Vatican II is far beyond the scope of our project here. Nevertheless, it is important to note briefly some of the major developments around the world, as these continue the trajectory set by Vatican II's account of the church's public and prophetic mission, while at the same time clarifying the depth of the challenges to this mission to be a witnessing sign and an instrument of harmonious community in society. Karl Rahner famously hailed Vatican II as the beginning of a truly world church, and indeed many of the deepest insights since the council have come from non-Eurocentric perspectives rooted in greater attention to the theological significance of widespread poverty and the necessity and difficulty of a noncolonial inculturation of the church.[43]

---

43. Karl Rahner, "Towards a Fundamental Theological Interpretation of Vatican Council II," *Theological Studies* 40 (1979): 718.

Latin American Liberation Theology

The development of the church's commitment to the poor was furthered by the 1968 Conference of Latin American Bishops (CELAM) meeting in Medellín, Colombia, and the development of Latin American liberation theology.[44] Striving to be a church of and for the poor, many in Latin America took up *Gaudium et Spes*'s challenge to consider the struggle against poverty and injustice to be integral to the mission of the church. Recognizing that God opts for the poor, the pioneers of Latin American liberation theology argued that the church too must opt for the poor and, in fact, become a church of and for the poor. If the church is to be a sign as well as an instrument of justice and liberation for the poor, then the poor must be subjects in the church as well as in society. As Leonardo Boff has notably argued in his liberation ecclesiology, the communion of persons in the Trinity is a model for a participatory community in church as well as society.[45]

One of the most energizing, if sometimes exaggerated, developments in Latin American ecclesiology is the *comunidades de base*, or ecclesial base communities. This movement, begun in part as a response to the lack of priests in the institutional church, evolved a structure of small, face-to-face communities that focused on growth in discipleship through prayer or Bible readings and social activism. As Michelle González has noted, these base communities brought the church closer to people's lives and strengthened community among the laity while also (and contrary to much criticism) increasing their connection to the institutional church.[46]

This ecclesial commitment to justice for the poor amid great economic inequality was apparently threatening enough to the established power structures that, especially in the decades following

---

44. Gustavo Gutiérrez, *A Theology of Liberation: History, Politics, and Salvation* (Maryknoll, NY: Orbis, 1988); William T. Cavanaugh, "The Ecclesiologies of Medellín and the Lessons of the Base Communities," *Cross Currents* 44, no. 1 (Spring 1994): 67–84; Roger Haight, *Christian Community in History*, vol. 2, *Comparative Ecclesiology* (New York: Continuum, 2005), 408–17; Michelle A. González, "Latin American Liberation Theology," in *The Oxford Handbook of Ecclesiology*, ed. Paul Avis (Oxford, UK: Oxford University Press, 2018), 583–93.

45. Leonardo Boff, *Trinity and Society* (Maryknoll, NY: Orbis, 1988).

46. González, "Latin American Liberation Ecclesiology," 584. See also Haight, *Comparative Ecclesiology*, 416–17.

Vatican II, the powerful defended their privileges with violence directed even against church leaders. El Salvador in particular suffered the martyrdom of its archbishop, St. Óscar Romero, and several of its priests and nuns, along with the many laypersons who sought justice and a more equitable society. Fr. Jon Sobrino, who survived the massacre of his Jesuit community because he happened to be away, has continued to argue that a church that follows its crucified Lord will risk itself on behalf of the suffering, crucified peoples of Latin America.[47]

A more recent development in Latin American ecclesiology involves appreciation for popular religious expressions and indigenous cultural traditions. Rather than continuing to reject popular religiosity as a distortion or failure of catechesis, more recently church leaders and theologians have endorsed an inculturation that is less dismissive of indigenous culture and of non-Eurocentric forms of Christianity. The development of an Afro-Brazilian style of worship in the Brazilian Catholic Church and the encouragement of rituals appropriate to the indigenous culture in Chiapas, Mexico, are examples of the inculturation that is essential to the unity-in-diversity the church espouses.[48]

Ecclesiologies in Asia

The ecclesiological challenges in Asia have been described similarly as comprising the three issues of liberation of the poor, inculturation, and interreligious dialogue.[49] As in Latin America, many countries in Asia experience widespread and often extreme poverty. This has led in Korea to the development of minjung theology, a theology that seeks to place the perspective of the masses of people

---

47. Jon Sobrino, *Witness to the Kingdom: The Martyrs of El Salvador and the Crucified Peoples* (Maryknoll, NY: Orbis, 2003).
48. González, "Latin American Liberation Ecclesiology," 588–89.
49. Simon Chan, "Asian Ecclesiologies," in *The Oxford Handbook of Ecclesiology*, ed. Paul Avis (Oxford, UK: Oxford University Press, 2018), 595–615; Peter C. Phan, "A Church in the Service of the Reign of God: Prophetic Dimensions of an Asian Ecclesiology," *Zeitschrift für Missionswissenschaft und Religionswissenschaft* 95 (2011): 104–15, esp. 108. See also Kwok Pui-lan, *Introducing Asian Feminist Theology* (Cleveland: Pilgrim Press, 2000), 98–112; and Norlan H. Julia, "Beyond Basic Ecclesial Communities (BECs): Challenges to the Reception of Communio Ecclesiology in Asia," *Landas* 26, no. 1 (2012): 127–38.

(*minjung*) rather than that of the elites at the heart of the church. Dalit theology in India has also arisen as a theological reflection from the perspective of the oppressed, so-called untouchable peoples.

An ongoing challenge for the church in Asia is to foster truly Asian forms of church that are not merely transplants of Eurocentric ecclesial practices. In particular, the church must learn how to be church in a way that is genuinely Christian while also being appropriate to cultures in which religion has traditionally been family based and the primary locus of religious life has been the home. When is the focus on being called out to form a new community a liberating act of the Spirit, and when is it a rejection of the centrality of the family that is central to Asian culture and a means of resistance to Western individualism?[50]

It is never simple to negotiate the tensions inherent in the demand for the church to be both public and prophetic, to engage cultures and societies positively but also critically. Certainly ancestral veneration is an element in the Asian focus on family that could enrich the Christian faith, especially in its appreciation of the communion of saints. Peter Phan points also to Asian insistence on the inseparability of yin and yang as a contribution to Christian understanding of the indispensability of diversity in any ecclesial unity.[51]

Another of the notable factors influencing Asian ecclesiology is that Christianity is a minority religion in most of Asia. Fostering interreligious cooperation and mutual respect is a daily practice when Christians are a minority and continually interact with non-Christians. Phan contends that this minority status has made Asian churches more outwardly directed and accustomed to collaboration with other religious traditions.[52] The church in Asia might then serve as a model of how to be a public church, seeking unity with non-Christians and engaging together with others in the transformation of society.

Ecclesiologies in Africa

Many of the issues the church has faced in Latin America and in Asia are also central to the church in Africa. Small Christian communities, for example, have emerged here too as a viable structure

---

50. Chan, "Asian Ecclesiologies," 597–98.
51. Phan, "Church in the Service," 114–15.
52. Phan, "Church in the Service," 108, 115.

through which the African church can be more thoroughly part of the lives of the people. The regional (Catholic) bishops of East Africa thus made the development of small Christian communities "a cornerstone" of their plans for the church in 1973, and there were over 110,000 Roman Catholic small Christian communities in Africa in 2012.[53]

Inculturation is also an ongoing concern here, especially as the Catholic Church continues to handle the affairs of the church in Africa through the Congregation for the Evangelization of Peoples, suggesting that the church in Africa is a dependent, or mission, church, despite its long tradition and enormous contributions to the development of Christianity.[54] Here as elsewhere, a Eurocentric church tends to suspect that non-European cultural forms will be inappropriate to the Gospel, thus imposing a cultural uniformity in place of the officially endorsed diversity. Given that many African Christians continue to find traditional African religious rituals more spiritually adequate for dealing with liminal situations and death, there is much work to be done to discern—and gain acceptance of—fully African forms of Christianity.[55]

One of the most inspiring African ecclesiologies is that of Fr. Elochukwu Uzukwu. Uzukwu contends that, in the African context, there is a pressing need to reconstruct human rights and democracy on the basis of the relational notion of the person and with the church as a model of respecting human rights.[56] The church's commitment to persons-in-community could thus be an important force in creating just African political structures that honor human rights while resisting Western individualism. Drawing on the Manja tribal tradition of the chief as the one with big ears who listens to all before speaking, Uzukwu defends a listening style of ecclesial leadership that truly respects the gift of the Spirit given to the whole people of God.[57]

---

53. Haight, *Comparative Ecclesiology*, 417–19; Stan Chu Ilo, "African Ecclesiologies," in *The Oxford Handbook of Ecclesiology*, ed. Paul Avis (Oxford, UK: Oxford University Press, 2018), 615–35.

54. Ilo, "African Ecclesiologies," 623.

55. Ilo, "African Ecclesiologies," 631.

56. Elochukwu E. Uzukwu, *A Listening Church: Autonomy and Communion in African Churches* (Maryknoll, NY: Orbis, 1996), 35.

57. Uzukwu, *Listening Church*, 127–30.

Many have suggested that the role of the African clan in particular has much to offer Christian ecclesiology. Mercy Amba Oduyoye draws on women's experience of mutual care and communion established through feeding to propose that the church be seen as the "hearth-hold" (i.e., all who are gathered and fed around this hearth) of Christ within the universal hearth-hold of God.[58] Uzukwu further suggests that the collegial communion envisioned between the pope and bishops in *Lumen Gentium* 23 is modeled in Africa by the eldest brother in the clan, who exercises concern for family harmony but refrains from meddling in the affairs of adult family members.[59]

Race and Culture in the United States

The decades following Vatican II have been an especially lively period for theology in North America. At the same time that liberation theology was developing in Latin America, James Cone was beginning black liberation theology in the United States. Cone argues that if God sides with the poor, then God is black, in solidarity with those oppressed because of their race in the United States.[60]

Bryan Massingale has more recently criticized the Catholic Church in the United States for its (often unconscious) self-identity as a white institution that marginalizes its nonwhite members. Since race is entangled with nearly every social problem in the United States, the church cannot truly be a church in solidarity with the poor and oppressed without relinquishing its own white privilege. Here again, we are reminded that to be an instrument of liberation and justice in society, the church must witness the inclusive unity it proclaims.[61]

Another major contribution is the development of Latinx (earlier known as US Hispanic) theology along with its rich ecclesiological

---

58. Mercy Amba Oduyoye, *Introducing African Women's Theology* (Cleveland: Pilgrim Press, 2001), 78–89.

59. Uzukwu, *Listening Church*, 142–43.

60. See especially James H. Cone, *A Black Theology of Liberation* (Philadelphia: Lippincott, 1970).

61. Bryan N. Massingale, *Racial Justice and the Catholic Church* (Maryknoll, NY: Orbis, 2010). Agbonkhianmeghe E. Orobator, SJ, reminds us that racism is a global issue in his "The Struggle against Racism and the Global Horizon of Christian Hope," in *Ecclesiology and Exclusion: Boundaries of Being and Belonging in Postmodern Times*, ed. Dennis M. Doyle, Timothy J. Furry, and Pascal D. Bazzell (Maryknoll, NY: Orbis, 2012), 125–29.

insights. The Anglo-identified US Catholic Church marginalizes not only black Catholics but also its near majority of Spanish-speaking members and their hybrid US–Latin American cultures. Virgilio Elizondo draws on the devotion to the mestiza image of Our Lady of Guadalupe in his argument that the church, called to witness to unity-in-diversity, must follow the Galilean Jesus in locating itself among the culturally and racially mixed people who are often rejected as impure by both of their parent cultures.[62] Proceeding from a commitment to Vatican II's definition of the church as the people of God, Orlando Espín's theology of tradition is centered on the *sensus fidelium* of ordinary Latinx peoples, in opposition to the idolatry of certain, fixed doctrines removed from people's experiences of the ultimately undefinable divine mystery.[63] Natalia Imperatori-Lee similarly defends an ecclesiology that seeks universality through deep particularity and an inductive, bottom-up approach that includes everyday Latinx experiences of what it means to be church.[64] Other contributions of Latinx theology include the emphasis on beauty, fiesta (celebration), and justice as integral to a Christian ecclesiology that truly celebrates the joys and hopes of all people.[65]

Pentecostalism and Women

Two significant developments in Christian ecclesiology are found throughout the world: the emergence of Pentecostalism and of women's voices. Pentecostalism is growing in Latin America, Asia, and Africa, offering a less structured form of Christianity that is

---

62. Virgilio P. Elizondo, *Galilean Journey: The Mexican-American Promise* (Maryknoll, NY: Orbis, 1983); and Virgilio P. Elizondo, *Guadalupe: Mother of the New Creation* (Maryknoll, NY: Orbis, 1997).

63. In addition to Espín, *Grace and Humanness*, see also Orlando O. Espín and Gary Macy, eds., *Futuring Our Past: Explorations in the Theology of Tradition* (Maryknoll, NY: Orbis, 2006).

64. Natalia Imperatori-Lee, *Cuéntame: Narrative in the Ecclesial Present* (Maryknoll, NY: Orbis, 2018).

65. Roberto S. Goizueta, *Caminemos con Jesús: Toward a Theology of Accompaniment* (Maryknoll, NY: Orbis, 1995). See also his article "Fiesta: Life in the Subjunctive," in *From the Heart of Our People: Latino/a Explorations in Catholic Systematic Theology*, ed. Orlando O. Espín and Miguel H. Díaz (Maryknoll, NY: Orbis, 1999), 84–99.

often more open to local cultural expressions along with strong community bonds and intense religious experiences.[66] The dynamism of Christian Pentecostal churches reveals the widespread hunger for religious community and less constrained religiosity. For the more structured forms of Christianity such as the Catholic Church, the strength of Pentecostalism is a challenging reminder that the institution must find ways to nurture local faith communities rather than stifle them.

Another global development in the decades following Vatican II has been the demand for attention to women's voices and experiences in theology and the church. Feminist ecclesiologies around the world are arguing for the full inclusion of women, whose voices are often marginalized from church leadership and decision-making, and whose experiences have been absent from the theological tradition until recently.[67] No true communion is possible without greater mutuality between women and men, beginning with the full inclusion of women in both church and society.

Conclusion

As these global movements and critiques indicate, the church is nowhere living its mission perfectly. This is not surprising; it is an article of faith that the goal of harmonious communion will be found in its completion only in the eschaton. In the meantime, the members of the church stand in need of the same redemption that the church is called to bring to the world. The church is not a gathering of the perfect but rather, as the Jesuit tradition acknowledges, a community of sinners called to be in the company of Jesus.

---

66. See especially Haight, *Comparative Ecclesiology*, 452–77; González, "Latin American Liberation Ecclesiology," 488–590; and Chan, "Asian Ecclesiologies," 610–11.

67. The literature here is vast. For a starting point, in addition to the works of Haight, González, and Chan, I recommend especially Natalie K. Watson, *Introducing Feminist Ecclesiology* (Cleveland: Pilgrim Press, 2002); Letty M. Russell, *Church in the Round: Feminist Interpretations of the Church* (Louisville, KY: Westminster/John Knox, 1993); and McBrien, *The Church*, 337–42.

Yet communion is never completely lacking in the church either. God's grace continues to empower mutual love and care within and beyond the church. The point is neither to deny the sinfulness and failures through which we know our need for God, nor to despair of the power of God's grace to overcome our limitations and continue to heal the church and the world.

There are many, many ways in which the church has fallen short of its mission to embody the loving communion it has been called to bring to the world. The clergy sexual abuse scandal—within and beyond the Catholic Church—is one such failure, and an egregious one. This scandal reminds us that internal reforms, including structures of mutual accountability and greater transparency, continue to be necessary to the church's ability to serve its mission as the loving, if imperfect, communion it is called to be. Too often and in more ways than can be recounted here, the church has witnessed to authoritarian uniformity rather than loving unity-in-diversity. Acceptance of our sin and our inclination to sin, within and as church, is integral to the church's function as sign and instrument of greater (but never perfect) harmony in the world.

Our focus here, however, will be on two major failures with regard to unity-in-diversity that have plagued the church from its beginnings and have continued to distort the development of the church throughout its history: religious anti-Semitism and misogyny. Both are already present in the New Testament, and both have become interwoven with essential church beliefs and practices to the extent that these distortions cannot be fully repudiated without considerable effort to disentangle them from fundamental aspects of ecclesial life. With its anti-Judaism, the church fails to embody loving unity-in-diversity with those outside of the church, denying any valid Jewish difference and seeking with sometimes lethal consequences to absorb Jews within the church. With its misogyny, the church fails to embody loving unity-in-diversity within the church, as the male gender is taken as the normative Christian identity against which women's sexual identity is measured and found inadequate to full membership in the church.

Before turning to the unprecedented challenges to—and opportunities for—genuine unity in the diverse twenty-first century, the church must first attend to its two primary failures to envision and embody the mutual community it proclaims. The church cannot witness to unity-in-diversity within the church without affirming the full membership of its women; the church cannot witness to unity-in-diversity with those outside the church until it makes theological room for the difference of Judaism, the church's principal other. It is to these challenges that we now turn, first to the need to rethink the church's relationship to Judaism and to Jews (chapter 2) and then to the project of overcoming the devaluing of women within Christianity (chapter 3).

Chapter 2

Overcoming Religious Anti-Semitism

Communion with the Church's External Other

A short story I once read began with a small Christian boy casually mentioning to his father that he and his friends had taunted and chased away a little Jewish boy who wanted to join their play that afternoon. The father, visibly alarmed, jumped up from his desk and demanded to know where the Jewish boy was last seen. If they hurried, the father said, perhaps they could find the boy and beg his forgiveness before it was too late. So off the father and child ran, up and down the streets of the neighborhood, searching unsuccessfully until finally darkness fell and the Christian boy was ready to drop with exhaustion. As they returned home in failure, the father sadly explained to his son that tormenting one of God's chosen people was a most serious offense. After putting his boy to bed, the father advised his wife that their son might sleep poorly and be a bit feverish that night. This was to be expected, the father said, since the boy had just that day been inoculated against a most serious virus—Christian anti-Semitism.[1]

---

1. I am retelling the story here as I remember it. Unfortunately, I have been unable after much searching to locate a written copy or source for this story.

This story is fictitious, at least as far as I know. Yet it raises challenging questions: what if Christians took seriously the biblically based claim that the Jewish people are God's chosen people, bound to God in an everlasting covenant? What if, rather than seizing on Jewish otherness as an occasion to reaffirm Christian superiority and even to persecute Jews, Christians had revered the people whose religious fidelity made possible the Christian faith?

Flipping on its head the longstanding Christian portrayal of Judaism as a contagious disease, this story rightly describes contempt for Jews as a persistent and grave Christian sickness. Indeed, religious anti-Semitism is not only a deep distortion of Christian faith but one that has dangerous, even lethal, consequences for Jews.[2] In the two millennia of Christianity's existence, Jews living in Christian-dominated societies have faced onerous restrictions, additional taxes, appropriation of their property, beatings, expulsion, murder, even genocide—and have had few legally protected rights. This oppression has been justified, even by some of the most revered Christian authorities, as an appropriate expression of Christianity.

The twentieth-century Nazi Holocaust of six million Jews was not, strictly speaking, a Christian program. The ideology of the Nazi Party incorporated elements of paganism, racism, and eugenics at odds with official Christianity. But Christianity is not thereby released from responsibility. Many of the perpetrators of the Holocaust were Christians in good standing with their churches, and centuries of explicitly Christian anti-Semitism paved the way for Nazi anti-Semitism.[3] Key Christian teachings have maligned Jewish

---

2. "Anti-Semitism" is commonly used for the denigration of or hostility to Jews, while "anti-Judaism" refers to denigration of or hostility to the religion and religious practices of Judaism. However, as I argue here, these two phenomena are too intertwined in most cases to be separable, especially in the history of Christianity. The term "religious anti-Semitism" is intended to express the interrelated reality of contempt for Jews and for Judaism, though my preference for the term "anti-Judaism" is due to my focus on the role of anti-Judaism in reinforcing contempt for Jews.

3. See *inter alia* Robert M. Selzer, *Jewish People, Jewish Thought: The Jewish Experience in History* (New York: Macmillan, 1980), esp. 661–71; Jack Bemporad, John T. Pawlikowski, and Joseph Sievers, eds., *Good and Evil after Auschwitz: Ethical Implications for Today* (Hoboken, NJ: KTAV, 2000); Judith H. Banki and

people as well as their beliefs and practices, while mainstream Christian churches continued well into the twentieth century to propagate pernicious stereotypes of Jewish people as greedy and evil, opponents of God, and a danger to Western society. As suggested by Jules Isaac's 1964 groundbreaking work on the teaching of contempt, the Christian tradition has represented Jews as *demonic* members of a *degenerate* religion who were *dispersed* from Jerusalem and *dismissed* from the covenant for their sin of *deicide*.[4] Without this history of Christian contempt for Jews, the ready acceptance of Nazi anti-Semitism, especially by so many German Christians, makes little sense.[5]

Those of us who are Christian might well ask, How did we get here? We follow a Jewish messiah, worship a Jewish God, pray with Jewish psalms, and honor as revealed the sacred writings of the Jewish Scriptures. One might expect Christians to revere Judaism as the foundation of their religion. Yet instead the Christian tradition has identified Judaism with spiritual blindness, evil, and opposition to God. How can it be that the Jewish people, who gave to Christianity its monotheism, the larger part of its Bible, Jesus, his mother, and the earliest disciples, are portrayed in classic Christian texts—including the New Testament—as demonic conspirators who oppose God and corrupt society? Are they not rather our spiritual benefactors whose struggle through millennia to remain

---

John T. Pawlikowski, eds., *Ethics in the Shadow of the Holocaust* (Chicago: Sheed and Ward, 2001), esp. 103–16; and Robert A. Krieg, *Catholic Theologians in Nazi Germany* (New York: Continuum, 2004).

4. Jules Isaac, *The Teaching of Contempt: Christian Roots of Anti-Semitism*, trans. Helen Weaver (New York: Holt, Rinehart, and Winston), 1964. See also the discussion of these "five Ds" as summarized in Elena Procario-Foley, "Liberating Jesus: Christian Feminism and Anti-Judaism," in *Frontiers in Catholic Feminist Theology: Shoulder to Shoulder*, ed. Susan Abraham and Elena Procario-Foley (Minneapolis: Fortress, 2009), 97–118.

5. See the discussion of German and Austrian Catholics, their religious anti-Semitic education, and their participation in Nazi politics and the Shoah in Robert Michael, *A History of Catholic Antisemitism: The Dark Side of the Church* (New York: Palgrave Macmillan, 2008), 112–14. See also the nuanced discussions in Kevin P. Spicer, ed., *Antisemitism, Christian Ambivalence, and the Holocaust* (Bloomington, IN: Indiana University Press, 2007).

faithful to their ancient covenant with God is a great witness and gift to the world, including to the Christian tradition?

The deeply regrettable reality is that, even while building on Jewish beliefs, texts, and practices, Christian identity has been constructed in opposition to Judaism and to Jews.[6] From its earliest days, the church found it helpful to define Christianity over against Judaism and to define what a Christian is by defining the Jew as what the Christian is not. Long before modernity began to defend the mastery of the normative, "white" Man over "his" devalued raced, sexed, and animal other, Christians learned to understand themselves as the inverse of their Jewish other, whom Christians described as the bestial opponent not only of God but also of Christian civilization.[7]

It should be obvious that Christians cannot fulfill their ecclesial mission to unite creation in its diversity without coming to terms with this long Christian history of rejecting, often violently, the difference embodied in Judaism and in Jewish people. How can the church be a credible prophetic voice against the world's divisions if some Christian beliefs and practices still—at least implicitly—malign the church's primary religious other? Will not the world respond to the church as forewarned in Matthew 7:5: "You hypocrite, first take the log out of your own eye, and then you will see clearly to take the speck out of your neighbor's eye"?

The ecclesiological issue here is not merely that Christians have failed, rather egregiously, to live up to the demands of their faith. The problem is more deeply rooted: Christianity has defined itself as having gotten right what Judaism, the abject other, got wrong. Although some may see this as simply an affirmation of Christian faith, I will argue that it is an obstacle to the church's mission: Christians cannot appropriately represent God's will for unity-in-diversity at the same time they are denigrating, even at times de-

---

6. This thesis is developed masterfully in David Nirenberg, *Anti-Judaism: The Western Tradition* (New York: W. W. Norton, 2013) but is presented clearly and concisely in the much earlier Rosemary Radford Ruether, *Faith and Fratricide: The Theological Roots of Anti-Semitism* (New York: Seabury, 1974).

7. Ellen T. Armour, *Signs and Wonders: Theology after Modernity* (New York: Columbia University Press, 2016).

monizing, the Jewish difference from Christianity. If the church is not able to make theological room for its Jewish other, the church will be neither a good model nor an effective agent of harmony amid the world's differences.

Overcoming Christian anti-Semitism is no easy task. Contempt for Jews and for Judaism is present throughout Christian history, in the thought of the greatest Christian thinkers, and even in the sacred writings of the New Testament, as will be explored below.

Indeed, anti-Judaism is so entrenched in Christianity that describing anti-Semitism as a Christian disease, as in the above story, may not be a strong enough metaphor. Contempt for Jews is more appropriately understood as Christianity's original sin. Instead of a mere illness that Christians might—or might not—contract, religious anti-Semitism is a corruption that has distorted belief and practice from the beginning of recorded Christian tradition. Demonizing of Jews and of Judaism has played such a deep and formative role in Christianity that Christians must guard against anti-Jewish tendencies for the rest of their history.

Recent official church statements repudiating past Christian teachings of contempt for Jews are significant and necessary, but they are not sufficient to ensure the end of such a deeply entrenched anti-Semitism. Denigration of Jews as well as of Judaism is explicit in Christian Scriptures and at least implicit in many expressions of Christian belief and practice, so that new generations of Christians continue, even if unconsciously, to understand Christianity against a stereotype that demeans both Judaism and Jews themselves. Not surprisingly, then, anti-Semitic attacks continue to erupt when Western society is under pressure, as is happening again in the United States and Europe as I write. Rosemary Radford Ruether's question of several decades ago must still unsettle any complacent Christianity: "Is it possible to say 'Jesus is Messiah' without, implicitly or explicitly, saying at the same time 'and the Jews be damned'"?[8]

Coming to terms with the religious anti-Semitism so deeply embedded in the Christian tradition is, of course, a very painful task. Learning that a beloved religious symbol like the cross has a history

---

8. Ruether, *Faith and Fratricide*, 246.

of inspiring violence against vulnerable people is spiritually distressing.[9] But as a Jesuit spiritual director once told me, to know one's sin is a great grace revealing one's need for God. So too, facing the evil in our religious traditions, soul-searing as this can be, should be welcomed as a gift, a grace that calls Christians to greater fidelity to the God beyond our institutions. After all, as the church has long taught, it is only with God's grace—and not by any human power—that we can serve God's plan for the redemption of the world.

While attention to overcoming anti-Semitism must be integral to any adequate ecclesiology today, it is particularly significant for a feminist ecclesiology. Notwithstanding its liberating intentions, feminist theology has contributed to anti-Judaism by portraying the Jewish tradition as an oppressively patriarchal religion repudiated by an egalitarian Jesus.[10] Christian feminists have critiqued the hierarchical thought that values men over women and humans over nature, yet some have deployed the same binary logic to set an egalitarian Jesus movement over against a patriarchal Judaism. To be truly liberating, feminist ecclesiology must come to terms with the ways in which Jews, along with women, have been positioned as the others against whom normative Christian identity has been defined since the church's first centuries.

There is, of course, a key difference here: while the Jewish difference was supposed to be erased, gender differences have been exaggerated in the church. Church authorities taught that Jews should give up their difference and become Christians, whereas Christian women must remain different and thus in a circumscribed role within the church. Fulfilling the mission of the church today requires that the church come to terms with the appropriate unity-in-diversity in the formation of Christian identity both with regard to this primary external other, the Jewish people, which is the topic

---

9. James Carroll reflects powerfully on this painful reality in *Constantine's Sword: The Church and the Jews* (Boston: Houghton Mifflin, 2001), esp. 3–12.

10. In addition to Procario-Foley, "Liberating Jesus," see Mary C. Boys, "Christian Feminism and Anti-Judaism," in Mary C. Boys, ed., *Seeing Judaism Anew: Christianity's Sacred Obligation* (Lanham, MD: Rowman and Littlefield, 2005), 70–79; and Katharina von Kellenbach, "Jewish-Christian Dialogue on Feminism and Religion," *Christian and Jewish Relations* 19 no. 2 (June 1986): 33–40.

of this chapter, and with regard to the primary internal other, Christian women, which is the topic of chapter 3.

The New Testament: From Disagreement to Demonization

The most serious obstacle to overcoming Christian anti-Semitism is that contempt for "the Jews" is embedded in the New Testament and has become intertwined with the Christian proclamation of Jesus as the messiah. Indeed, the major stereotypes of Jewish people that have done so much harm throughout history—portrayals of Jews as spiritually blind, as bearing a collective guilt for the crucifixion of Jesus, and as consistently in defiance of God's will—are all found in the New Testament. The Christian teaching of contempt, with its description of Jews as degenerate, demonic, dismissed, and dispersed for the crime of deicide, is rooted in the sacred texts of the church.[11]

To be sure, the New Testament contempt for Judaism is not a racial anti-Semitism. Often Jewish themselves, as St. Paul was, and certainly knowing that Jesus and his earliest disciples were Jews, the New Testament authors did not intend to revile all who share the lineage of the people of Israel. But at the same time, this was no mere theological dispute over Jewish rejection of messianic claims for Jesus. The New Testament authors not only vigorously defended Jesus' messianic identity against Jewish rejection of this claim, as might be expected; they went further and denigrated Jews themselves—that is, at least those who did not join the Jesus movement—as a people.

This calumny against "the Jews" emerged as the followers of Jesus of Nazareth struggled, despite the disagreement of the majority of first-century Jews and the problems posed by the unexpected crucifixion, to defend their belief in Jesus as the messiah who fulfilled Jewish hopes. Taking Hebrew Bible quotations out of context, the gospels describe events of Jesus' life as consistent with ancient prophecies and thus evidence that Jesus was and is truly the awaited

---

11. See Isaac, *The Teaching of Contempt,* and Procario-Foley, "Liberating Jesus."

messiah.[12] The Gospel of Matthew, for example, applies the reference to the Exodus event in Hosea 11:1 to the story of the escape of the Holy Family into Egypt: "This was to fulfill what had been spoken by the Lord through the prophet: Out of Egypt I have called my son" (Matt 2:15). The Gospel of John, which omits stories of Jesus' birth, focuses instead on details of the crucifixion—the gambling for Jesus' tunic, the offer of sour wine, the thrusting of a spear into Jesus' side rather than breaking his bones—presenting these details as evidence that Jesus satisfied predictions from the Hebrew Bible (John 19). And still today Christians usually hear a prediction of the birth of Jesus in the prophet Isaiah's sign to the eighth-century BCE King Ahaz: "Look, the young woman is with child and shall bear a son, and shall name him Immanuel. . . . For before the child knows how to refuse the evil and choose the good, the land before whose two kings you are in dread will be deserted" (Isa 7:14-16).

This use of the Hebrew Bible serves a significant theological purpose: it connects the Christian community's hopes in Jesus to the hopes of the Jewish people. Unlike Marcion who rejected the Hebrew Bible, these evangelists emphasize the continuity between the Jesus movement and the Hebrew Bible, which they recognize as authoritative. Christians could thus present their messianic faith to the Gentile world not as a "new superstition," but as the truest version of the ancient religion of Judaism, whose privileges they claimed.[13]

As a defense of messianic beliefs about Jesus, however, this strategy of proof texting is unlikely to convince any who are not already inclined to be persuaded. After all, biblical passages taken out of context can support a great many different conclusions. Further, as John Dominic Crossan has noted, many of these supposed events from Jesus' life are not history remembered—there is little evidence they actually occurred—but rather prophesy historicized: that is, they are details taken from the Hebrew Bible and written into the

---

12. See the thoughtful discussion of reinterpreting memory to give meaning in Carroll, *Constantine's Sword*, 122–24.

13. See especially the discussions in Nirenberg, *Anti-Judaism*, 66–86, 102; Ruether, *Faith and Fratricide*, 64–116; and William Nicholls, *Christian Antisemitism: A History of Hate* (Northvale, NJ: Jason Aronson, 1993), 153–75.

narration of Jesus' life.[14] While for Christians Jesus is indeed properly understood in relation to the hopes of the Hebrew Bible, these scriptural citations are far from compelling evidence that Jesus was foreseen by the prophets.

Another and more serious problem is the supersessionism—the idea that Christianity has replaced, or superseded, Judaism—implicit in the assertion that Jesus fulfills the prophecies and hopes of the Hebrew Bible. If Jewish hopes are completed in Christianity, then it would seem to follow that Judaism has achieved its historical purpose and that its role in God's plan is ended.[15] As history has shown, the conviction that Judaism should no longer exist leads far too easily to the horrific conclusion that Jews themselves no longer ought to exist.

Moreover, the New Testament authors were not satisfied simply to argue that Judaism is completed by and in Jesus. With claims to Jesus' messiahship bolstered by quotations from the Hebrew Bible (however dubious the connection), a troubling question inevitably arose: Why have so many Jews failed to see what seemed obvious to the followers of Jesus? After all, while belief in Jesus spread among the Gentiles, the majority of Jews did not join this Jesus movement. Indeed, throughout Christian history, the church has continued to be unsettled by the fact that the "evidence" that Jesus fulfilled ancient biblical prophecies has been largely unpersuasive to Jews. Could it be that Jesus is not, after all, so clearly the fulfillment of the hopes of the Hebrew Bible? Or must it rather be that Jews who refuse to accept Jesus are peculiarly blind to the meaning of their own faith?

It is, of course, the latter position—Jewish spiritual blindness—that has been held most commonly in Christian history. St. Paul provided an early articulation of this idea: in his second letter to

---

14. John Dominic Crossan, *The Birth of Christianity: Discovering What Happened in the Years Immediately after the Execution of Jesus* (New York: HarperCollins, 1998), 518–23.

15. Among the numerous writings on the problems of Christian supersessionism, see especially John T. Pawlikowski, *Christ in the Light of the Christian-Jewish Dialogue* (Ramsey, NJ: Paulist Press, 1982), 8–35, for an excellent overview of Christian theological proposals. See also Boys, *Seeing Judaism Anew*.

the Corinthians, he argued that Jews reject Jesus because "a veil lies over their minds" (2 Cor 3:15); and in his letter to the Romans he ascribed to the people of Israel "a sluggish spirit" that resulted in "eyes that would not see / and ears that would not hear" (Rom 11:8). St. Paul further explained to the church in Rome that God had afflicted this people with a temporary blindness to allow for the conversion of Gentiles (Rom 11:7-32).

This idea of Jewish religious obtuseness is reinforced by the gospel stories of Jesus' conflict with Pharisees, who are presented as legalistic and hypocritical in their interpretation of the Torah. Jesus as depicted in the gospels is participating in lively first-century Palestinian Jewish debates about how strictly the law should be applied. Without knowledge of first-century Palestinian Judaism, later generations of Christians have assumed that Jesus was a lone voice against legalistic Jewish authorities who were blind to the true, spiritual intent of the law and that these Jews must be the children of the flesh enslaved by the law, in contrast with the Christian children of promise living in freedom, as described by St. Paul in Galatians 4. Judaism appears as a misguided and oppressive—to use Isaac's term, degenerate—religion. It makes sense to a Christian audience that Jews, who so mistake God's will with regard to the law, would also misunderstand their own biblical prophecies and would fail to "recognize God's moment when it came," as alleged by the Second Vatican Council document *Nostra Aetate* (NA 4).

As noted above, there is, unfortunately, more to the story. It is one thing to defend messianic claims for Jesus through vigorous debate, even if that includes the uncharitable insistence that one's religious opponents are not merely wrong but spiritually inept. It is quite another thing to call your rivals murderers, malevolent killers of Jesus as well as of the prophets. Yet this is precisely what the New Testament texts do. While the Gospels of Mark and Luke blame Jesus' crucifixion primarily on Jewish authorities, the Gospels of Matthew and John blame Jesus' crucifixion on the Jewish people. In Matthew, the "crowds" in Jerusalem demand Jesus' crucifixion, willingly cursing themselves and their descendants in order to achieve the desired execution: "His blood be on us and on our children!" (Matt 27:25). The Gospel of John explicitly identifies the people clamoring for Jesus' death as "the Jews," a group who are defined in this gospel by their evilness or, in terms of the "five *D*s," as demonic. They are presented not only as opponents of Jesus but as children of the devil, and like the devil, they are liars and murderers.[16] In the Gospels of Matthew and John, Pontius Pilate not only recognizes Jesus' innocence but tries unsuccessfully to persuade the bloodthirsty Jewish people to accept the release of the obviously innocent Jesus.[17]

While this shifting of responsibility for Jesus' crucifixion from the Romans to the Jewish people is most pronounced in the Gospel of John, the last canonical gospel to be completed, Jews are already assigned this guilt in what is possibly the earliest extant letter of St. Paul. In 1 Thessalonians, which likely predates the canonical gospels by more than twenty years, we find this unambiguous declaration: "the Jews . . . killed both the Lord Jesus and the prophets, and drove us out; they displease God and oppose everyone by hindering us from speaking to the Gentiles so that they may be saved. Thus they have constantly been filling up the measure of their sins; but God's wrath has overtaken them at last" (1 Thess 2:14-16). Some scholars argue that this passage is a later interpolation and was not actually written by St. Paul.[18] Nevertheless, its presence in a canonical text contributes to the New Testament portrayal of Jewish guilt for Jesus' death. In 1 Thessalonians, Jews are clearly described not merely as mistaken but as murderous sinners who deserve severe punishment for opposing God and killing his messengers, including Jesus. The foundation is thus laid for the charge of deicide, which was first articulated explicitly by Melito of Sardis (d. 180 CE).[19]

The accusation that "the Jews" killed Jesus has incited violence against Jews for two millennia, yet it is a strange accusation.[20] After all, crucifixion was a Roman means of execution, and even though

---

16. See especially John 8:44.

17. See Matthew 27 and John 18–19. An excellent discussion is available in Gerard S. Sloyan, *Jesus on Trial: A Study of the Gospels*, 2nd ed. (Minneapolis: Fortress, 2006).

18. See the discussion in Werner Georg Kümmel, *Introduction to the New Testament*, rev. ed., trans. Howard Clark Kee (Nashville: Abingdon, 1975), 260–62.

19. Melito of Sardis, *On Pascha: With the Fragments and Other Material Related to the Quartodecimans*, translated, introduced, and annotated by Alistair Stewart-Sykes (Crestwood, NY: St. Vladimir's Seminary Press, 2001), esp. 52–62.

20. See especially Isaac, *The Teaching of Contempt*; Ruether, *Faith and Fratricide*, 84–91; and Sloyan, *Jesus on Trial*.

there are a few rather obscure references to the killing of prophets in the Hebrew Bible, the biblical stories generally describe the prophets as ignored or rejected and occasionally harassed, but not killed. How and why did this emphasis on murderous Jews develop?[21]

The reality is that, despite gospel passages in which Jesus foretells his death, his crucifixion was apparently unexpected and as such must have been significantly disorienting for Jesus' followers. James Carroll suggests that Jesus' disciples likely turned to their sacred texts, the Hebrew Bible, to come to terms with the unexpected and confounding event of Jesus' execution. Sifting through Hebrew Bible passages and combining the descriptions of Isaiah's suffering servant with hopes for a messiah, the nascent Christian community concluded that the Bible had in fact predicted a suffering messiah who would not only be rejected by the people but also killed.[22]

At the same time, according to Ruether, a Jewish cult of prophets as martyrs had arisen in Jerusalem since Herod had installed the tombs of the prophets there. It is a short step from honoring supposedly martyred prophets to determining that martyrdom is in fact the sign of a true prophet.[23] Thus, instead of Jesus' crucifixion being an embarrassment to those who made messianic claims about him, his execution became further evidence that Jesus is indeed the Christ. Not only was Jesus foretold in the Hebrew Bible, then, but so were his rejection, suffering, and death—at the hands of his countrymen and women, who were said to have a habit of violently rejecting God's messengers. In a theological jujitsu move, the stubborn facts of Jesus' brutal death and the widespread Jewish rejection of Jesus as the messiah were turned from reasons for doubt into further evidence of Jesus' messiahship. But the cost of this defense of Christian faith was the denigration of Jews, who, instead of being revered as the descendants of the prophets, are reviled as particularly inclined to repudiate and even kill prophets.

Of course, the Jesus movement in the Roman Empire had very good reasons to downplay the all-too-evident reality that they followed a man who was crucified for challenging the power of Rome. These

---

21. See especially Ruether, *Faith and Fratricide*, 90–95.
22. Carroll, *Constantine's Sword*, 122–24.
23. Ruether, *Faith and Fratricide*, 91–94.

early followers of Jesus were understandably eager to emphasize that theirs was a religious movement, not a political rebellion against Roman authority. With the shift of primary responsibility for Jesus' execution from the Roman governor to the Jewish people, the Roman crucifixion of Jesus as "the king of the Jews" could be portrayed as an unfortunate misunderstanding in which the Roman political authorities were misled into intervening in a religious conflict.

Given the context of contradiction, conflict, and competition between the emerging traditions of rabbinic Judaism and what would become Christianity, the deployment of invective against "the Jews" was unfortunate but not surprising. Of course, what matters for our purpose is less that we plumb the depths of why this contempt for Judaism—and for Jews—came about than that we recognize that this contempt is a nonessential but real development and is present in the New Testament. Still today, those who read the New Testament will find problematic assumptions about Jews: they are depicted as legalistic, spiritually obtuse, and with a history of violent opposition to God's messengers, including Jesus. Whatever is valid in the Judaism that nurtured Jesus and his earliest disciples has been claimed by and for the church, while those who remain Jews are considered the stubborn enemies of God, of Jesus, and of Christianity. Even though St. Paul's letter to the Romans affirms that Jews "are beloved [by God], for the sake of their ancestors" and that Jews will be regrafted into the covenant that now belongs to the church, Jews are predominantly defined in the New Testament by their supposed opposition to God rather than by their divine election.[24]

The Early Church: Developing a Christian Identity against "the Jews"

As influential as this scriptural calumny against the Jewish people has been and continues to be, the New Testament is far from the

---

24. Romans 11:28-29. See also Romans 11:17-24. While this letter definitely supports a Christian theology recognizing that the Jewish covenant continues, we must also acknowledge the supersessionism implicit in the claim that Jews who do not accept Jesus are currently cut off and will be restored by accepting Jesus as the Christ, even if only at the end of time.

sole source of Christian anti-Semitism. The post–New Testament church, in its work to establish the fundamentals of Christian belief and practice, amplified Christian contempt for Jews.

This early church period, from the second to sixth centuries of the Common Era, was a critical stage in the development of Christianity. During this time, the church determined the contents of the Christian Bible, formulated the essential doctrines of what would become orthodox Christian faith, and so successfully spread this new religion that it became the official religion of the Roman Empire. Christian perspectives on Jews and Judaism, building on the New Testament portrayals of Judaism as fulfilled in Christ and of Jews as murderous opponents of God, were integral to these developments.

A Supersessionist Narrative of Salvation History

As suggested above, the affirmation of the Hebrew Bible as sacred and revelatory for Christians poses a hermeneutical challenge: that is, what came to be known as the "Old Testament" must be interpreted in a manner that is consistent with faith in Jesus as the Christ. There was, of course, the option to reject the Hebrew Bible altogether. This was the path taken by the second-century figure Marcion, who posited the existence of two gods: the Hebrew Bible's evil creator of the material world and the New Testament's good and spiritual savior.[25] In refusing this Marcionite approach, the early Christian community had to determine, then, how to read the Hebrew Bible through a Christian lens and, once the New Testament writings were also given the status of Sacred Scripture, how to unite these two distinct canons into a coherent perspective.[26]

The common Christian solution has been to unify the varied texts of this unwieldly Bible through a supersessionist narrative of redemption. As R. Kendall Soulen demonstrates, the early church constructed an overarching story that became basic to Christian self-understanding. In this account, God's good creation was disrupted by the fall of humanity, to which God responded first by

---

25. Nirenberg, *Anti-Judaism*, 97–100. See also Nicholls, *Christian Antisemitism*, 178–81.

26. R. Kendall Soulen develops this point especially clearly in *The God of Israel and Christian Theology* (Minneapolis: Fortress, 1996), 12–17.

preparing the people for salvation through the events of the Hebrew Bible and finally by making the promised salvation available through the life, death, and resurrection of Jesus, the Christ.[27] Expanding beyond the New Testament interpretation of specific Hebrew biblical passages as prophecies of Jesus, then, the early Church encouraged typological readings in which the Hebrew Bible was understood as prefiguring Christian salvation.[28] The crossing of the Red Sea was thought to point to Christian baptism, for example, while Moses's raising of the snake was viewed as foreshadowing Jesus' healing death on the cross.

Reducing the Hebrew Bible to a prefiguration of Christ and Christianity reinforces supersessionism to the point that, as David Nirenberg argues, "these theologians have deprived the Jews of their scripture, and the scriptures of their Jews."[29] That is, the supersessionist narrative not only excludes the Jewish reading of these texts but, in fact, as Soulen concludes, erases the theological significance of God's history with the people of Israel. The role of the Hebrew Bible is limited to proclaiming a universal Creator God, acknowledging the universal fall of humanity, and preparing for the coming of Jesus to redeem all of humankind. God's covenant with the descendants of Abraham becomes truly an "old" covenant, replaced with the new, improved, and universal covenant with the church, the "new Israel."[30]

Theologians have pointed out that this failure to provide a positive account of God's history with the Jewish people has caused theological problems even beyond the obvious supersessionism that renders Judaism and Jews superfluous in a Christian era. Besides failing to account for the biblical assurances of God's everlasting fidelity to the Abrahamic covenant, this neglect of the theological significance of Israel inclines Christianity toward an otherworldly and privatized spirituality. As Soulen contends, when the history of the Jewish people is judged to have no value beyond pointing to a universal salvation now available to all through Jesus, then history

---

27. Soulen, *God of Israel*, 25–34.
28. Soulen, *God of Israel*, 38–39; Nirenberg, *Anti-Judaism*, 100–120.
29. Nirenberg, *Anti-Judaism*, 120.
30. Soulen, *God of Israel*, esp 27–33.

itself—except for the event of Jesus Christ—becomes religiously irrelevant.[31] Rosemary Radford Ruether has similarly observed that there simply is no further historical hope if Jesus' messianic work is complete without the fulfillment of Jewish hopes for history.[32]

This neglect of history helps explain why the development of Christian social thought is so often treated by Christians as of secondary importance, at best. The persistence of an individualistic and ahistorical faith, one that reduces the mission of the church to getting souls into heaven, is rooted in the Christian supersessionist narrative and its failure to accord any revelatory value to the ongoing history of the people of Israel.

Against "the Evil Jews"

Along with articulating a more explicitly supersessionist narrative in which the Jewish people are dismissed because their covenant is now given to Christians, the early church period also magnified the New Testament portrayal of the malevolence of "the Jews" in their supposed opposition to God, Christ, and the church. As early as Melito of Sardis (d. 180), Jews were accused of deicide—that is, of killing the one who came not only as the messiah but as the eternal Son, God incarnate.[33] Indeed, as Ruether has shown, the Gospel of John's presentation of Jews as sons of Satan is further developed in the traditional anti-Jewish polemics known as the *Adversus Judaeos* texts, even to the point that Jews are described as particularly bent toward evil since their time in Egypt. In these early Christian writings, "the Jews are not only prophet killers, but idolaters, law breakers, and sinners of every description," Ruether notes. They "assume the status of a people on probation who fail all the tests and finally are flunked out" when they reject Jesus as the Christ.[34]

Among the more vicious of the harangues in the Adversus Judaeos texts are those of the fourth-century archbishop St. John Chrysostom, who refers to Jews as animals who deserve to be slaughtered: "Although such beasts are unfit for work, they are fit for killing.

---

31. Soulen, *God of Israel*, 17, 54–56.
32. Ruether, *Faith and Fratricide*, 246–51.
33. Nicholls, *Christian Antisemitism*, 176–78.
34. Ruether, *Faith and Fratricide*, 125, 137.

And this is what happened to the Jews: while they were making themselves unfit for work, they grew fit for slaughter. This is why Christ said, 'But as for my enemies, who did not want me to be king over them, bring them here and slay them.' "[35] Chrysostom further inveighs against Christian socializing with Jews, telling his audience that God is repulsed by Jews and they should be too: "If a man were to have slain your son, would you endure to look upon him, or to accept his greeting? . . . They slew the Son of your Lord; do you have the boldness to enter with them under the same roof?"[36]

While it is often assumed that this anti-Jewish invective arose due to the competition between Jews and Christians in the early church period, Nirenberg has demonstrated that something more was going on here. After all, the anti-Jewish polemics of Chrysostom originated long after Jews had become a "twice-defeated people without political power."[37] There may still have been rivalry between Christians and Jews in some places, but the claim that the persecuted Jewish minority was a threat to Christians in the Christian empire of St. John Chrysostom's day is not credible. As Nirenberg's analysis shows, these diatribes, ostensibly against Jews and Judaism, are more accurately viewed as a rhetorical tool deployed primarily against Christian opponents—not Jews!—in disputes over church teachings. Since Jews rejected the idea of Jesus of Nazareth as both divine and human, then anyone who disagreed with one's formulation of Jesus' dual natures could be accused of falling into a "Jewish" error.[38]

So when St. John Chrysostom interrupted his promised series of sermons against the Anomoean heresy to deliver his public lectures against "the Jews," his reason for this deviation was probably not the reason he gave, which was that Jews were the more pressing

---

35. John Chrysostom, *Discourses against Judaizing Christians*, trans. Paul W. Harkins (Washington, DC: Catholic University of America, 1979), 1.2.6. Both Nirenberg and Ruether discuss this passage; see Nirenberg, *Anti-Judaism*, 11; and Ruether, *Faith and Fratricide*, 179.

36. Chrysostom, *Discourses*, 1.7.5. Ruether discusses this passage in Ruether, *Faith and Fratricide*, 130. Given Nirenberg's analysis, one wonders if the socializing Chrysostom warns against might be with Arians rather than Jews.

37. Nirenberg, *Anti-Judaism*, 86.

38. Nirenberg, *Anti-Judaism*, esp. 93, 112–17.

threat. Nirenberg contends that Chrysostom, a master rhetorician, was more likely making a powerful rhetorical move here that would allow him further to vilify the Arians, and particularly the Anomoean subgroup of Arians, by associating them with the putative evils of Judaism, on which Chrysostom then elaborated at length. Chrysostom himself confirms this connection between his rhetorical opponents when, in the midst of his first discourse against Jews, he declares that "the Jews and the Anomoeans make the same accusation. . . . That He [Jesus] called God His own Father and so made Himself equal to God."[39] Nirenberg has persuasively concluded, "We can accurately paraphrase John's 'this is why I hate the Jews' as meaning 'this is why you should hate those that I call Judaizers: Arians, pagans, and any others who disagree with me about the nature of Jesus' divinity and thereby become God's enemies.' "[40]

As this analysis suggests, Christian opponents were not treated as simply mistaken in their understanding of Christian doctrine. Instead, those whose position could be identified as somehow "Jewish" were thereby accused not only of rejecting the essence of Christianity but also of aligning themselves with the supposed evil that had cost Jews their salvation. Denouncing their adversaries as Jewish, Christian debaters tarred these Christian opponents with all of the evil that had been and was being ascribed to Jews, including being carnal, overly literal, spiritually blind and denying the Incarnation. As Ruether has also noted, "The *adversos Judaeos* literature was not created to convert Jews or even primarily to attack Jews, but to affirm the identity of the Church, which could only be done by invalidating the identity of the Jews."[41]

This is, of course, an all-too-familiar phenomenon. As René Girard's work on scapegoating clarifies, a communal identity is very often strengthened through the creation of an enemy, who is then assailed as a threat to the group's norms and perhaps to its very existence.[42] Abusing a weak minority so that people fear to be as-

---

39. Chrysostom, *Discourses*, 1.6; Nirenberg, *Anti-Judaism*, 115.
40. Nirenberg, *Anti-Judaism*, 115.
41. Ruether, *Faith and Fratricide*, 181.
42. René Girard, *The Scapegoat*, trans. Yvonne Freccero (Baltimore, MD: Johns Hopkins University Press, 1989).

sociated with that minority is a common human strategy, from the playground to the nation-state, for shoring up a community's identity and policing its boundaries.

Influential Christian thinkers in the early church period deployed this scapegoating strategy in their efforts to develop and defend Christian doctrine. Building on the depiction of "the Jews" in the New Testament, the early church developed a binary that defined the church as the true, spiritual, and faithful people of God, whereas Jews were the false, carnal, and utterly unfaithful and so rejected ones.

This is obviously a serious failure and impediment to the mission of the church. The church cannot be an honest and effective witness against the world's violent divisions without coming to terms with the fact that the church's identity has itself been based on an oppositional, binary logic in which the good side of every polarity is claimed as proper to Christians and the negative side is assigned to Jews. This abjection of Judaism and of Jews is thus a major challenge to the church's mission of increasing unity-in-diversity, as well as a powerful reminder that the Christian church has some work to do to overcome its deeply rooted triumphalism, which precludes a mission of building communion with those outside of the church.

Persecution of Jews in a Christian Empire

It is important to recognize that, even if the *Adversus Judaeos* tradition was primarily a rhetorical strategy wielded against Christian opponents in the construction of Christian orthodoxy, these writings had real consequences for Jews, who were—and are—real people of flesh and blood and not merely a rhetorical trope. Those consequences became evident in the fourth century, especially when Christianity became the official religion of the Roman Empire. It was now Christians who would decide what rights and privileges to allow their beleaguered religious kin, Jews. For many in the church, a Christian empire meant not only the vindication of Christianity's truth but also the achievement of the final stage of history, with Christ ruling on earth. Should Jews, increasingly defined as the archetypal opponents of Christianity and the source of all heresy, continue to have the ancient privileges accorded them under the pagan Roman Empire?

One might have hoped that, having experienced some persecution themselves, Christians would exercise power magnanimously. Unfortunately, this was not the case, as the Theodosian Code and the Code of Justinian increasingly restricted Jewish rights.[43] Furthermore, violence broke out against Jews, with riots and burning of synagogues, often led by zealous monks.[44] Regrettably, the response of influential church figures, including St. Simeon Stylites and St. Ambrose, was not to denounce this persecution of Jews but to vehemently condemn imperial efforts to exact restitution or to rebuild the burned synagogue. St. Ambrose even refused to continue to celebrate the Eucharist unless the emperor agreed to no restitution to Jews for the property destroyed or stolen.[45]

While St. Ambrose favored the expulsion of Jews from the Christian empire, it was not his view but rather the position of St. Augustine of Hippo that became the dominant policy of Western Christendom.[46] St. Augustine argued that Jews should remain in the Christian empire, though under considerable restrictions, in order to demonstrate through their suffering the consequences of denying Christ. St. Augustine found support for this position in Psalm 59: "Slay them not, but scatter them in your might, lest your people forget your Law."[47] So while Augustine defended Jews against expulsion and massacre ("Slay them not"), he also endorsed their oppression as a minority whose punishment confirms the truth of Christianity.

The belief that Jewish suffering witnessed to the truth of Christianity justified legal restrictions that officially positioned Jews as "others," aliens with limited rights in Christian societies. Jews were banned from public office and forbidden to own Christian slaves, since Jewish authority over Christians was seen as inconsistent with the triumph of Christ on earth (and might perhaps incline Christians under that authority to convert to Judaism). In a largely slave economy, Ruether points out, such laws prevented Jews from owning

---

43. Ruether, *Faith and Fratricide*, 184–95.
44. Nirenberg, *Anti-Judaism*, 117–18; Ruether, *Faith and Fratricide*, 192–95.
45. Ruether, *Faith and Fratricide*, 193–94.
46. Nirenberg, *Anti-Judaism*, 119.
47. Nirenberg, *Anti-Judaism*, 131; Ruether, *Faith and Fratricide*, 132.

economic enterprises of any size. Additionally, they were often required to pay additional taxes, not allowed to build or repair synagogues, forbidden to proselytize, and banned from intermarriage and other social interaction with Christians.[48]

The early church period thus intensified the anti-Jewish rhetoric begun in the New Testament. During these formative centuries, Christian thinkers developed an explicitly supersessionist story of salvation, erased the theological significance of Israel's history, and described the Jewish tradition as one of recurring evil and error in contrast to Christian goodness and truth. By the end of this foundational era of Christianity, the understanding of Jews as demonic members of a degenerate religion who were dismissed from the covenant and dispersed for the sin of deicide (as summarized by Isaac) was firmly established in the Christian imagination. Jews were consistently depicted as the archetypal enemy of Christianity, opponents of Christ, and the source of all Christian heresy.

The Reviled Jewish Other, From Christendom to the Shoah

Limitations on Jewish rights and roles in society continued and even increased in Europe during the Middle Ages. In the feudal society that followed the fall of the Roman Empire in the West, Jews were able to reside in a territory only with the permission and protection of the ruler, to whom they and their property then "belonged."[49] Bans on Jews' holding positions of authority over Christians were extended, so that Jews were prohibited not only from holding civic or governmental positions but even at times from employing Christian servants. The explicitly Christian character of the medieval guilds precluded Jewish membership and, along with laws against Jewish ownership of land, severely limited Jews' options for making a living. The Fourth Lateran Council in 1215 sought to increase Jewish social isolation further by requiring Jews to reside in ghettos and to wear special dress, including badges

---

48. Ruether, *Faith and Fratricide*, 187–91.
49. Nirenberg, *Anti-Judaism*, 191–93.

identifying them as Jews.[50] These and other legal restrictions were supported by church leaders as consistent with the Augustinian resolution that Jews should not be killed or expelled from Christendom but be kept in subjection and misery as a living testimony to the consequences of rejecting Christ.

The belief that Jews were an evil influence grew along with the constraints on Jewish participation in society. Already portrayed in authoritative Christian documents of the New Testament and early church as the "other," or opposite, to Christian identity, Jews came to be seen as a danger not only to Christian faith but also to the society constituted by that faith. Jews became the ever-available scapegoat, attacked both as the cause of society's problems and, sometimes, simply because to assault Jews expressed the "pious" desire to defend Christ.

As history demonstrates, Augustine's "Slay them not, but" was inherently unstable. With Jews defined as evil and a threat to all that is good and sacred, it was nearly inevitable that physical—and even murderous—violence would break out against Jews. In hindsight, it seems obvious that Crusaders, responding to Pope Urban II's plea for a "defense of Christianity" against Muslims in the distant Holy Land, would also rampage against the more proximate enemy, Jews. It made little sense to Crusaders to travel so far to fight Muslims and bypass Jews, whom they had learned to identify as God's worst enemies. Though some ecclesiastical authorities attempted to intervene, they were not always able to protect European Jews against inflamed Crusaders. Indeed, Ruether observes that the Crusades revealed the impotence of authorities in the face of mob violence, thus clearing the way for the waves of pogroms in subsequent centuries.[51]

It was perhaps inevitable that the period of intense societal stress caused by the fourteenth-century Black Death, which killed about one-third of Europe's population, would lead to allegations that

---

50. Ruether, *Faith and Fratricide*, 210–12. See also Carroll, *Constantine's Sword*, 281–83.

51. Ruether, *Faith and Fratricide*, 205–7. See also Michael, *History of Catholic Antisemitism*, 67–69; and Carroll, *Constantine's Sword*, 237–77.

Jews had caused the plague by poisoning wells.[52] There is often a strong emotional need for an enemy to blame—and attack—when people are dying from mysterious diseases.

Yet the earlier and persisting accusations of ritual murder (commonly known as blood libel) and of desecration of the sacred eucharistic host were probably the most outrageous and persistent expressions of the Jew-as-threat in the Middle Ages. Having long been defined as murderers of Christ, medieval Jews were further accused of reenacting that murder by desecrating hosts and killing innocent Christian children at Passover. To be sure, church leaders and Christian political authorities often objected to these unwarranted accusations and tried to protect the Jewish communities from the mob violence and even massacres that frequently resulted. Nevertheless, by later authorizing devotions honoring the presumably martyred Christian children, church officials contributed to the perpetuation of this calumny.[53] The belief that Jewish law commanded the Passover murder of a Christian child spread until it became common "knowledge" that was taken for granted among even educated Catholics well into the twentieth century, appearing as late as 1914 in the influential Jesuit periodical *La Civiltà Cattolica*.[54]

It was arguably in Catholic Spain in the fifteenth century, following the brilliant Jewish culture made possible by the *Convivencia* under Islamic rule, that the hatred of Jews first became clearly racial and not merely religious and ethnic. According to Nirenberg, the English word *race* derives from the Spanish word *raza*, used at this time to refer to Jews as a distinct people.[55] There is, I believe, an incipient racism against Jews already in the New Testament descriptions of Jews as a disobedient and even demonic people who are collectively guilty of Jesus' death and who pass that guilt on to their biological descendants. Nevertheless, there is no doubt that this contempt for Jews became more explicitly racist during the Inquisition in Spain,

---

52. Michael, *History of Catholic Antisemitism*, 72.

53. Michael, *History of Catholic Antisemitism*, 69–73. See also Ruether, *Faith and Fratricide*, 213–14; Nirenberg, *Anti-Judaism*, 202–7; and Carroll, *Constantine's Sword*, 268–77.

54. Michael, *History of Catholic Antisemitism*, 166–69.

55. Nirenberg, *Anti-Judaism*, 238–39.

when even the efficacy of baptism to counteract the putative Jewish propensity for evil was called into question. Originally due to the fear of false conversions, Christians with Jewish forebears were banned from religious as well as civic office. This prohibition was evidently racial and not merely religious, since candidates for such offices were required to provide genealogical evidence that they had had no Jewish ancestor for several generations. Further, as Nirenberg reports, the biologically transmitted taint of Judaism was also thought to be inherited through the breast milk of a wet nurse if she had even a distant, perhaps unknown, Jewish ancestor.[56] As can be imagined, this led to considerable anxiety among the Christian population about possible Jewishness.

Ecclesiastical authorities at first resisted this racist denial of the power of baptism to incorporate all peoples into the Body of Christ. However, the church hierarchy (including popes) eventually came to tolerate such laws in some places, so that some religious orders had barriers against the admission of any Christian with Jewish parentage well into the twentieth century.[57]

The Christian othering of Jews thus reached its peak. In the earliest days of the church, Jews had been welcomed as fellow monotheists whose conversion did not necessitate the lengthy catechumenate required of pagans. Later, as the church increasingly defined Jews to be murderers of Christ and opponents of God, the catechumenate of Jews was lengthened beyond that of other converts, and their baptismal rites included an additional curse on Judaism and on themselves if they reverted to their earlier faith. Finally, at least in the practice of some parts of the church, the idea that the corruption of Judaism would remain despite baptism was embraced.[58]

---

56. Nirenberg, *Anti-Judaism*, 243–44; see also Ruether, *Faith and Fratricide*, 202–3.

57. Ruether, *Faith and Fratricide*, 203. A Jesuit priest I met in the 1980s confirmed that when he entered the Society of Jesus, questions in the interview process included whether one had a Jewish parent. They skipped these questions in his case because he was himself a Jewish convert to Catholicism. Apparently when this man had joined the society some decades earlier, the rules against members having Jewish lineage were still on the books but were not enforced.

58. Ruether, *Faith and Fratricide*, 191–92, 203.

By the time of the Enlightenment, the centuries of pogroms, expulsions, and harassment had left few Jewish communities in Western Europe. Yet Christian anxiety about Jewishness persisted. The political revolutions of modernity restored citizenship rights and ended many of the laws limiting Jewish rights, yet Europeans continued nonetheless to debate the appropriate place of Jews in society. Proponents of the Enlightenment, for example, tended to oppose Jewish ethnic identity and to consider Judaism a foreign and superstitious allegiance that had no place in a modern Europe. Jews must then give up their Jewishness and assimilate to become part of the new social order.[59]

At the same time and notwithstanding the evident contradiction, others rejected the Enlightenment altogether as a Jewish plot. Catholic churchmen, who were especially dismayed by secularism, democracy, liberalism, and the concomitant loss of the church's power, viewed the Enlightenment as a conspiracy to weaken the church—a conspiracy they alleged was instigated by Jews, long considered the epitome of opposition to the church.[60]

Given the tendency to treat modern secular anti-Semitism as unrelated to the tradition of Christian anti-Jewish rhetoric, it is crucial to recognize that Christian contempt for the Jewish people continued through the late nineteenth and early twentieth centuries (if not later).[61] The Catholic Church in France, for example, was a staunch supporter of anti-Semitic movements at this time and incited further anti-Semitism during the Dreyfus affair as a means of strengthening Catholic identity.[62] In the nineteenth century, Jews in the Papal States were still required to live in ghettos, barred from some professions, and ordered to wear identifying badges.[63] Devotions honoring the children supposedly killed in ritual murder by Jews, along with the scripted vilification of their alleged Jewish murderers, continued with ecclesial support even through the

---

59. Nirenberg, *Anti-Judaism*, 344–86.
60. Nirenberg, *Anti-Judaism*, 376–83; Ruether, *Faith and Fratricide*, 214–25.
61. Michael, *History of Catholic Antisemitism*, 2.
62. Michael, *History of Catholic Antisemitism*, 128–29. See also Carroll, *Constantine's Sword*, 450–71.
63. Michael, *History of Catholic Antisemitism*, 164–65.

mid-twentieth century.⁶⁴ And, of course, churches and seminaries continued to speak of Jews as demonic members of a degenerate religion, dismissed from the covenant and dispersed for the crime of deicide.⁶⁵

This is the historical context in which Nazi anti-Semitism must be understood. Up to the point of the Final Solution of genocide, Hitler's vile and racist campaign against Jews would not have seemed especially outrageous to people accustomed to similar ideas and practices in their Christian tradition. For centuries, Christian authorities had depicted Jews as a danger to religious, moral, and physical health, and had sought to limit their participation in society. Indeed, Hitler himself defended his policies of identifying, isolating, and expelling Jews as modeled on what the church had itself often said and done.⁶⁶ Nor did it help that the Catholic hierarchy in Germany lifted the ban on Catholic membership in the Nazi Party in 1933 or that the pope never excommunicated any Catholic-born Nazi—not Goebbels, not Himmler, and not even Adolf Hitler, whose name remained on the rolls of the Catholic church where he was baptized. Yet Pope Pius XII excommunicated all Communists in 1949, leaving no doubt where the Catholic Church stood on communism.⁶⁷ Instead of seeing Hitler's anti-Semitism as an affront to Christian belief in the dignity of all humanity, many Christians, as Ruether aptly notes, found that "the fact that the Nazis declared themselves anti-communist, anti-liberal, and anti-Semitic was enough to guarantee that they were on the side of Christianity and the restoration of Christendom, despite their worship of Wotan."⁶⁸

This ongoing history of hatred also sheds light on the international resistance to Jewish refugees, including in the United States, where Fr. Coughlin's openly anti-Semitic radio program was popular in the 1930s.⁶⁹ In polls taken from 1939 to 1946, a majority of Americans

---

64. Michael, *History of Catholic Antisemitism*, 166–67.
65. See especially Michael, *History of Christian Antisemitism*, 101–92.
66. Ruether, *Faith and Fratricide*, 224.
67. Carroll, *Constantine's Sword*, 498, 437.
68. Ruether, *Faith and Fratricide*, 224.
69. Carroll, *Constantine's Sword*, 437–38.

consistently identified Jews as the greatest threat to the United States—even while the US armed forces were fighting against the Axis powers in both Europe and the Pacific and the alliance with Stalin's USSR was uneasy at best.[70] It is unfortunately necessary to keep in mind that staunch and even heroic opposition to Nazi Germany was not primarily based on, nor did it always include, concern for the lives and well-being of Hitler's Jewish victims.

There can be no doubt that the Nazi Holocaust (Shoah) was sui generis, particularly in the sheer scale of mechanistic killing made possible by technology. All the same, the Nazi program of anti-Semitism makes little sense apart from the contempt for Jews coded in the sacred texts of the Christian faith and developed through two millennia of Christian opposition to the Jewish other, to the point that Christian society had long learned to identify nearly every physical, moral, or social danger as somehow "Jewish." The persistence of Judaism had been deemed a threat—often an intolerable one—throughout Christian history, and the people who embodied this supposed threat were frequently isolated, harassed, persecuted, violently attacked, expelled, or massacred.

Yet, as Nirenberg has demonstrated, the otherness of Jews has been essential to Christian identity. Christians understood themselves through opposition to "the Jew," the religious, ethnic, racial, and bestial other whose difference clarified Christian identity. The church was defined as the New Israel, whose spiritual virtue and truth stood in contrast to the legalistic materialism, vices, and errors of the Old Israel. What would it mean to be a Christian if not to be the opposite of a Jew?

Dismantling Christian Anti-Semitism: Toward a Christianity without Contempt for Jews

Horrified by the Nazi Holocaust of six million Jews, many Christian denominations have renounced their explicitly anti-Jewish teachings. This is not to say that the churches have fully acknowledged their part in making the Holocaust possible. In fact, Christian

---

70. Nirenberg, *Anti-Judaism*, 457–58.

leaders have tended to exaggerate the distance between the modern racism of neopagan Nazism and a presumably long-past Christian dislike of Jews. Nevertheless, after the Nazi effort to exterminate Jews, church leaders were embarrassed by their traditional Christian descriptions of Jews as evil and of Judaism as an obsolete religion, especially as Jews (such as Jules Isaac) and Jewish Christians (like Msgr. John Oesterreicher) challenged these Christian teachings of contempt in the postwar era.[71] Simply put, after the actual massacre of two-thirds of European Jewry, the Good Friday tradition of killing Jews in effigy no longer seemed like an appropriate Christian devotion.[72]

In 1958, Pope St. John XXIII removed the word *perfidis* (faithless) from the Good Friday prayer for the conversion of Jews. He also convened Vatican II, which addressed Christian attitudes toward Judaism and other religions in its document *Nostra Aetate*. Here the Catholic Church officially repudiates the "deicide" charge, declaring that neither all Jews at the time of Jesus nor later generations of Jews are to be blamed for Jesus' crucifixion. In addition, *Nostra Aetate* retrieves St. Paul's belief, expressed in his letter to the Romans, "that the Jews remain very dear to God, for the sake of the patriarchs" and "God does not take back the gifts he bestowed or the choice he made" (NA 4; cf. Rom 11:28-29). Contradicting millennia of Catholic teaching, *Nostra Aetate* further declares that "the Jews should not be spoken of as rejected or accursed" by God (NA 4).

Other churches have similarly renounced the deicide charge and affirmed that the Jewish covenant with God continues.[73] The Jewish people are no longer (at least publicly) defined as an evil other

---

71. John Connelly, *From Enemy to Brother: The Revolution in Catholic Teaching on the Jews, 1933–1965* (Cambridge, MA: Harvard University Press, 2012).

72. Nirenberg, *Anti-Judaism*, 188. Unfortunately, this ritual hanging of a Jew (perhaps intended to represent Judas) was reenacted in Poland on Good Friday in 2019.

73. See, for example, the 1967 statement of the Faith and Order Commission of the World Council of Churches, "The Church and the Jewish People," https://www.bc.edu/content/dam/files/research_sites/cjl/texts/cjrelations/resources/documents/protestant/WCC1967.htm; and the more recent World Council of Churches, *The Theology of the Churches and the Jewish People: Statements by the WCC and Its Member Churches* (Geneva: WCC Publications, 1988).

threatening Christianity but rather as having a special bond and even a common mission with Christians.[74]

These developments are essential. The Christian portrayal of Jews as deicides who lost the covenant for their wickedness in crucifying Jesus has caused much harm—to Jews and to Christianity. It is, of course, historically inaccurate, since Rome alone had the authority to impose the death penalty. The deicide charge is also a serious theological distortion of the Christian belief that Jesus died for the sins of all humanity. Yet this persistent—and widespread—allegation of deicide has provoked centuries of Christian violence against Jews in retribution for their supposed murder of Jesus, the ultimate defiance for which this disobedient people was held to be rejected by God, dismissed from the covenant, and dispersed from their land.

This punitive supersessionism, in which the covenant is taken from the Jewish people for their failures and given instead to the Christian church, is a corruption of Christianity as well as grossly unfair to the Jewish history of fidelity to God. No covenant with God will be secure if it depends on fallible humanity rather than on unfailing divine grace. Hence, a supersessionist church has minimized and even denied its own sinful failures while interpreting the prophetic self-criticism in the Hebrew Bible not as exemplary spiritual honesty but as evidence of a specifically Jewish tendency to evil.[75] Breaking with this history by denouncing both the deicide charge and the punitive supersessionism, Christian leaders have made room for a more theologically adequate perspective on the unmerited grace of redemption in Jesus' life and death for a universally sinful humanity. They have also laid the foundation for deconstructing the ancient binary that opposes Christian fidelity to Jewish infidelity.

---

74. See especially the Anglican-Jewish statement by Reuven Silverman, Patrick Morrow, and Daniel Langton, *Jews and Christians: Perspectives on Mission*, The Lambeth-Jewish Forum, https://www.woolf.cam.ac.uk/assets/file-downloads/Jews-and-Christians-Perspectives-on-Mission.pdf. See also Interfaith Consultative Group of the Archbishop's Council, *Sharing One Hope? The Church of England and Christian Jewish Relations* (London: Church House, 2001); and Michael Ipgrave, "Remembering the Covenant: Judaism in an Anglican Theology of Interfaith Relations," *Anglican Theological Review* 96 (1), http://www.anglicantheologicalreview.org/static/pdf/articles/ipgrave.pdf.

75. Ruether especially develops this critique in *Faith and Fratricide*, 228–32.

Yet if the church is to end its tradition of portraying Jews as evil Christ killers and the special objects of divine wrath, Christians must grapple with the New Testament texts that make just these claims. While better translations, especially those substituting in places the more accurate "some Jewish leaders" for the less nuanced "the Jews," are helpful, there remain passages that cannot be translated or explained away. These include 1 Thessalonians' celebration of God's punishment of the Jews, the Gospel of John's representation of Jews as the enemies of Christ and children of Satan, and Matthew's depiction of the crowd claiming the guilt for Jesus' crucifixion for themselves and their offspring. These passages cannot be ignored and so must be engaged as teachable moments, occasions for reflecting on the contempt for Jews that has distorted Christianity from its early days and remains an ever-present temptation.

Fortunately, there is a long and developed Christian tradition of rejecting textual literalism in favor of the ecclesial community's discernment of the meaning of Scripture. Moreover, the Bible itself witnesses to self-criticism and correction, not only throughout the Hebrew Scriptures but also in the New Testament's acknowledgment of the failures of Jesus' key disciples. If St. Peter can be described in the New Testament as betraying Jesus (Luke 22:54-62) and as hypocritical toward Gentile Christians (Gal 2:11-14), Christians today ought to be able to summon sufficient spiritual honesty to acknowledge the flaws of later New Testament authors and to criticize those aspects of our Sacred Scriptures that represent the church's early efforts to defend itself at the expense of rabbinic Judaism. The polemics of the first century should not be confused with the truth revealed for our salvation but rather should be seen as indicative of the reality that all revelation is expressed contextually.

While some fear that a critical engagement with biblical texts leaves Christianity without a secure source of truth and standard of judgment, official Catholic doctrine maintains that the inerrancy of the Bible extends only to its portrayal of God's self and will for our salvation as discerned by the church with the guidance of the Holy Spirit.[76] The revealed truth in the Bible does not include New Testament claims

---

76. Vatican II, Dogmatic Constitution on Divine Revelation (*Dei Verbum*), esp. 12, 19.

about God's wrathful punishment of deicide Jews, as many churches have acknowledged by officially repudiating this teaching.

Yet still more work must be done. Underlying the obviously problematic *punitive* supersessionism which holds that the Jewish people have lost the covenant because of their sins, there remains the more tenacious *economic* supersessionism in which the role of Judaism in the economy of God's dealing with humanity is over, its task complete with the coming of Christ. Jews may still be divinely beloved because of their ancestors and may even retain a covenantal relationship with an ever-faithful God, but if Jesus is the fulfillment of Jewish prophecies and hopes, Judaism itself would seem to have no further purpose. Even if Jews are no longer understood as condemned to demonstrate through their suffering the consequences of denying Jesus' messiahship, are not Jews *as Jews* relegated at best to serving Christianity as extraecclesial witnesses to the biblical texts preparing for the coming of Christ?

A first step toward a Christian theology in which Judaism exists on its own terms and not merely as preparatory to Christianity is to make room for Jewish readings of our common Scriptures. Biblical scholarship can be of great help in this task, since studying Hebrew Bible passages in their contexts underscores that these texts are not properly interpreted as Nostradamuslike predictions of Jesus. However, most important here is to engage, and learn from, Jewish interpretations of these texts. Their meaning is certainly not exhausted by the reductionistic readings in which Jesus is their fulfillment. But the Hebrew Bible also has further meaning beyond the views of the ancient Israelites. There is every reason to believe that the Jewish growth in understanding through millennia of religious experience is a deepening led by the Holy Spirit no less than the development of doctrine in Christianity.

Rosemary Ruether and, more recently, Pope Benedict XVI, further remind Christians that their doctrine of the Second Coming indicates that neither Christian nor Jewish hopes have been achieved. Jews, then, are not wrong to continue to wait for the messiah.[77]

---

77. Ruether, *Faith and Fratricide*, 246–51; and Pontifical Biblical Commission, *The Jewish People and Their Sacred Scriptures in the Bible* (Vatican City: Libreria Editrice Vaticana, 2002), 21, vatican.va/roman_curia/congregations/cfaith/pcb_documents/rc_con_cfaith_doc_20020212_popolo-ebraico_en.html.

Christians too look forward to a messianic redemption of history when God's reign of peace and justice will be fully established, while disagreeing with Jews over whether this will be the first or the second appearance of the messiah on earth. The New Testament citations of Hebrew Bible passages in relation to Jesus thus present an occasion for reflecting on how the expectations of Israel, understood historically as well as in the ongoing Jewish experience and interpretation, might deepen and enrich the Christian vision of and hope for the fullness of the world's redemption in the reign of God.

As Soulen astutely notes, Christians cannot—and should not—avoid constructing their own overarching narrative to integrate the Hebrew Bible with the New Testament. Christians have to find some way to give meaning to the whole Christian Bible, and the New Testament provides a context that changes the understanding of the Hebrew Bible. Nevertheless, a better narrative is needed than the currently common story that reduces the history of Israel to a prelude to Christianity. Soulen rightly contends that this economic supersessionism is inadequate to the Hebrew Bible and yields Christian doctrine virtually uninformed by the Hebrew Bible and the history of Israel, as well as by "such 'middle range' dimensions of human life as public history, economics, politics, and so on, all of which are of central concern to the Hebrew Scriptures."[78]

The narrative framework Soulen proposes is a promising approach for integrating the testaments into a nonsupersessionist Christianity. Noting that God's covenant with Israel is presented in the Hebrew Bible as an everlasting blessing not only for Israel but for "all the nations," Soulen argues that the Christian church should understand itself as another development in the divine plan for a diverse creation of mutual blessing. Along with the unity-in-diversity of male and female, parent and child, nature and humanity, and even God and humans, the Hebrew Bible reveals God's will for harmony between Israel and the nations, between Jews and Gentiles.

---

78. Soulen, *God of Israel*, 50. See also Ruether, *Faith and Fratricide*, 246–51; John T. Pawlikowski, *Jesus and the Theology of Israel* (Wilmington, DE: Michael Glazier, 1989), 88–99; and Pawlikowski, *Christ in the Light*, 119.

God desires a creation of mutual blessing enriched by the diversity of human history, cultures, and ethnicities, including the distinction between Jews and Gentiles.[79]

Soulen proposes that Christians view the gracious act of God in Jesus of Nazareth as a further revelation of God's intent to bring the world to the consummation in mutual blessing begun in creation and furthered through the blessings of the Abrahamic covenant. For Christians, the salvific event of Jesus Christ reveals the depth of God's steadfast commitment to establish the world in harmonious mutuality. As Pawlikowski maintains, the event of Jesus Christ reveals an unforeseen degree of divine-human unity and offers a universal covenant that incorporates Gentiles in explicit relation to—but not, as Soulen rightly insists, in replacement of—God's covenant with Jews.[80] God's history with Israel is not finished; rather, it continues as the "permanent and enduring medium of God's work as the Consummator of human creation, and therefore it is also the permanent and enduring context of the gospel about Jesus."[81]

A Christian triumphalism in which the church replaces Judaism is not God's plan, then, but a sinful human construct. Soulen points out that, in the Hebrew Bible, "sin seeks blessing apart from its source in the divine Other and apart from life with the human other. As a consequence, sin transforms the divine blessing into curse and the relationship with the human other into a source of enmity and discord."[82] To eclipse the ongoing history of God's relation to the people of Israel, as Christian supersessionism does, is just such an effort to seek blessing at the expense of Jews, and this has indeed resulted in a horrific history of enmity and discord.

Current official Catholic teaching, as well as that of many other Christian churches, maintains that God's covenant with the Jewish people continues and has not been superseded by the covenant in Jesus Christ. However, there is much theological debate about whether these covenants are best understood as two distinct covenants or as

---

79. Soulen, *God of Israel*, 142–44.
80. Pawlikowski, *Christ in the Light*, 109–16; Soulen, *God of Israel*, 156–77.
81. Soulen, *God of Israel*, 110.
82. Soulen, *God of Israel*, 144.

two forms of one covenant.[83] While this debate continues, I believe what is most important for the witness and mission of the church is the affirmation of covenantal unity-in-diversity. According to Christian Scripture, both Jews and Christians have an everlasting covenantal relationship and call from God through which the one God is working differently to redeem the whole world.

Given their shared Scriptures and the Jewish origins of Christianity, the Jewish people remain the church's primary religious other—that is, Christians cannot not think about Jews. Christian dialogue with Jews—at all levels of the church—is therefore imperative to ensure that Judaism is understood on its own terms rather than as a negative projection of Christianity. In addition to making room for a Jewish reading of Scripture, Christians must seek to learn from the ongoing history of Judaism as willed by God, *in its differences from* as well as in its similarities to Christianity. A practice of consulting the wisdom of our elder brothers and sisters in faith would be a more effective way to witness against the belief that Judaism is superseded than any number of ecclesial statements, of which the vast majority of church members remain largely unaware. Furthermore, working together for the redemption of the world is the context in which Christians and Jews can nourish the relationship of mutual blessing called for by their common Scriptures.

Conclusion

A prophetic, public church cannot fulfill its mission to be a sign and instrument of unity in the world without publicly repenting of the church's "original sin" of anti-Semitism. If the church is to witness against the discriminations and rejections that plague today's society at all levels, the church must come to terms with its own scapegoating of—and, frankly, campaign of terror against—its Jewish other. Indeed, the modern Western construction of the person over against "his" raced, sexed, and bestial other echoes the long-

---

83. For an excellent overview of some of the theological discussion on the relationship between God's covenant with the people of Israel and the covenant in Jesus of Nazareth, see Pawlikowski, *Jesus*, 15–47.

established Christian othering of the Jew as the negative foil that opposes and threatens, but also defines, Christianity.

A beginning has been made with the repudiation of explicit church teachings of contempt and, more recently, with Pope St. John Paul II's 2000 public apology for the harm members of the church have caused to Jews throughout history.[84] But this is truly only a beginning. Repentance is incomplete without the hard work of reform and restitution. Christians will need to exercise continual vigilance to overcome the supersessionism implicit in the triumphalism that represents Judaism as inherently flawed in comparison to Christianity. Christians will also need a better story of the church and its faith, one that weaves together the Hebrew Bible and the New Testament without implying that Judaism is degenerate or that the Jewish people are dismissed from the covenant. A church able to make theological room for Judaism without denying its own Christian revelation might be able to make room as well for other religions that witness to the mystery that exceeds the grasp of human culture or construct.[85]

A public and prophetic church is, then, an open and humble church. The attractive mirage of a pure ecclesial community witnessing in perfect holiness against the external evils of the world is neither spiritually healthy nor honest. Nor is it likely to fool many outside of the church. Instead of fearing that acknowledging the sinful distortions of the Christian tradition will impede the church's mission, a truly prophetic public stance requires that the church embrace—and apply to itself—the Good News of repentance for the forgiveness of sins. After all, a church that denies its own sins is not a very good witness to the joy of repenting and receiving forgiveness from God and from our offended brothers and sisters,

---

84. Alessandra Stanley, "Pope Asks Forgiveness for Errors of the Church Over 2,000 Years," *New York Times*, March 13, 2000, https://www.nytimes.com/2000/03/13/world/pope-asks-forgiveness-for-errors-of-the-church-over-2000-years.html.

85. Peter Phan develops this point in his "Jesus as the Universal Savior in the Light of God's Eternal Covenant with the Jewish People: A Roman Catholic Perspective," in Boys, *Seeing Judaism Anew*, 127–37.

with whom we might then more fully embody the relationships of mutual blessing that God intends.

John Pawlikowski retells a story that asks us to reimagine Jewish-Christian relations eschatologically. In this tale, attributed to Rabbi Zalman Schachter-Shalomi, the messiah arrives on earth to establish his reign and is greeted by both Jewish and Christian faithful. Eager to settle their differences once and for all, they ask the messiah if he has been here before. The messiah smiles but otherwise refuses to answer. They are then able to realize that the point after all was the kind of lives they had lived together.[86]

---

86. Pawlikowski, *Sinai and Calvary: A Meeting of Two Peoples* (Beverly Hills, CA: Benziger, 1976), 228–29.

Chapter 3

Overcoming Misogyny

Communion with the Church's Internal Other

Women around the world continue to do more than their share of work while receiving less than their fair share of the world's resources. Global statistics indicate that women work an hour more per day than men, yet women receive less pay, hold less political power, and have less access to education.[1] On average, women are paid 23 percent less than men are paid, even though women's wages have been shown to increase family well-being more than men's wages do.[2] Women also comprise two-thirds of the world's illiterate population, as girls are often denied the education available to

---

1. Ceri Parker, "It's Official: Women Work Nearly an Hour Longer than Men Every Day," *World Economic Forum*, June 1, 2017, https://www.weforum.org/agenda/2017/06/its-official-women-work-nearly-an-hour-longer-than-men-every-day/; see also UN Women, "Fact Sheet–Global," in *Turning Promises into Action: Gender Equality in the 2030 Agenda for Sustainable Development* (2018), https://www.unwomen.org/-/media/headquarters/attachments/sections/library/publications/2018/sdg-report-fact-sheet-global-en.pdf; and Ana Revenga and Sudhir Shetty, "Empowering Women Is Smart Economics," *Finance and Development* 49, no. 1 (March 2012), https://www.imf.org/external/pubs/ft/fandd/2012/03/revenga.htm.

2. UN Women, "Facts and Figures: Economic Empowerment," July 2018, https://www.unwomen.org/en/what-we-do/economic-empowerment/facts-and-figures.

boys.³ Nobel Prize winner Malala Yousafzai's extraordinary courage and commitment have drawn international attention to this injustice, but her defense of girls' education nearly cost her her life when she was shot at the age of fifteen by a would-be assassin seeking to end her outspoken advocacy on this issue.⁴

While various factors contribute to the unequal treatment of women, the underlying reality is clear: women and girls are too often "discounted human beings," considered to be of less value than men and boys. When resources such as food and medical care are scarce, those resources often go to the males in the family.⁵ In covering human rights violations in China, Pulitzer Prize–winning reporters Sheryl WuDunn and Nicholas Kristof discovered that the number of infant girls dying *each week* in China from lack of adequate medical care was about 750, roughly the same as the number of prodemocracy protestors killed in the Tiananmen Square massacre.⁶ These infant girls are among the approximately 100 million missing girls and women uncovered by economist Amartya Sen's analysis of global demographics.⁷ The multiple causes of the absence of these girls and women include abortion and infanticide of female offspring because boys are preferred and the consistent allocation of scarce resources such as food and medical care to male rather than female members of a family.

To put it simply, the sociocultural devaluing of women has lethal consequences. Women and girls die from unequal access to resources

---

3. Liz Ford, "Two-Thirds of World's Illiterate Adults Are Women, Report Finds," *The Guardian*, October 20, 2015, https://www.theguardian.com/global-development/2015/oct/20/two-thirds-of-worlds-illiterate-adults-are-women-report-finds.

4. "Malala Yousafzai Biographical," Nobel Prize website, accessed September 24, 2019, https://www.nobelprize.org/prizes/peace/2014/yousafzai/biographical/.

5. "C. Inequalities in Access to Health and Related Services," *Linkages*, International Institute for Sustainable Development, accessed September 24, 2019, http://enb.iisd.org/4wcw/dpa-028.html#top.

6. Nicholas D. Kristof and Sheryl WuDunn, *Half the Sky: Turning Oppression into Opportunity for Women Worldwide* (New York: Alfred A. Knopf, 2009), xiv.

7. While estimates vary depending on methodological assumptions, Sen's groundbreaking work has drawn attention to an important gender disparity. See Amartya Sen, "More Than 100 Million Women Are Missing," *New York Review of Books*, December 20, 1990.

but also from sustained patterns of violence and abuse directed at them simply because they are women. One of every three women in the world today suffers intimate partner violence or nonpartner sexual abuse.[8] Human rights advocate and former US president Jimmy Carter describes some of the egregious yet widespread forms of violence against women around the world: "unpunished rape and other sexual abuse, infanticide of newborn girls and abortion of female fetuses, a worldwide trafficking in women and girls, and so-called honor killings of innocent women who are raped."[9] This list should be expanded to include bride burnings (which may be as frequent as one every two hours), domestic violence, and routine genital mutilation.[10]

This global violence against women is unfortunately so common as to be perceived as unremarkable, even normal. In their work as journalists, Kristof and WuDunn came to realize that the arrest of a single political dissident would merit a front-page newspaper article, but "when 100,000 girls were routinely kidnapped and trafficked into brothels, we didn't even consider it news."[11] In fact, women and girls comprise 71 percent of the world's trafficked persons, an enslavement made possible (as slavery usually is) by the fact that women are so little valued that their abuse is seen as perhaps regrettable but not a truly significant matter.[12]

Americans may prefer to think of the abuse of women and girls as a major problem only in other countries and cultures, but the reality is that women and girls are harassed, abused, and even trafficked in the United States. In addition, US citizens are among the "sex tourists" who make the sexual slavery of girls abroad such a lucrative

---

8. World Health Organization, "Violence against Women: Key Facts," November 29, 2017, https://www.who.int/en/news-room/fact-sheets/detail/violence-against-women.

9. Jimmy Carter, *A Call to Action: Women, Religion, Violence, and Power* (New York: Simon and Schuster, 2014), 4.

10. Kristof and WuDunn, *Half the Sky*, xiv.

11. Kristof and WuDunn, *Half the Sky*, xiv.

12. United Nations Sustainable Development Goals, "Report: Majority of Trafficking Victims Are Women and Girls: One-Third Children," December 22, 2016, https://www.un.org/sustainabledevelopment/blog/2016/12/report-majority-of-trafficking-victims-are-women-and-girls-one-third-children/.

business.¹³ Unfortunately, Americans are deeply involved in the business of buying and selling female bodies around the world.

The American self-image of leadership in women's rights is further challenged by the fact that the United States ranks only 51st out of 149 countries in gender equity according to metrics of economics, politics, health, and education. In education, US women are doing quite well, receiving more college and graduate degrees than men do, and this helps to boost the United States' rank overall. Yet, despite their education, women do not fare well in the United States economically or in politics, where they are significantly underrepresented. Much of the public realm is controlled by men, especially government, employment, and media, with the result that male perspectives and interests dominate the public sphere.¹⁴ Further, as the #MeToo movement has reminded us, women at all levels of professional attainment continue to be treated as instruments for fulfilling male desires. The pornographic gaze is prevalent in Western society and a great deal of the world: women and girls are for sale nearly everywhere, and the public display of female bodies for male pleasure is commonplace.

But what does the abuse of women have to do with ecclesiology? Is this misogyny not simply one more among the many social problems that the church must—and often does—resist?

Feminist thinkers have analyzed the connections between the devaluation of women and other forms of oppression that plague our world today, especially racism, colonialism, and environmental devastation. These feminists have demonstrated that the dualistic hierarchy that values males over females is an essential element in a broader pattern of thought that also esteems white Western culture

---

13. Kristof and WuDunn, *Half the Sky*, 24. It should be noted that Kristof and WuDunn find Americans involved in the sex trade overseas as "sex tourists," but they are not a large percentage of those buying sex in these countries. However, Americans do foster an unfortunately thriving sex trade in trafficked women and girls in the United States.

14. World Economic Forum, *The Global Gender Gap Report 2018*, http://www3.weforum.org/docs/WEF_GGGR_2018.pdf. See also Saadia Zahidi, "America Is Falling Behind Other Countries in Gender Equality. The Next President Must Fix That," World Economic Forum website, October 27, 2016, https://www.weforum.org/agenda/2016/10/global-gender-gap-2016-usa-saadia-zahidi/.

at the expense of other races, cultures, and the earth itself.[15] As early as 1975, Rosemary Radford Ruether had already noted that "our present Western type of society . . . is based on the exploitation of people by people and the rape of the earth . . . . All the crises of history are converging: racism, sexism, colonialism, the technological depletion of the earth."[16] If this assessment is accurate, and I believe it is, then misogyny is not merely one among the many injustices in the world today, even if it is one that affects nearly half of the human race. Instead, sexism and, in its stronger form, misogyny, are inseparable from other societal problems that the church must address as it seeks to be a sign and instrument of unity among humanity.

Also to our point, the Christian church is itself implicated in the oppression of women. Throughout Christian history, church leaders have interpreted Scripture and church tradition as evidence that the subjugation of women is divinely willed, part of God's intended order for the world.

This is not to deny that women have at times found opportunities in the church that were unavailable to them elsewhere, especially alternatives to patriarchal marriage. Moreover, most mainstream Christian churches no longer oppose women's right to vote, to work outside the home, to own property, or even to have equal authority with their husbands in the family. Many Christian denominations now ordain women and set no official restrictions on women's leadership within the church. Although there is still a good deal of Christian opposition to women's full equality in family, society, and church, there can be no doubt that official church teachings have shifted considerably in the past hundred years with regard to women's public and legal rights.

---

15. See *inter alia* Rosemary Radford Ruether, *New Woman, New Earth: Sexist Ideologies and Human Liberation* (New York: Seabury Press, 1975; Boston: Beacon Press, 1995), esp. 78–79, 132, 204–5 (citations refer to the Beacon Press edition); Mary Ann Hinsdale, "Heeding the Voices: An Historical Overview," in *In the Embrace of God: Feminist Approaches to Theological Anthropology*, ed. Ann O'Hara Graff (Maryknoll, NY: Orbis, 1995), 26; and Elizabeth Johnson, *Women, Earth, and Creator Spirit* (Mahwah, NJ; Paulist Press, 1993), 10–22.

16. Ruether, *New Woman*, 182–83.

But the question remains as to whether the devaluation of women has been so deeply interwoven throughout the history of Christian thought and practice that sexism remains embedded in the life of the church. Certainly male terms and symbols are prevalent in much Christian liturgy and prayer, so that both God and the Christian worshiper are often described as male. Women are still banned from the priesthood and other clerical offices in the Catholic and Orthodox Churches, as well as in some of the more conservative forms of Protestant and nondenominational Christianity. However strenuously these practices may be defended as somehow consistent with respecting the true value of women, it is hard to escape the implication that women's voices and views have little to contribute to the church and that men are in some way more representative of the divine than women.

Underlying the dominance of male imagery and leadership in the church is, of course, the deeper and thornier issue of the role of gender in theological anthropology—that is, how are Christians to understand what it means to be female or male human beings or, for that matter, what it means to be a person who fits into neither category or both categories?[17]

The perspective supported by influential (male) theologians throughout most of Christian history affirms that there is one human nature, but that that nature is fully developed only in males, as taught in Aristotelian philosophy. More recently, an anthropology of gender complementarity has emerged, with the differences between male and female emphasized even to the point of eclipsing a common human nature. The question remains as to whether gender complementarity continues—despite its best intentions—to assume that the male is primary and normative, with females still discounted as the projected opposite of male humanity.

The argument of this chapter is that the church cannot fulfill its mission to be a sign and instrument of the union of all in God without coming to terms with its history of positioning women as the other to the normative, and therefore male, Christian. In the

---

17. I have developed this topic further in Mary Doak, "Sex, Race, and Culture: Constructing Theological Anthropology for the 21st Century," *Theological Studies* 80, no. 3 (2019): 508–29.

preceding chapter, we explored the church's failure to imagine a unity-in-diversity that could encompass non-Christians. Instead, Christian identity was constructed in opposition to the otherness of Jews, whose differences—some imagined more than real—clarified what it means to be a Christian. The current chapter is concerned with how normative Christian identity came to be constructed over against the otherness of women, whose differences—again, some imagined more than real—illustrate what the ideal, male Christian should *not* be (i.e., bodily, emotional, morally and intellectually weak). While Jews exemplify the abject external other, Christian women have provided an internal and similarly abject other.[18] This long-standing sexism is thus, like religious anti-Semitism, a very early and systematic failure that has distorted Christian faith and continues to be an obstacle to the church's mission.

To be a sign and instrument of unity-in-diversity in our deeply divided world, the church must undo these two fundamental refusals to celebrate diversity within as well as beyond the Christian community. Just as the church cannot overcome its anti-Semitic history without serious revision of church thought and practice, so also the church cannot ignore Christian sexism or relegate misogyny to a side issue without significantly damaging the church's witness to and work in the world. What kind of a church, and what kind of people, would consider the often violent and frequently deadly oppression of women a minor concern?

An adequate ecclesiology cannot be built on the sexist foundations of Christian tradition, as though the devaluation of women is a minor issue of little consequence for the church's mission. Unless and until we come to terms with Christian sexism, the church cannot fulfill its role as the sacrament of unity-in-diversity that the world so desperately needs.

The project of this chapter is briefly to trace the process through which women's alterity within the Christian tradition developed to the point that women have been positioned as not fully Christian and, more importantly, to explore Christian resources for overcoming this sexism. Women's full humanity, along with their capacity for

---

18. For a profound discussion of the abject, see Julia Kristeva, *Powers of Horror: An Essay on Abjection*, trans. Leon Roudiez (New York: Columbia University, 1982).

complete and exemplary Christian discipleship, ought to be affirmed and celebrated, with sexual differences valued as a contribution to the enrichment of the church. Undoing the ecclesial history of defining women as the devalued other to the normative (male) Christian is essential to the church's mission to witness to unity-in-diversity.

A Brief History of Official Church Views on Women

New Testament

The New Testament provides a record of early ambivalence about the place of women in the nascent Christian Church. On the one hand, these Scriptures witness to women's leadership in positions that far exceed what would be allowed in later centuries. On the other hand, some passages prohibit women from engaging in precisely the preaching and teaching they are praised for in other parts of the New Testament.[19] Apparently, the marginalization of women was already well underway within a few decades of Jesus' death. As Elisabeth Schüssler Fiorenza observes, there was clearly a struggle over the role of women in the church's formative years.[20]

All four of the New Testament gospels suggest that women were significant members of the Jesus movement. To be sure, no women are named among the symbolic twelve disciples who represent the twelve sons of Jacob and thus a renewed Israel. Other than this, however, the traditions passed down in the gospels give little support for the idea that Jesus treated female disciples differently from male disciples. On the contrary, the gospels describe women as included among those who are active in hearing and spreading the Good News, as is evident in the Gospel of Luke's account of Mary of Bethany learning "at the Lord's feet" (10:38-42) and in the Gospel of John's story of the interaction between Jesus and the Samaritan woman who was convinced to bring many other Samaritans to believe in Jesus (4:1-42).

---

19. For historical context and insightful interpretations of the New Testament texts on the role of women, see especially Ross Shepard Kraemer and Mary Rose D'Angelo, eds., *Women and Christian Origins* (Oxford and New York: Oxford University Press, 1999).

20. Elisabeth Schüssler Fiorenza, *In Memory of Her: A Feminist Theological Reconstruction of Christian Origins* (New York: Crossroad, 1986), esp. 285–94.

The gospels do portray Peter, James, and John as having a degree of priority among the disciples. But they also present Martha, Mary, and Lazarus as special friends of Jesus and, more significantly, all four of the canonical gospels indicate that Mary of Magdala, who is not described in the New Testament as a repentant prostitute, was an important disciple. She is most often identified as the one who—whether alone, as in the Gospels of John and Mark, or with another Mary, as in the Gospel of Matthew—first experienced Jesus as risen from the dead.[21]

It should be further noted that, although the male disciples figure prominently as select companions of Jesus in the Garden of Gethsemane, where they nap while Jesus struggles with his approaching death, this male priority is certainly more than offset by the fact that women disciples (again, Mary of Magdala along with other women) are described as remaining faithfully present during Jesus' crucifixion and as the first to witness the risen Lord.[22] As Mary Malone observes, "the women stories in the gospels are often used

---

21. See John 20:1-18; Mark 16:9; Matthew 28:1-10. As depicted in the Gospel of Luke (24:1-35), Mary of Magdala, Joanna, and another Mary are the first to be told by an angel of Jesus' resurrection, but Simon and the two disciples on the road to Emmaus are perhaps the first to see the risen Lord. See Mary Rose D'Angelo, "Reconstructing 'Real' Women from Gospel Literature," in Kraemer and D'Angelo, *Women and Christian Origins*, 105–28.

Following the tradition that Mary of Magdala was first to see the risen Lord, the editorial board of *America* magazine has concluded that before Mary of Magdala reported Jesus' resurrection to the other disciples, she alone *was* the church! See Editors, "When Only Mary Magdalene Knew of the Resurrection," *America: The Jesuit Review*, March 19, 2013, https://www.americamagazine.org/faith/2013/03/19/when-only-mary-magdalene-knew-resurrection.

22. See the emphasis on Peter, James, and John in Matthew 26:36-46 and Mark 14:32-42. For the women at the crucifixion, see especially Matthew 27:55-56 and Mark 15:40-41. John 19:25-27 includes an unnamed male disciple among the women at the foot of the Cross.

It is commonly argued that Jesus did differentiate between men and women because he only ordained men. This is an unsupportable claim since there is no evidence that Jesus ordained anyone, male or female. The argument is based on two unsubstantiated assumptions: (1) that the Last Supper is to be understood as an event of ordination, a claim for which there is no evidence; and (2) that only men were at this Last Supper, again a claim that extrapolates beyond the textual—or any other—evidence.

to contrast the faith and full discipleship of the women with the cowardice and mutterings of the male disciples."[23]

That women were active not only as faithful disciples but also as leaders of the nascent Christian Church is evident in the letters of St. Paul as well as in the later Acts of the Apostles. Paul praises many women with whom he worked closely in growing the church. These include Junia, whom Paul describes as "prominent among the apostles" (Rom 16:7), and Prisca, who, along with Aquila, traveled considerably and led house-churches in various cities. In Paul's letter to the Romans, Prisca and Aquila are said to have the gratitude of "all the churches of the Gentiles" (Rom 16:3-4); this couple is also described in the Acts of the Apostles as having taught a more nuanced understanding of Christianity to the prominent preacher Apollos (Acts 18:26). Interestingly, Prisc(ill)a's name is usually listed before her male partner Aquila's name in both Acts and Paul's letters, suggesting Prisc(ill)a's greater prominence.[24] Paul also commends Phoebe to the church in Rome, referring to her as a "deacon of the church at Cenchreae" (Rom 16:1).

In expressing his esteem for these (and other) women, St. Paul gives no indication that their active leadership in the Jesus movement is in any way remarkable or controversial. This acceptance of the authority of women who had the means to travel and to host congregations was probably well within the sociocultural norms for elite women in the Roman Empire at this time.[25] Furthermore, this female leadership would seem to be consistent with Paul's often-cited assertion of equality in his letter to the Galatians. His repetition of what may have been an established baptismal formula is still striking in its apparent egalitarianism: "As many of you as were baptized into Christ have clothed yourselves with Christ. There is no longer Jew or Greek, there is no longer slave or free, there is no

---

23. Mary T. Malone, *Women & Christianity*, vol. 1, *The First Thousand Years* (Maryknoll, NY: Orbis, 2000), 53.

24. See also the reference to Prisca and Aquila in 2 Timothy 4:19.

25. Jouette M. Bassler, "Limits and Differentiation: The Calculus of Widows in 1 Timothy 5:3-16," in *A Feminist Companion to the Deutero-Pauline Epistles*, ed. Amy-Jill Levine with Marianne Blickenstaff (New York: T&T Clark International, 2003), 124.

longer male and female; for all of you are one in Christ Jesus" (Gal 3:27-28). Later church authorities would insist that this equality is purely spiritual and eschatological, having no implications for the obvious inequality and even slavery that continued within the church as well as in the larger society.

Yet the New Testament, even in St. Paul's letters, also demonstrates an early concern to restrict women's leadership. First Corinthians 14 states rather unequivocally that women should be silent in church gatherings, a directive that seems to contradict Paul's command to women a few chapters earlier in the same letter to keep their veils on while praying or prophesying, activities that presumably involved speaking in the public assembly. This inconsistency has generated considerable attention from exegetes trying to determine what this letter might have meant in its context, with some arguing that the passage silencing women is a later interpolation.[26] However that may be, it is a significant testimony to ambivalence about women's roles in the church that Paul's letters, as passed down in the New Testament, include praise for women's work in public teaching and preaching along with prohibitions on just this kind of female activity.

We also find in 1 Corinthians an inchoate form of the hierarchical dualism that associates men with Christ and with the divine, setting them above women, who represent humanity and creation. In casting about for reasons why women should not engage in the indecorous behavior of removing their veils, St. Paul asserts: "I want you to understand that Christ is the head of every man, and the husband is the head of his wife, and God is the head of Christ" (1 Cor 11:3). He further argues, "Neither was man created for the sake of woman, but woman for the sake of man" (1 Cor 11:9). Apparently not fully satisfied with this asymmetrical description of the male-female relationship, Paul adds, "For just as woman came from man, so man comes from woman; but all things come from

---

26. See, for example, the discussion in Philip B. Payne, *Man and Woman, One in Christ: An Exegetical and Theological Study of Paul's Letters* (Grand Rapids, MI: Zondervan, 2009), 217–67. See also Jerome Murphy-O'Connor, "1 and 2 Corinthians," in *The Cambridge Companion to Paul*, ed. James D. G. Dunn (Cambridge: Cambridge University Press, 2003), 82.

God" (1 Cor 11:12); he thus qualifies his depiction of male priority with an affirmation of the interdependence of the sexes. Even so, and regardless of whether this "headship" is understood merely as source or as authority, men are still portrayed as related to Christ and God in a way that women are not.[27]

The household codes of behavior in the deutero-Pauline letters to the Ephesians and the Colossians further develop the claim to Christlike authority for the male head of the patriarchal household. Wives are told to submit to their husbands, and slaves to their masters, as though they are obeying Christ.[28] It is arguable that these letters propose a greater mutuality in Christian marriage than was common in the Greco-Roman world, since the husband is directed to love his wife, even to the point of giving his life for her as Christ did for the church.[29] Nevertheless, the development of this connection between the authority of men and that of Christ and of God has been used to support the oppression of women, with the Bible cited as commanding women's submission to male dominance not only in marriage but in church and in society as well.

Perhaps the most repressive New Testament position on women in the church is found in the first letter to Timothy, which is a fairly late New Testament text, perhaps written in the second century. This letter states, "Let a woman learn in silence with full submission. I permit no woman to teach or to have authority over a man; she is to keep silent. For Adam was formed first, then Eve; and Adam was not deceived, but the woman was deceived and became a transgressor. Yet she will be saved through childbearing, provided they continue in faith and love and holiness, with modesty" (1 Tim 2:11-15). Notably, St. Paul in 1 Corinthians and Romans describes Adam as the one whose sin introduced death into the world,[30] whereas the

---

27. See the discussion of head as source, not authority, in Virginia Ramey Mollenkott, "Emancipative Elements in Ephesians 5:21-33: Why Feminist Scholarship Has (Often) Left Them Unmentioned and Why They Should Be Emphasized," in Levine, *A Feminist Companion*, 50–51.

28. Ephesians 5:21–6:9; Colossians 3:18-25. See also 1 Peter 2:18–3:7, where slaves are commanded to obey even harsh and unjust masters!

29. See Mollenkott's developed argument for marital mutuality in Ephesians in her "Emancipative Elements in Ephesians 5:21-33."

30. See 1 Cor 15:21-22; Rom 5:12-14.

author of 1 Timothy focuses on Eve as the first sinner and implies that all women inherit Eve's specific moral weakness, so that women cannot be trusted to teach or otherwise exercise authority over men.

The author of 1 Timothy stretches the point further with the odd and theologically problematic statement that women will be saved through childbearing. However this puzzling claim is intended, it must be noted that no comparable qualification is placed on men's salvation. At the very least, this suggests that, for this author, the salvation of women poses problems that the salvation of men does not. This is quite a difference from the assertion in Galatians 3:28 that "there is no longer male and female; for all of you are one in Christ Jesus!" And, as we will see, the idea that women are especially inclined to evil has had deeply unfortunate consequences in Christian history.

As this brief review of the New Testament indicates, women's roles in the church were contested in the decades following Jesus' death. That women were active in public service as teachers, missionaries, and leaders of local communities is confirmed both by the New Testament references that praise their work and in the proscriptions against their public activity. There would have been, after all, little need to repeat prohibitions against women teaching and speaking in church if women had not in fact been engaging in these ministries. By the time of the later New Testament letters, some important Christian voices were insisting that women must be kept from positions of authority, not only because such public activity is unseemly for women but because women are morally weaker and inclined to lead men astray.

Increasing Restrictions on Women

As Christianity grew into an institution with established offices, the public leadership of women that St. Paul apparently took for granted became much less common. By the end of the second century, the historical record suggests that males largely monopolized the positions of bishop and priest and that even the female diaconate was rare in Western Christianity.[31]

---

31. The repeated prohibitions on women in office (along with occasional, but rare, records acknowledging their existence) suggest that there were women in these offices even while the emerging institutionalized church opposed and

Women's public contributions and activities were, of course, never completely suppressed, especially in the centuries before the church developed sufficiently effective and centralized authority structures to impose uniform practices. Women continued to exercise some degree of official ministry as deacons or deaconesses, particularly in Eastern Christianity (where the order of deaconesses still continues) but also in some parts of Western Christianity as late as the eleventh century.[32] Interestingly, there is more evidence of women priests in Western Christianity than in Eastern Christianity during the first millennium.[33] In addition to some ancient tombs and other inscriptions referring to women *presbyterae* or even *sacerdotae*, extant letters from the fifth-century pope Gelasius and again from the eighth-century pope Zachary complain that some bishops are allowing women to minister at the altar in ways these popes insist is to be reserved to the male sex.[34]

The historical record indicates that the "order of widows" provided women with a formal ecclesial role for some centuries. However, the third-century document *Didascalia Apostolorum* expresses considerable interest in curtailing the ministry of these women. This text maintains that enrolled widows should be confined to a life of prayer at home. However, there is so much attention here to forbidding widows to teach and baptize that we must assume that many of these widows were engaged in just these activities, though obviously not without some official resistance.[35] The *Apostolic Constitutions*, a fourth-century document from Syria, similarly sought to diminish the status of enrolled widows and to prohibit them from

---

marginalized women's leadership. See *inter alia* Francine Cardman, "Women, Ministry, and Church Order in Early Christianity," in Kraemer and D'Angelo, *Women and Christian Origins*, 300–29; and Kevin Madigan and Carolyn Osiek, eds., *Ordained Women in the Early Church: A Documentary History* (Baltimore: Johns Hopkins University Press, 2005).

32. Madigan and Osiek, *Ordained Women*, 145, 147–48.
33. Madigan and Osiek, *Ordained Women*, 9, 163–98.
34. Gary Macy, *The Hidden History of Women's Ordination: Female Clergy in the Medieval West* (Oxford and New York: Oxford University Press, 2008), 61–62. See also Madigan and Osiek, *Ordained Women*, 186–88, 193–98.
35. Cardman, "Women, Ministry, Church Order," 308–14. See also Malone, *First Thousand Years*, 128–31.

teaching and baptizing. As Francine Cardman observes about this later text, "Ultimately, the argument is about the nature of ministry, of women and men, even of God. This is evident in the almost seamless way in which the argument slips from the practice of women baptizing to the headship of men over women and the maleness of priesthood."[36]

The increasingly effective male monopoly of official church ministry in the offices of bishop, priest, and (in the West) deacon continued to marginalize female leadership through the Middle Ages. Yet at the same time, abbesses emerged as powerful ecclesial figures. The ritual installation of abbesses during these years was sometimes described as an ordination, and in at least one official rite the new abbess was given a miter and staff, symbols of episcopal authority. Within their monasteries, abbesses were known to read the Gospel, to preach, to hear confessions, and to give absolution—activities otherwise associated with ordained ministry.[37] They also held an episcopal level of authority over the territory of their monasteries, which may have some relation to the legend that St. Brigid of Ireland, a noteworthy abbess, was ordained a bishop by divine intervention.[38]

Even while there is solid evidence that women were not as uniformly and thoroughly excluded from ecclesial leadership and ministry as the standard church histories have assumed, the limits imposed on women were nevertheless extensive. They were banned from official office and public ministry in most spheres of ordinary parish life. The contributions of countless women who managed to shape the history of Christianity as writers, mystics, teachers, and exemplars were substantial, but so too were the obstacles such women faced in a church whose official leaders considered women's teaching and active authority to be suspect if not utterly unacceptable.

Furthermore, the marginalization of women in the church was by no means limited to women's exclusion from church offices and official ministry. The restrictions that would keep widows silent, submissive, and at home reflect ecclesial beliefs about the proper role of Christian women. For much of Christian history, women who sought

---

36. Cardman, "Women, Ministry, Church Order," 315.
37. Macy, *Hidden History*, 80–86, also 37.
38. Macy, *Hidden History*, 54.

freedom from the patriarchal household were enclosed in the convent and, like the enrolled widows before them, were often allowed to teach only the most rudimentary levels of catechism to other girls.[39] Even as great a mystic, saint, and reformer as Teresa of Ávila felt compelled to excuse her writing from within the cloister as an exercise in obedience to her spiritual director.[40] Contemporary Catholics accustomed to the "nuns on the bus" and other religious women's public campaigns for social justice may be surprised to know that, well into the modern era, all Catholic religious women were officially cloistered, confined to the convent or monastery, and prohibited from active work in the world, including such work as teaching elementary subjects or caring for the poor and sick in society.[41]

Many women, of course, resisted these limitations, working diligently and creatively to find ways to put their various talents at the service of the pressing needs of the world and the church, despite official prohibitions. The stories of the Ursulines, of Mary Ward and the English Ladies, of the Sisters of the Visitation, and of so many others demonstrate the resilience of women religious who developed strategies that successfully resisted the imposition of cloister—at least for a time—so that they could respond as they saw fit to the needs around them.[42] Other women, seeking to avoid altogether the limits set by church authorities, formed religious groups without asking for official recognition or approval from the church, but even these groups—such as the Beguines—were usually dispersed and banned.[43] Apparently, all Christian women who were not governed by fathers, brothers, or husbands were to be kept under the supervision of male ecclesiastical authorities.

Our concern here with this summary history is not principally with the exclusion of women from ordination and official leader-

---

39. Mary T. Malone, *Women & Christianity*, vol. 2, *From 1000 to the Reformation* (Maryknoll, NY: Orbis, 2001), 127–28. See also Mary Daly, *The Church and the Second Sex: With the Feminist Postchristian Introduction and New Archaic Afterwords by the Author* (Boston: Beacon Press, 1985), 102–6.

40. Mary T. Malone, *Women & Christianity*, vol. 3, *From the Reformation to the 21st Century* (Maryknoll, NY: Orbis, 2003), 77.

41. Daly, *Church*, 102–3.

42. Malone, *From the Reformation*, 95–125.

43. Malone, *From 1000*, 128–32.

ship, a story that has been thoroughly studied by many others. Of primary interest for our present purposes is the ecclesial marginalization of women that went along with their exclusion from positions of leadership. Barred from church office and prohibited from publicly preaching, interpreting the Scriptures, or engaging in theological debates, women had no direct voice in the doctrinal debates through which the foundations of Christian thought were established and developed in an increasingly hierarchical church. Considering how impoverished Christian doctrine would be without the distinct voices of Augustine, Anselm, Aquinas, and Bonaventure, we can only imagine how the perspectives of equally brilliant women throughout these centuries might have further enriched Christian faith. Alas, as Mary Malone has noted, the loss of these contributions leaves a void that can never be filled.[44] Furthermore, these centuries of suppressing women's voices make it possible still for many scholars to consider adequate histories of the church and of church doctrine that include (at best) only minor mention of women from the biblical period until modern times.

Women as the Inferior, Dangerous, Abject Other

Unfortunately, the marginalization of women and their voices was only one aspect of the ecclesial developments that positioned Christian women as the abject other to the normative Christian man. Another significant factor was the idea that men are naturally holier and more fully symbolic of Christ and God than women are. We have already seen an early version of this viewpoint in St. Paul's first letter to the Corinthians. In addition to suggesting that husbands hold the place of Christ in relation to their wives, this letter describes men as the image and reflection of God while women are the reflection of men (1 Cor 11:3-7). This idea was repeated by patristic and medieval theologians who apparently considered themselves on firm biblical grounds in concluding that the female body is simply not the image of God as the male body is, even if women may somehow spiritually represent the divine. St. Augustine, for example, maintained that "in their corporeal sex . . . it is said that

---

44. Malone, *First Thousand Years*, 245–46.

man only is the image and glory of God," while Aquinas similarly determined that "God's image is found in man in a way in which it is not found in woman; for man is the beginning and the end of woman, just as God is the beginning and end of all creation."[45]

These influential Christian thinkers do not seem disturbed by the implication that, if men more directly represent God and Christ, then it might follow that women are, by nature, less suited not only to ministry but even to being Christians.[46] To the contrary, there is much in the patristic and later traditions that unabashedly emphasizes the maleness of the ideal Christian. Virtue, for example, was assumed to be a male characteristic; the etymological connection between the Latin *vir* for man and *virtus*, meaning valor or moral excellence, is surely no accident. Since women were seen as more inclined to evil than men, holy women, especially virgins and martyrs, were praised for having overcome their female nature. Their moral excellence was taken as evidence that, by the grace of God, they had become spiritually male. At the same time, men were shamed for lagging behind holy, virginal woman in the spiritual development that was thought to come more naturally to men.[47]

Women, it seems, stood in need of what Mary Malone has described as a "double redemption," in which "the first, the choice of virginity, raised them to the level of men; the second redemption,

---

45. Augustine, *De Genesi ad Litteram*, XI, xlii, 58, as translated by Prudence Allen and cited in Prudence Allen, *The Concept of Woman: The Aristotelian Revolution 750 BC–AD 1250* (Grand Rapids, MI: William B. Eerdmans, 1997), 222; and Thomas Aquinas, *Summa Theologiae* (New York: McGraw, 1967), I, q. 28, a. 4. See also the discussion in Allen, *Concept of Woman*, 387–88.

46. Interestingly, contemporary Catholic ecclesial arguments, especially by Pope St. John Paul II, affirm that women are fully the image of God but nevertheless insist that women cannot represent Christ, even while sometimes claiming that women are more inclined by nature to Christlike behavior than men are! See Rosemary Radford Ruether, "*Imago Dei*, Christian Tradition and Feminist Hermeneutics," in Kari Elisabeth Børrsen, ed., *The Image of God: Gender Models in Judaeo-Christian Tradition* (Minneapolis: Fortress Press, 1995), 267–91.

47. See Mary Daly's discussion and especially the quotations from Jerome and Augustine in Daly, *Church*, 85–89. Similarly, the medieval scholar Gratian asserted that the Latin words for man and woman are derived, respectively, from the phrases "strength of soul" and "soft of mind or character" (Macy, *Hidden History*, 118). See also the discussions in Malone, *First Thousand Years*, 110, 146, 160, 158.

then, helped them to attain to the transformation offered to the perfect."[48] Or as Rosemary Radford Ruether puts it: "Males were 'naturally spiritual.' . . . [Women] must transcend, not only their bodily, but their 'feminine' nature in order to be saved."[49]

Church leaders also drew on 1 Timothy 2:11-15, with its allusion to Eve's role in the first sin, as biblical support for their insistence on women's greater inclination to sin. Tertullian pronounced women "the Devil's gateway," maintaining that all women bear the guilt for the first sin and thus also for the death of the Son of God that brought redemption.[50] This idea that women inherit from Eve a greater inclination to sin and to lead men astray added further justification for male authority over females and for banning women from preaching and teaching. As St. John Chrysostom contends, the author of 1 Timothy did not permit a woman to teach because the woman taught the man once . . . and wrought our ruin," and so, for this reason, males must "have the preeminence in every way."[51] Indeed, according to Malone, St. Ambrose recommends that women should weep "for the fault of being a woman."[52]

This abjection of women became more entrenched at the beginning of the second Christian millennium as the Gregorian Reforms sought to institutionalize clerical celibacy. Of course, as many have noted, these reforms were fundamentally about ecclesial power over church property and over secular authority.[53] Yet the campaign to convince priests and laity of the superiority of a celibate clergy involved serious misogyny. St. Peter Damian's tirade against clergy wives is an example of the abhorrence of women and sexuality: "I speak to you, O charmers of the clergy, appetizing flesh of the devil . . . you bitches, sows, screech-owls, night-owls, bloodsuckers,

---

48. Malone, *First Thousand Years*, 140.

49. Ruether, *New Woman*, 92.

50. Elizabeth A. Clark, *Women in the Early Church* (Collegeville, MN: Liturgical Press, 1983), 39.

51. John Chrysostom, "Homily 9 on 1 Timothy," accessed November 16, 2019, http://www.newadvent.org/fathers/230609.htm. See also the discussion in Clark, *Women in the Early Church*, 157. See Macy, *Hidden History*, 122–24, for further medieval views on women and the sin of Eve.

52. Malone, *First Thousand*, 157.

53. Macy, *Hidden History*, 112–14.

she-wolves . . . harlots, prostitutes, with your lascivious kisses, you wallowing places for fat pigs, couches for unclean spirits."[54] In another sermon, he further insults the wives (not the mistresses!) of priests by insisting, "the hands that touch the body and blood of Christ must not have touched the genitals of a whore."[55]

While Damien's visceral disgust with women and sex is certainly extreme, his focus on women as an impure source of defilement is consistent with the growing medieval emphasis on cultic sacramentality. As Madigan and Osiek attest, "the motif of blood as uncleanness unworthy of the purity of the altar was one of the most common reasons given for the exclusion of women from altar service."[56] Women were even discouraged from receiving Communion—or in some cases from entering a church at all—while menstruating or after childbirth due to their presumed state of pollution.[57] In their femaleness, women represent not holiness but defilement.

The denigration of women is reinforced by the late medieval embrace of Aristotelianism, including its view of women as defective, or "misbegotten," males.[58] This idea that women are essentially incomplete men is a further argument against women's ability to represent the divine, since women then symbolize imperfection, not eminence. Furthermore, the defective nature of women extends to their moral and intellectual capacities. Women's female embodiment in itself—and not only the inheritance from Eve's transgression—is said to render women more inclined to sin and stupidity: women possess a weakness of will and intellect such that women can never be fully mature adults. Even adult women require male supervision, then, because they remain inherently immature, at least until grace perfects the defect of their sex in heaven.

---

54. Peter Damian, "*Contra Intemperantes Clericos*," as translated in Anne Llewellyn Barstow, *Married Priests and the Reforming Papacy: The Eleventh Century Debates* (New York: Edwin Mellon Press, 1982), 60–61.

55. Peter Damian, "*De Celibatu Sacerdotum*," as translated in Barstow, *Married Priests*, 119. See also Malone, *From 1000*, 49, 30; and Macy, *Hidden History*, 112–15.

56. Madigan and Osiek, *Ordained Women*, 139, 205.

57. Malone, *First Thousand Years*, 122–66; Macy, *Hidden History*, 114.

58. Macy, *Hidden History*, 119–21; Allen, *Concept of Woman*, 361–473.

Macy aptly sums up the implications of medieval arguments about gender: "Women were reconceived as the quintessential danger to men: irrational, unclean, sinful, passive, morally and physically weak, victims who at the same time tempted men to violate them. . . . This redefinition of women also redefined men as rational, pure, salvific, active, morally and physically strong, constantly having to fight off the temptations of women."[59] Macy astutely draws our attention to the cultural work this rhetoric about women did. The norms of Christian life were both clarified and made attractive through contrast with the repulsive flaws attributed to women. In other words, women's nature reveals what a Christian (including Christian women) should strive to overcome. Just as Jews served as the non-Christian other whose projected difference defined Christian identity, Christian women served as the Christian other whose putative defects represented the opposite of the ideal, or exemplary, Christian.

Yet there is more. Women, inclined by nature to lead good (male) Christians astray, are thereby positioned as an internal danger to the church. They are a threat that must be contained no less than the supposed menace of Judaism, though with the difference that women remain necessary for the future of society and church. As we saw in chapter 2, the demonizing of the Jew as the Christian's quintessential other led not only to legal oppression but to centuries of abuse, beatings, and pogroms that were all justified as reasonable and even honorable ways of defending the Christian community. The culmination of centuries of demonizing rhetoric and violent actions in the twentieth-century massacre of 6,000,000 Jews is seared into the history of the West. Alas, the positioning of women as an internal threat has also generated physical violence to match the rhetorical violence. Recent studies have determined that, between 1560 and 1760, at least 200,000 women were burned to death as witches, with uncounted others dying in prison, from torture, or because they were lynched before they could be burned by the authorities.[60] One bishop in Germany was so thorough that,

---

59. Macy, *Hidden History*, 126–27.
60. Malone, *From the Reformation*, 32.

according to Ruether, he left several villages with only one woman remaining alive.[61]

The extent of this misogynist violence is horrifying, and yet such savagery against the threat of the other is very difficult to resist in times of social anxiety. Violence against the scapegoated other, as René Girard has shown, fosters group cohesion through the common action taken to reaffirm the group's ideals and boundaries.[62] Through expelling (usually violently) the dangerous other—in this case, presumably disobedient women—anxieties are allayed, the group is unified, and shared norms are reinforced.

As I write this, there is much angry rhetoric in the United States and abroad about the dangers that various ethnic, racial, and sexual minorities pose. The ease with which public sentiment is whipped up against those who have been defined as a threat (whether to jobs, physical security, or cultural norms) is increasingly evident, as is the violence this rhetoric inspires. Every social group, including the church, faces the perennial temptation to secure its identity through the creation and vilification of a supposedly threatening other, whether that other be external or internal to the group. This is why the church's mission of witnessing to the divine gift and call to peaceful harmony amid diversity is so critical. It is also why the church cannot fulfill this mission without coming to terms with its own history of defining Jews and women as the paradigmatic others in opposition to whom the ideal Christian is defined.

Hierarchical Dualism and Systemic Oppression

Christianity did not, of course, invent the practice of defining males as the exemplary form of humanity. As Simone de Beauvoir demonstrates in her classic *The Second Sex*, male normativity has been taken for granted in much of human history; it would be surprising if this male-centric thinking had not been replicated in Christianity.[63] The habit of considering men to be the default and superior

---

61. Ruether, *New Woman*, 102.
62. René Girard, *The Scapegoat*, trans. Yvonne Freccero (Baltimore, MD: Johns Hopkins University Press, 1989).
63. Simone de Beauvoir, *The Second Sex*, trans. and ed. H. M. Parshley (New York: Random House, 1952). See also the discussion in Ruether, *New Woman*, esp. 4.

human being, with women as an inferior—if necessary—variant is entrenched in many languages and cultures. And so, in what is often an unconscious process, women are devalued, given less access to resources, and have fewer opportunities, while violence against them somehow seems less objectionable and more "normal" than if it were against the more valued male sex. A prophetic, public church must oppose this mistreatment of half of the world's population, but the church cannot provide the prophetic witness the world needs without coming to terms with its own traditions that position women as the inferior other to the normative male Christian.

The extent of the needed reform becomes clearer when we understand how interwoven sexism is with other forms of systemic oppression. In her classic 1974 essay "Is Female to Male as Nature Is to Culture?," anthropologist Sherry Ortner argues that women's subordination is rooted in the association of women with nature, presumably because of their evident involvement in birth and usually in child-rearing.[64] The realm of "culture," more highly esteemed because it is constructed rather than given, is then assumed to be the province of men.[65] This foundational insight has been expanded and developed by feminist theorists into an analysis of the underlying system of binary thinking, or hierarchical dualism, that structures the Western construal of how humans relate to the divine, to each other, and to the natural world.[66]

Elizabeth Johnson explains that hierarchical dualism divides reality into two opposing categories, with one category judged as superior and the other as inferior. God is thus opposed to world, male to female, reason to emotion, culture to nature, spirit to body, and even "white" people to people of color. A further aspect of this

---

64. Sherry B. Ortner, "Is Female to Male as Nature Is to Culture?," in *Woman, Culture, and Society*, ed. Michelle Zimbalist Rosaldo and Louise Lamphere (Stanford, CA: Stanford University Press, 1974), 68–87.

65. Kwok Pui-lan argues that Ortner's analysis at this point is not as universally valid as Ortner claims, since some Asian cultures deeply value nature but still devalue women. See Kwok Pui-lan, *Introducing Asian Feminist Theology* (Cleveland: Pilgrim Press, 2000), 114–15.

66. As Elizabeth Johnson argues, "These three relationships—human beings to the earth, among each other, and to God—are profoundly interconnected. . . . [A]ll three have been conceived primarily according to the values of patriarchy" (*Women, Earth, and Creator Spirit* [New York: Paulist Press, 1993], 3).

hierarchical dualism is that all of the "top" or more highly valued categories are associated with each other, so that the male is more closely related not only to culture (as Ortner argues) but also to God, reason, spirit, and "white" or Euro-American civilization. Similarly, the less valued categories of the world—including female, emotion, nature, body, people of color, and the Global South—are understood as sharing characteristics. It follows then that white or Euro-American men represent God more accurately, are more reasonable, are creators of culture and, like God, are the appropriate rulers over the world and especially over inherently irrational women, nature, and people of color.[67]

This contrastive approach to defining the value of humanity is developed by Ellen Armour in her analysis of the concept of the modern "Man" (the white male as normative human being) clarified through opposition to Man's raced, sexed, animal, and divine other. These latter categories form what Armour calls the "modern fourfold," in which nonwhite people, women, and animals clarify what the normative human person (the Man) is not, as well as what that Man must be defended against.[68] Armour's work further elucidates what Rosemary Radford Ruether and others have also noted: that sexism cannot be separated from other forms of oppression because their justifications are systemically interrelated. Indeed, Ruether has argued in her groundbreaking analysis of the connection between sexism and racism that "sexism was the first and basic model for this subjugation of one part of the race to bodily work, so that the other part could be free to create and enjoy."[69] It can never be sufficient, then, to seek to liberate the few, elite Euro-American women from sexism. A truly liberating feminism recognizes that sexism, racism, colonialism, and ecological destruction are intertwined in the system of hierarchical dualism that undergirds much of Western thought, including Christianity.

Particularly important today is the development of ecofeminism, with its commitment to overcoming the destruction of the earth and climate as well as the subjugation of women and other op-

---

67. Johnson, *Women, Earth, Creator Spirit*, 10–22.

68. Ellen T. Armour, *Signs and Wonders: Theology after Modernity* (New York: Columbia University, 2016).

69. Ruether, *New Woman*, 182.

pressed peoples. As will be discussed in chapter 5, the looming climate crisis threatens the conditions of life on this planet and is already making life more difficult for the poor, and especially women, in many places. Ecofeminists contend that hierarchical and dominating habits must be replaced with mutuality and interdependence in our relations with each other and with nature.[70] This task poses a significant challenge to the Christian tradition, which has not only largely neglected nature as a moral concern but also has a long history of supporting social hierarchies thought to mirror the rule of God. To be a prophetic sign and instrument in the world today, Christianity must espouse a unity-in-diversity that celebrates mutuality in all aspects of human life, including our connection to the sustaining earth.

Women in the Church Today

Given the evident devaluation of women in the Christian tradition, we must ask how much this history continues to affect contemporary Christianity. Is Christian misogyny appropriately consigned to the past, dismissed as an element of a patriarchal time that mainstream Christianity, at least, has outgrown, even if women continue to suffer at the hands of others around the world?

Certainly the worst of the vitriol against women is no longer commonly espoused by church leaders. Public sermons in mainstream churches are not likely to rage against women as evil temptresses, and menstruation and childbirth are not generally thought to render women unfit for church attendance or for Holy Communion. Moreover, as Catherine Keller has noted, church authorities no longer condemn women who dare to preach or teach to be burned alive, since, as she rather sardonically quips, Rome has "had its matches confiscated."[71]

---

70. Ruether, *New Woman*, esp. 204–5. See also Anne M. Clifford, *Introducing Feminist Theology* (Maryknoll, NY: Orbis, 2001), 222–54; and Irene Diamond and Gloria Feman Orenstein, eds., *Reweaving the World: The Emergence of Ecofeminism* (San Francisco: Sierra Club Books, 1990).

71. Catherine Keller, *Apocalypse Now and Then: A Feminist Guide to the End of the World* (Boston: Beacon, 1996), 112.

But has this othering of women not been encoded in the Christian tradition, in its ongoing language, teachings, and patterns of thought? Don't women continue to be defined (if in subtle ways) as other to the normative, male Christian? Are European and Euro-American Christians no longer inclined to the dualistic thinking that assumes that God, male, reason, culture, spirit, and white belong together?

In the concluding volume of her magisterial study of the history of women in Christianity, Mary Malone observes that three major aspects of women's position in the church remain problematic: (1) the entrenched patriarchal leadership, especially in the Catholic and Orthodox Churches, that prohibits women from holding ordained office; (2) the ongoing dominance of male language and imagery in worship and prayer, with both God and humanity represented as male; and (3) the understanding of sexual difference, especially in relation to the common humanity of men and women.[72]

In my judgment, this third aspect—concerning the anthropology of sexual difference—is the key issue, since interpretations of sexual difference provide the rationale for both the patriarchal structures of church leadership and the dominance of male language. The marginalization of women in church life on the traditional grounds that they are essentially defective males who lack intellectual and moral maturity, being biologically and morally indefensible, is of course no longer credible. However widespread this view has been in the Christian tradition, there are fortunately not many now who will publicly maintain such an explicit denial of the full humanity of women.

But gender complementarity is an alternative account of sexual difference that has become prominent especially in official Catholic teachings in recent decades.[73] Drawing on the work of Hans Urs

---

72. Malone, *From the Reformation*, 253–54.

73. John Paul II, *Man and Woman He Created Them: A Theology of the Body*, trans. Michael Waldstein (Boston: Pauline Books and Media, 2006); John Paul II, On the Dignity and Vocation of Women (*Mulieris Dignitatem*), http://w2.vatican.va/content/john-paul-ii/en/apost_letters/1988/documents/hf_jp-ii_apl_19880815_mulieris-dignitatem.html; Prudence Allen, *The Concept of Woman*, vol. 3, *The Search for Communion of Persons: 1500–2015* (Grand Rapids, MI: Eerdmans, 2016), 442–87; and Susan Ross, *Anthropology: Seeking Light and Beauty* (Collegeville, MN: Liturgical Press, 2012), 99–101.

von Balthasar, Pope St. John Paul II identifies essential psychological and spiritual differences between men and women based on their different biological contributions to human reproduction. With the laudable goal of defending the equality-in-difference of men and women, gender complementarity insists that neither sex is more human than the other; rather, both sexes are needed not only for physical fertility but also for any truly loving and creative community. Most commonly, the analysis defines maleness as essentially initiatory whereas femaleness is inherently receptive, though Prudence Allen prefers to emphasize that men have a biologically based inclination to protect others, while women have a "genius" for nurturing persons in their particularity. Each is fully human, Allen explains, but she insists that together they comprise a communion greater than the sum of the parts.[74]

If love necessarily involves a dynamic interaction of initiation and reception, and God is love, then it is not surprising that complementarian Christian theologians would seek to apply this analysis of sexual love to the inner life of the divine. Doing so allows both male and female to represent the divine, although only through a dizzying degree of shifting in the gender roles assigned to the persons of the Trinity. The Father takes the initiative and so is male in begetting the Son who, despite the masculine noun, is feminine in being begotten by the Father. Yet the Son joins the Father in their male activity of spirating the Spirit, who is female in being spirated. But then the Father is, as Father, conditioned by the relation to Son and Spirit, who then are masculine in relation to the feminine/receiving Father. The final outcome is that both male and female humans, in different ways, can be said to reflect the image of God.[75]

But there is a catch here: the Trinitarian God always takes the initiative with regard to humanity, while humans are, in relation to the divine, inherently receptive or female. So God must continue to

---

74. Allen, *Search for Communion*, 8, 464–71.

75. See the discussion of this Balthasarian approach as set forth and defended in David L. Schindler, *Heart of the World, Center of the Church: Communion Ecclesiology, Liberalism, and Liberation* (Grand Rapids MI: Eerdmans, 1996), 242–55; cf. Ruether's discussion of the earlier form of gendered Trinity as developed by Karl Barth in Ruether, "*Imago Dei*," 267–91.

be represented predominantly as male in ecclesial worship, where the focus is on God's relation to humanity and to creation. Furthermore, Jesus, as the incarnation of God, could only be male because this is a divine initiative to save humanity.[76]

The implications of this gender complementarian theory for Christian leadership are even more clearly articulated and strenuously defended. God must be predominantly referred to as male in worship because God takes the initiative with regard to humanity, and only men can be priests for the same reason that Jesus had to be male: the incarnation and the priesthood are instruments of the divine initiative in salvation. Pope St. John Paul II acknowledged that God can be imaged at times as female, but the divine femininity remains marginal in public worship, which focuses on God's initiatory, or male, relation to humanity.[77] The historical justification for patriarchal leadership and the dominance of male imagery based on the explicit denigration of women has been replaced, but the practices remain the same—and men are still somehow more like God than women are.

A male-only clergy is further defended on the grounds that the church, like all (heteronormative) productive love, requires the interactive cooperation of both of these male and female activities. In the church, these are embodied in a "Petrine" principle of initiatory leadership and a "Marian" principle of receptive and loving response to that leadership. Together, these principles constitute the church as a fertile, creative community of love, the image of God's saving action and humanity's graced response.[78] Clergy, representing God's initiative, are thus inherently male, while female receptivity is paradigmatic of the laity. Allowing female clergy would distort the important symbolism through which the male represents not only God's proper priority in relation to humanity but also the indispensability of a feminine receptivity to the leaders' initiatives.[79]

---

76. Allen, *Search for Communion*, 481; Sacred Congregation for the Doctrine of the Faith, Declaration on the Question of Admission of Women to the Ministerial Priesthood (*Inter Insigniores*), http://www.vatican.va/roman_curia/congregations/cfaith/documents/rc_con_cfaith_doc_19761015_inter-insigniores_en.html; and Ruether's insightful critique in "*Imago Dei*," 267–91.

77. *Mulieris Dignitatem* 6–8.

78. *Mulieris Dignitatem* 27.

79. *Mulieris Dignitatem* 26; Allen, *Search for Communion*, 481.

This complementarian anthropology, though developed only in the nineteenth and twentieth centuries, is currently the most plausible (or least implausible) theological basis for excluding women from ordained office and official leadership in the Catholic Church. As the Pontifical Biblical Commission determined in 1976, arguments that Jesus did not ordain women fail, since there is no scriptural or other historical evidence that Jesus ordained anyone.[80] The ordained priesthood as a Christian practice began in the early church and has continued to develop in meaning and practice over the millennia since then.[81] The argument from tradition—the church didn't ordain women in the past so it can't do so now—has weight to the extent that long-standing practices have a claim to serious consideration and should not be changed lightly. Yet the authority of past practices cannot be and has never been absolute, or the church would be denied the possibility of growing in understanding, as it clearly has with regard to the issue of slavery after nearly two thousand years despite scriptural warrants in support of this practice. Moreover, Christian history does not witness to a blanket rejection of women's ordination but rather shows that this has been a contested issue for much of the Christian tradition, as we have seen above.

There is also, of course, an argument from sacramentality, which holds that the priest stands in for Christ and so must bear a physical likeness to Jesus of Nazareth.[82] This too is finally unpersuasive because it is a circular argument, depending on the assumption that gender is crucial to the representation of Jesus' humanity, the very issue at stake here.[83] What is it about gender that alone must be maintained, while age, race, or other aspects of human embodiment—things that can make one quite unlike a young, first-century Palestinian Jew—are considered insignificant?

---

80. Pontifical Biblical Commission, "Can Women Be Priests?," *Origins* 6 (1 July 1976): 92–96. See also "Women and Priestly Ministry: The New Testament Evidence," *Catholic Biblical Quarterly* 41, no. 4 (October 1979), https://www.jstor.org/stable/43715611?seq=1#metadata_info_tab_contents.

81. For the complex history of development in the meaning of ordination, see Macy, *Hidden History*, esp. 3–22.

82. *Inter Insigniores* 5.

83. See especially Elizabeth Groppe, "Women and the *Persona* of Christ," in *Frontiers in Catholic Feminist Theology: Shoulder to Shoulder*, ed. Susan Abraham and Elena Procario-Foley (Minneapolis: Fortress, 2009), 153–71.

The singular importance of gender is, of course, precisely the point that gender complementarity intends to defend. Biological sex is not merely a matter of physiology; it determines one's position in a fundamental psychospiritual binary that is essential not only to physical reproduction but, according to this theory, to all relations of generative love, including the divine-human relation. Gender complementarity maintains that men and women differ essentially in their ways of being and loving and, as such, represent different poles of the God-human relationship. The binaries of hierarchical dualism—at least the primary binaries of God/world, male/female, ruler/ruled—are reinforced as reflective of one of the deepest truths of human life. To be sure, the binary should not be oppressive and presumably will not be, as long as good Christian men exercise their leadership in the loving manner of divine rule and good Christian women are appropriately and lovingly responsive to male initiative. Of course, one need not strain much to hear here a suppressed echo of the deutero-Pauline insistence that all will be well if husbands love their submissive wives and rule justly over their obedient slaves.

While patriarchal leadership in the church is thus consistently and rather strenuously defended by gender complementarians, the continuation of male language to describe the normative Christian would seem to be quite problematic on complementarian grounds. If sexual difference is to be acknowledged and celebrated, if all acts of generative love must have both a male and a female component, then it should follow that the language of worship would emphasize a gender balance in which both male and female terms are used for the congregants. Indeed, if God is to be represented as male in relation to humanity, then shouldn't the normative Christian be described as female in order to emphasize the human role of responding to God's prior initiative? Yet even while official church teachings assert a complementarian anthropology that in principle rejects the presumption of the male as the normative human, church leaders continue to insist that male (and not female!) language is liturgically appropriate to represent both male and female worshipers. One might suspect that the defense of traditional practices trumps the commitment to a complementarian anthropology.

Gender complementarity is certainly preferable to the definition of women as defective men, especially when the defects in question are intellectual and moral. And if we must have binaries, it is clearly better that the poles should be united in mutual love than locked in mutual antagonism. Whether a binary approach to humanity can be retained without continuing the othering of women that devalues and marginalizes sexual and gender diversity, however, remains a key question that we'll discuss below. But first it is worth noting that gender complementarity fails in three other significant ways: it cannot take embodiment seriously, it cannot support coherent societal or ecclesial practices, and it cannot be rendered consistent with essential Christian beliefs.

Gender complementarism claims to take embodiment seriously by maintaining a causal connection between biological sex and psychospiritual inclinations. Yet this theory ignores the lack of biological evidence supporting any such universal, noncultural distinctions between the characteristics and inclinations of men and women, especially when the gender differences are so construed that women are understood to be inherently less inclined to take initiative or to protect their offspring than men.[84] If there are biologically based personality differences, they are surely not the ones asserted by gender complementarians. Furthermore, complementarism does not do justice to the pluriformity of human sexual and gendered experiences that do not fit into two clear and distinct categories, whether considered biologically or psychoculturally. The reality is that nature is more inclined to continuums than to stark binaries, and taking embodiment seriously requires acknowledging this fact.

Gender complementarism is also disturbingly incoherent in its practical implications for church and for society. As a matter of practice within the church, there is an irresolvable inconsistency in the teaching that women cannot liturgically represent God because they embody the receptivity of the laity while men, whose sexual embodiment symbolizes the initiative of God, can and often do represent the receptive laity. Why is the essential symbolism destroyed if a woman stands in a position of initiative as clergy, but not when men are among (or, as in monasteries, may be the entirety of) the receptive

---

84. Ross makes this critique in her *Anthropology*, 101.

laity? This point is never adequately explained and is a major point of inconsistency in gender complementarian ecclesiology.

The implications of gender complementarity for women's roles in society are especially disturbing. To be fair, Catholic Church teachings invoking gender complementarity generally (now) accept women's leadership in society, even arguing that room should be made for women's particular genius in directing society toward the care of persons. Prudence Allen clearly maintains that gender complementarity does not limit the roles women take in society but rather appreciates and protects the different gifts that that men and women bring to their shared social roles.[85] However, it is not at all clear why, if women's receptive or nurturing nature keeps them from clerical leadership in the church, women should not be as strenuously discouraged from leadership in society and in the family as well. Indeed, this conclusion is explicitly drawn by many Christian complementarians.[86] If women and men truly have distinct "geniuses," then it would seem to follow that they should take the roles in society and family that most draw on their putative strengths, lest their natures be frustrated and the roles performed badly. Even if what is at stake is primarily a matter of symbolizing true mutuality, through maintaining diverse roles, why isn't it just as important to maintain this symbolism in society and in the family as in the church? Conversely, if gender does not limit one's roles in society but only determines that women and men fulfill them differently, why doesn't this also hold in the church? Why couldn't women bring their care for persons to clerical leadership (which sorely needs such qualities), just as men bring their genius for protection and initiative to their roles as laity?

Gender complementarity's insistence on maleness in representing Christ is especially problematic theologically, as it contradicts the essential Christian belief that all of humanity is offered salvation through the event of Jesus Christ, as reflected in the practice of

---

85. See especially Allen, *Search for Communion*, 469.

86. Julia Baird, "Is Your Pastor Sexist?," *New York Times*, April 19, 2017, https://www.nytimes.com/2017/04/19/opinion/is-your-pastor-sexist.html. As Baird quotes from another writer on Christian complementarism in US churches, "women are told that if they meet a man they want to marry, they will have to submit their hopes, dreams, and opinions to him or risk being an outcast in their families and churches."

baptizing all Christians, male and female, into the Body of Christ that they may be Christ to the world. If, in Jesus, God's salvific initiative required a specifically male incarnation such that women cannot symbolically represent Christ, then it would seem to follow that women are not saved by the event of Jesus Christ. As Gregory Nazianzen declared in the fourth century, "that which He has not assumed, He has not healed; that which is united to His Godhead is also saved."[87] At the very least, it would seem that women need a separate, gender-specific baptism ritual if they are called not to be sacraments of Christ to the world as men are but rather to be sacraments of receptivity to the grace of Christ in the world.[88]

Despite its stark differences from the Aristotelian view of women as defective males, then, gender complementarity results in the same patriarchal leadership and male language (especially for God) as the earlier denigration of the full humanity of women, though it does so with less coherence. What is of most concern here, however, is the manner in which gender complementarity deals with the otherness of women in the church. Does gender complementarity succeed at least in supporting genuine difference, as it claims, so that women and men are accepted as distinct but interdependent in a mutuality of love, with neither positioned as the norm or as the other?

Notwithstanding its claim to affirm difference, complementarism not only leaves the binary structure of hierarchical dualism in place but also fails to make this binary a mutuality, an equality-in-diversity, as intended. After all, when God, men, and initiative remain juxtaposed to humanity, women, and receptive response, the binary is still hierarchical, with greater power and greater value on the side of the divine and male initiators (who, it follows, are surely then the leaders and rulers).[89]

---

87. Gregory Nazianzen, "To Cledonius the Priest against Apollinarius (Ep. CI)," in *Nicene and Post-Nicene Fathers: Cyril of Jerusalem, Gregory Nazianzen*, ed. Philip Schaff and Henry Wace (Peabody, MA: Hendrickson, 1994), 440.

88. See also the argument of Elizabeth A. Johnson, *She Who Is: The Mystery of God in Feminist Theological Discourse* (New York: Crossroad, 1992), 69–75, 153.

89. See also the critiques of gender complementarism in Ruether, "*Imago Dei*," 267–91; and Mary Catherine Hilkert, "Cry Beloved Image: Rethinking the Image of God," in Graff, *In the Embrace*, 190–205.

I would further argue that the binary of gender complementarity continues, despite its best intentions, to position men as the primary referent and to define women as men's other, thus denying the very difference it supposedly celebrates. After all, there is a logical priority to initiative: the initiator determines what action is taken and when, whereas receptivity is only exercised in response to a prior initiative. Furthermore, except for the case of physical reproduction, male initiative does not require a female respondent. An initiative can occur regardless of whether it is received, for example, but the reception cannot exist apart from the initiative. The relations of the sexes are thus asymmetrical, with women defined by their relation to men in ways that men are not defined by their relation to women. This leaves us finally not with difference but with sameness, and even an implicit violence, as Tina Beattie has argued in her analysis of Hans Urs von Balthasar's gender complementarity: women are erased by male sameness and perhaps even displaced by the male who seeks to take the female place in responding to God.[90]

This asymmetry and its erasure of women is obvious in the case of the church. A community of men can form a complete worshiping community and celebrate all necessary rituals because men can be both clergy and laity. A group of women, on the other hand, can never be a full ecclesial community in the Catholic Church, as they would lack priests, the Eucharist, bishops, and pope. In fact, as Susan Ross has noted, except for marriage, all the sacraments in the Catholic Church can take place without the presence of women.[91]

Despite gender complementarity's praise for women's putative "feminine genius," the reality is that men remain normative while women, defined in terms of their receptivity to men, are not really essential, except for physical reproduction.

---

90. Tina Beattie, *New Catholic Feminism: Theology and Theory* (London & New York: Routledge, 2006), 208. For an alternative view defending a Balthasarian complementarity, see Michelle A. González, "Hans Urs von Balthasar and Contemporary Catholic Feminist Theology," *Theological Studies* 65 (2004): 566–95.

91. Susan A. Ross, *Extravagant Affections: A Feminist Sacramental Theology* (New York: Continuum, 2001), 26.

Becoming the Church We Are Called to Be

To resist the global oppression of women, the church must recognize and unambiguously affirm women's full humanity. This involves explicitly supporting women's equal value and their right to develop and express the full range of their abilities within and beyond the ecclesial community. Women and girls possess the same human dignity as men and boys and deserve the same opportunities to develop themselves, to share in the world's resources, to shape the future, and to contribute to the good of humanity. And they should have these opportunities regardless of whether it is completely convenient for men and boys.

This ought to be uncontroversial, and as a theoretical statement it usually is. The devil, of course, is in the details. The Universal Declaration of Human Rights affirmed in 1948 that women have equal rights as persons, yet in fact women are still denied resources, still overworked and underpaid, still trafficked, and still targeted by sexual harassment and violence.[92] Books like Kristof and WuDunn's *Half the Sky* and Jimmy Carter's *A Call To Action* testify to the ongoing oppression of women around the world.

The question for us, then, is this: How can the church better witness to a commitment to the full dignity of women in church and also work more effectively for women's full equality in the world?

Beyond a doubt, we need to deconstruct the hierarchical dualism that has such powerful, if often unconscious, impact in making the subjugation of women along with the devaluing of nature and non-Western cultures seem normal, natural, and even good. This dualism needs to be dismantled in the language, thought, and practice of the church. A good beginning is to reject the theological anthropology that, however much it explicitly affirms women's equality, nevertheless defines men as normative and more aligned with God, while

---

92. United Nations, "Universal Declaration of Human Rights," December 10, 1948, un.org/en/universal-declaration-human-rights/index.html. According to the declaration, all people, regardless of sex, race, or creed, possess these rights, yet race, ethnicity, and religion (among other factors) continue to be the basis, along with sex, for their denial.

women are the others whose difference is valued for its receptive contribution to male-initiated projects.

Gender complementarity cannot help us here. Rather than offering a true mutuality, gender complementarity reinforces a binary, essentialist, gendered embodiment in which women remain defined as men's other. Further, gender complementarity insists, without evidence, that these binary categories are not products of culture and history but rather are inscribed in our bodies and determinative of our psychosexual natures.

There is hope, though, in the fact that resistance to women's marginalization and otherness is at least as deeply rooted in the Christian tradition as is women's alterity. The Hebrew Bible includes female images of God as well as stories of women of great initiative like Tamar and Ruth, who are claimed in Matthew 1:3-5 as ancestors of Jesus. Jesus seems to have had no trouble treating women as equal among his disciples, and he is remembered as having sent women as well as men to teach others his Good News. We also know that women in the New Testament period (as well as later) served the church as leaders of their local communities, as missionaries, deacons, and apostles. Finally, women throughout the history of the Christian Church have resisted their marginalization and worked heroically for the life and growth of the church. Many of these women have been officially canonized and are celebrated by later generations, even by those who would deny similar opportunities to women today.[93]

In addition to this rich history of women's active, creative, and nonconformist contributions to the church, there is support in fundamental Christian beliefs and practices for the full dignity and equality of women. As mentioned above, the church's official teaching maintains that in the incarnational event of Jesus Christ, God assumed a human nature for the salvation of all people. It is a denial of this essential Christian belief to allow sexual differences to eclipse the shared human nature. Furthermore, the tradition of baptizing all, male and female, into the Body of Christ to be Christ to the

---

93. See especially the stories of women saints in Robert McClory, *Faithful Dissenters: Stories of Men and Women Who Loved and Changed the Church* (Maryknoll, NY: Orbis, 2000).

world stands as a testimony to Christian gender equality, including an equality in ability to represent Christ.

The ongoing challenge for the church is to affirm the full equality of women and men on the one hand, while also making room for genuine difference, including differences that do not fit into a gender binary, on the other hand. As Daly astutely observed decades ago, there are two alternatives to be avoided: (1) an androgyny modeled on male experience, and (2) a binary that construes female as the inverse or complement of male experience.[94] In either approach, any true difference is disallowed because sexual diversity is defined in terms of a single, dominant, male norm. The church cannot serve as a witness to unity-in-diversity if it cannot allow real differences, especially in the experience of embodied sexuality.

Elizabeth Johnson has rightly identified what is needed as an "anthropological model of one human nature [that] moves beyond the contrasting models of either sex dualism or the sameness of abstract individuals toward the celebration of diversity as entirely normal."[95] The point is not to deny sexual and gender differences but to embrace the full variety of healthy sexual embodiment as experienced across race, class, culture, ethnicity, and time. There is, as Nancy Dallavalle notes, "no unconstructed human access to the meaning of our creation as male and female."[96] A true ecclesial witness to unity-in-diversity is one that affirms gender plurality as a dimension of human embodiment in a way that reinforces rather than eclipses the fundamental Christian commitment to a common human nature and the equality of baptism.

---

94. See *inter alia* Daniel P. Horan, "Beyond Essentialism and Complementarity: Toward a Theological Anthropology Rooted in *Haecceitas*," *Theological Studies* 75 (2014): 94–117; Daly, *Church*, 100–117; and the excellent overview in Hinsdale, "Heeding the Voices."

95. Elizabeth Johnson, "The Maleness of Christ," in *The Special Nature of Women*, ed. Anne Carr and Elisabeth Schüssler Fiorenza (Philadelphia: Trinity International, 1991), 108–16 at 111.

96. Dallavalle nevertheless maintains that there are inherent sexual differences underlying cultural interpretations. See her "Neither Idolatry nor Iconoclasm: A Critical Essentialism for Catholic Feminist Theology," *Horizons* 25 (1998): 23–42 at 29.

Such an ecclesial witness to gender equality requires not only a more adequate theory of gender but also more egalitarian practices and structures than the Catholic Church currently has. Assumptions of male normativity continue to be expressed in Catholic liturgies, prayers, and documents, especially in the use of male nouns and pronouns to refer to the entirety of the Christian community. "Man" is not the full human or the essential Christian, and "woman" is not appropriately described in terms that assume male normativity. Nor should we continue to allow male imagery to dominate our talk about God. If God is male, it may not follow that the male is God, but certainly the male is more like God, and so the most valued, Godlike characteristics will be ascribed to men. As Pope St. John Paul II has acknowledged, the church needs to recover the many female metaphors of God that are found in the Bible and in the Christian tradition—and, as feminist theologians argue, these female images must include nonmaternal aspects of women's experience, since mothers are not the only women who image God.[97] The argument that female images ascribe sex or gender to God in a way that male images do not is, of course, precisely the norming of the male as the fundamental form of humanity that must be resisted. While God is not sexed and remains beyond any and all of our images, the divine mystery is best reflected in a variety of always partial analogies and metaphors, including the fullest possible variety of gendered experiences.

Ultimately, of course, a church that witnesses to a unity-in-diversity that values men and women equally must end all of the exclusionary practices that ignore, marginalize, or curtail women's contributions to the church. Whatever differences women (and other-gendered) Christians bring, the full range of their insights and gifts must be welcomed and celebrated in the church as well as in society. At a time when the Catholic Church so clearly lacks quality vocations to ordained ministry and offices of leadership, to reject evidently qualified women is a self-defeating act of discrimination. Women are devalued, the church is diminished, and the church's mission is compromised. Further, the church continues to enact the hierarchical

---

97. *Mulieris Dignitatem* 8.

binary that not only oppresses women but also is colonialist, racist, and destructive of the earth. All binaries that disregard the dignity of some aspects of creation, including the fundamental male/female binary, must be deconstructed.

The history of the Catholic Church suggests that it may be some time before women are ordained again, even as minor clergy. Yet as has been widely noted, qualified women could be appointed now to the ecclesial leadership roles that do not require ordination. Indeed, many women are ably serving as parish administrators and as nonordained pastoral caregivers, though the idea that they are second best is reinforced by their dismissal whenever ordained priests become available for these roles. Women also can and should be included in representative numbers in every position open to the laity in parish and diocesan life, as well as in roles of international administration and consultation in the Vatican. Such inclusion is consistent with the full valuing of women that all sides on the women's ordination debate claim to support. Thus welcoming women's gifts, including their gifts for leadership, would benefit the church as well as its work in the world, increasing the official church's attention to the many, many manifestations of the global oppression of women. There is no good reason to delay appointing women to diocesan, regional, and Vatican positions that do not require ordination.

It will likely take a good while to achieve consensus in the Catholic Church on women's full inclusion through ordination. In the meantime, dialogue on this issue must continue. The role of women in the church is a matter central to the church's mission to witness to the equal dignity of all humanity. How can the church witness to unity-in-diversity in the world if it cannot incorporate women's diversity fully into all levels of the church?

Respectful dialogue rather than polarization on such a momentous topic would itself witness prophetically to a commitment to diverse inclusivity in a way that authoritarian silencing of debate does not. In the current context, nothing is easier than to separate from and even vilify those with whom we disagree on important topics. To affirm unity-in-diversity, however, requires recognition that we need each other in our differences, including our theological and political differences—even over the proper significance of sexuality and gender. After all, no one perspective is sufficient to include all truth, and in any case every person contributes to the whole, even those with ideas that may turn out to be wrong. The Holy Spirit will continue to lead the church toward greater truth as long as we remain open in love to the Spirit speaking in and through each other.

Conclusion

The argument of this chapter has been that the church needs to reconstruct its self-understanding with regard to women, the other within the church, no less than with regard to Jews, the paradigmatic religious other outside of the church. The recent embrace of a Christian theology of gender complementarity is evidence that the practice of treating women as second-class citizens within the church is no longer self-justifying, especially since the traditional view of women as defective males is unacceptable. Yet superficial changes will not suffice to overcome either religious anti-Semitism or misogyny. Both issues require revision of church practices (for example, the portrayal of Jews in passion narratives and the absence of women in ecclesial leadership). Both issues also require rethinking what it means to be church, given the importance of the theological construction of Jews/Judaism and of women in ecclesial self-understanding. The church fails in its mission when it defines itself in supersessionist terms as the "New Israel" taking the place formerly held by the Jewish people. Similarly, the church fails to witness to the equality-in-diversity of all humanity when it construes the church as comprising a male clergy representing God to a subservient female laity.

It is not the goal, of course, to construct a Jewish-Christian identity against the rest of the world's religions, nor is it the goal to include a few women in a clericalism that continues to devalue the contributions of the laity. Instead, reconstructing the church's relations to Jews and to women is an essential but only initial step toward a more profound unity-in-diversity with all others within and beyond the church.

Such ecclesial reforms would enable the church to be a better instrument as well as a more faithful witness to the unity-in-diversity it proclaims. Openness to Jewish insights and those of other religions contributes to a more accurate vision of the world's current distortions than Christians alone can provide. Similarly, when the male is no longer the unconscious norm in ecclesial thinking, the church's social analysis will be less likely to neglect the specific sufferings and exclusions of women in the world. To be an agent of healing amid the world's divisions, the church must begin to heal its own deep divisions, starting with its abjection of Jews as the others outside of the church and of women as the others within the church.

Chapter 4

A Prophetic, Public Church in a Global Economy

In his recent book *The World Is Flat,* Thomas Friedman describes the global economy through an old African story about the lion and the gazelle. A lion who wants to eat must outrun the slowest gazelle, while the gazelle who wants to survive has to outrun the fastest lion. The point, we are told, is that regardless of whether you are a lion or a gazelle, when the sun comes up, you'd better start running.[1]

In other words, Friedman contends that the contemporary global economy is a competition of each against all for economic survival. Those who work longer, harder, and smarter will succeed by producing goods or services more efficiently—thus driving other businesses into bankruptcy.

Friedman sees a positive side to this economic reality: the global competition enables people in some of the world's poorest countries to compete—and to succeed—in ways previously denied them. People in India, for example, no longer have to migrate to find good jobs as intellectual workers, since they can provide consumer services to people around the world via telephone or send their engineering designs through the internet from sites in their home country.[2] Competition also lowers costs, at least in the short term, as the more

---

1. Thomas L. Friedman, *The World Is Flat: A Brief History of the Twenty-First Century,* rev. ed. (New York: Farrar, Straus and Giroux, 2006), 137.
2. Friedman, *World Is Flat,* esp. 50–200.

efficient displace entrenched but less efficient producers. It is arguable that this globalization has not only led to less costly goods and services for consumers but has been the predominant force behind the dramatic decrease in the numbers of destitute people in the world, a decrease that is certainly to be celebrated.[3]

Yet there are reasons to see this economy as deeply problematic. Even if global capitalism is lifting many out of extreme poverty, there can be no doubt that the economy as currently structured has increased inequality to an almost unimaginable degree. The abundance of the earth is not evenly shared: By the end of 2016, 8 men together owned as much as the poorest 50 percent of the world—that is, more than 3.6 billion people![4] Additionally, as the drive for greater profits supplants other concerns in this worldwide race to be among the economically successful, globalization is also undermining local cultures and many of the traditional values that have sustained human communities for centuries if not millennia. Moreover, this global economy is unsustainable in its rate of resource depletion and is creating massive environmental problems, including the life-threatening global climate crisis caused by the release into the atmosphere of high levels of carbon dioxide and other greenhouse gases (the topic of our next chapter).

There are other issues here as well. The pace and extent of work in this 24/7 economy is absorbing all nonwork time. If global capitalism requires that "when the sun comes up, you'd better start running," what kind of life is that? Where in the midst of an economic life-and-death competition is there time for love, for prayer, or for strengthening community bonds? It is surely no wonder that

---

3. Extreme poverty, defined as living on less than $1.90 per day, has decreased in absolute numbers as well as in percentage of the growing world population. See World Bank, "Decline of Global Extreme Poverty Continues but Has Slowed: World Bank," press release, September 19, 2018, https://www.worldbank.org/en/news/press-release/2018/09/19/decline-of-global-extreme-poverty-continues-but-has-slowed-world-bank.

4. Deborah Hardoon, "An Economy for the 99%," Oxfam International, January 16, 2017, https://www.oxfam.org/en/research/economy-99. See also Oxfam International, "An Economy That Works for Women," March 2017, https://www-cdn.oxfam.org/s3fs-public/file_attachments/bp-an-economy-that-works-for-women-020317-en.pdf.

globalization is fostering not only international cooperation among economic elites but also more open xenophobia and tribal hostility on the part of those worried about being left out or left behind when production moves somewhere with lower costs.[5]

The current globalization of the capitalist economic system cannot be a matter of indifference to the church, which is charged to work for the unity of all in God. The global economy is knitting the whole world together more thoroughly than ever before in a complexly interconnected flow around the planet of goods, services, and capital. This could and should be a contribution to the human community, a means of increasing the unity of the human family through an economic system in which the earth's resources benefit the whole world. Unfortunately, such a harmonious economic unity is far from our reality, as global competition in a system seemingly controlled by market forces increases the opportunities for inequality, division, and oppression.

The church has long been concerned with the economic conditions that cause unnecessary human suffering and deny impoverished people the means to a life with dignity. God's preferential option for the poor is unmistakable in the laws and prophets of the Hebrew Bible, in the incarnation of God as a poor peasant preaching the beginning of God's reign from among the discounted and discarded in Galilee, and in the care for those in need that has been acclaimed a central virtue throughout the church's history. Modern Catholic social teaching has further developed this central concern for the poor and vulnerable in response to the injustices of industrial and postindustrial society, proclaiming the option for the poor, the dignity and priority of labor, and a social mortgage on the right to private property.

But contemporary global capitalism is a new reality, as Pope Francis recognizes, and one that begs for sustained attention to how global economic processes and structures affect unity among

---

5. United Nations General Assembly, "Racism, Xenophobia Increasing Globally, Experts Tell Third Committee, amid Calls for Laws to Combat Hate Speech, Concerns over Freedom of Expression," press release, November 1, 2016, https://www.un.org/press/en/2016/gashc4182.doc.htm.

humans and with creation.⁶ What does it mean to be a sign and instrument of communion in this global reality? What can and should Christians do, as church and as disciples of Christ, to witness to and work for a just and humane economy, especially when our current economy operates according to complex global forces that no one seems able to direct?

The question of this chapter is what it means to be a public and prophetic church serving the reign of God amid the unprecedented challenges of our global economy. However, as argued in the previous chapters, the church cannot be a genuine sign and instrument of unity-in-diversity without paying particular attention to the diversity of people of other religions and of women—the church's external and internal others. Aspects of the church's sacred texts, history, and structures continue to incline the church toward an ecclesial triumphalism and an androcentrism that contradict the church's mission to be a sacrament of communion enriched by difference. This is especially relevant to the task of being church in the current global economy because women have higher rates of poverty than men and often experience their poverty differently, with fewer options and more family responsibilities. Given that advances in a region's economic prosperity do not necessarily increase the economic well-being of women, a just and humane economy cannot be established without taking into account the specific economic challenges that women face.⁷ At the same time, and as generally acknowledged in Catholic social teaching, constructing a better world depends upon considerable cooperation among people of all faiths and none. Religious perspectives are critically important to

---

6. Pope Francis develops his astute criticisms of global capitalism especially in his apostolic exhortation, On the Proclamation of the Gospel in Today's World (*Evangelii Gaudium* [EG]), http://w2.vatican.va/content/francesco/en/apost_exhortations/documents/papa-francesco_esortazione-ap_20131124_evangelii-gaudium.html. See also the essays in Gerard Mannion, ed., *Pope Francis and the Future of Catholicism: Evangelii Gaudium and the Papal Agenda* (New York: Cambridge University Press, 2017).

7. Bureau of International Information Programs, "Chapter 1: Women and Poverty," in *Global Women's Issues: Women in the World Today* (US Department of State, 2012), https://static.america.gov/uploads/sites/8/2016/05/Global-Womens-Issues_Women-in-the-World-Today_English_508.pdf.

a public that has lost its capacity to consider any value greater than profit, so Christians must bring, and encourage others to bring, their particular religious perspectives to the public work of developing a humane globalization.

This is not a task for the church alone, because creating a more just global economy requires the concerted efforts of governments and international organizations. Moreover, the church cannot be a witness to the unity-in-diversity of the reign of God by mimicking the separatist tribalism so common today; it can do so only by reaching out to form community beyond the church.

Of course, many other issues beg for attention. Justice includes overcoming racism, which is a global reality as well as an especially virulent force of division and dehumanization in the United States. Indigenous peoples continue to be marginalized in their own homelands. Sexual minorities regularly have their rights and dignity denied, as do others who are discounted because they do not fit the norm of the healthy, able-bodied adult. The reign of God must be truly inclusive, celebrating the diversity of all humanity and, finally, of all creation.

An adequate treatment of all of these issues of exclusion and division is beyond the scope of this work, unfortunately.[8] The specific focus here will be on women, who comprise approximately 50 percent of the world's population, yet too often remain invisible when their gender difference is dismissed as unimportant by society and by male-dominated church teachings and practices. We will also attend to the challenges of working not only within but beyond the Christian community. The history of Christian abjection of the original Christian other, Judaism, stands as a reminder of the ongoing imperative to affirm a distinct Christian identity that stands in loving unity-in-diversity with—rather than vilifying—the religiously different.

To explore what it means for the church to be a prophetic and public sacrament of unity in the current global economy, this chapter will begin with Catholic social teaching, as this body of thought

---

8. A good beginning in exploring contemporary exclusions is available in Dennis M. Doyle, Timothy J. Furry, and Pascal D. Bazzell, eds., *Eccesiology and Exclusion: Boundaries of Being and Belonging in Postmodern Times* (Maryknoll, NY: Orbis, 2012).

provides carefully argued consensus positions around which Catholics and most other Christians ought to be able to unite in their ecclesial work and witness. Pope Francis's perceptive analysis of the idolatry of global capitalism, especially in his apostolic exhortation *Evangelii Gaudium*, is an especially significant recent addition to this tradition. We will then turn to some further questions that have not been dealt with adequately in ecclesial teaching, particularly with regard to the economic situation of women and the difficulties of maintaining a healthy subsidiarity that balances local initiatives with national and global concerns. This will provide a basis for underscoring the importance of what Christians can and must do, as church and as disciples of Jesus, to be more fully prophetic signs and public instruments of a truly humane economy.

Catholic Social Teaching, Pope Francis, and the Idolatry of the Market

Modern Catholic social teaching begins with Pope Leo XIII's reflections on the ethical demands of industrialization and the rights of workers in his 1891 encyclical *Rerum Novarum*.[9] This is the first of many papal and episcopal documents addressing the issues raised by industrialization and by the development of modern economic systems. Prior to the Second Vatican Council, as Charles Curran aptly describes, this body of modern Catholic social teaching assumed a two-missions approach in which the clergy had the important task of divinizing the world, while the laity had the less significant responsibility to humanize it.[10] Many Catholics continue, unfortunately, to think along these lines of primary and secondary missions, with the result that the church's social teachings are frequently considered peripheral to a life of Christian faith. Vatican II, however, reframed these purposes as one ecclesial mission of uniting all in God through building up that unity within the church

---

9. Leo XIII, On Capital and Labor (*Rerum Novarum*), http://w2.vatican.va/content/leo-xiii/en/encyclicals/documents/hf_l-xiii_enc_15051891_rerum-novarum.html.

10. Charles E. Curran, *The Social Mission of the U.S. Catholic Church: A Theological Perspective* (Washington, DC: Georgetown University Press, 2011), esp. 57.

(the clergy's primary vocation) and in the world (the proper focus of the laity). Justice is no longer "preevangelization," or "pre" anything, but rather is a constitutive dimension of the harmonious unity-in-diversity Christians are called to witness to and to work for in history.[11]

Gaudium et Spes articulates some of the fundamental principles of Catholic social teaching regarding the kind of economy consistent with the communion of all in God. Instead of seeking one's own benefit (or "voting one's pocketbook"), Christians should work for policies they judge will best serve the common good and enable everyone to have a share in the world's resources. The right to personal property is endorsed as integral to human freedom, dignity, and responsibility, but this right comes with a social mortgage such that this property must not be used contrary to the good of others in the community. Since all people have a right to what they need to live with dignity, those who refuse to pay a just wage or to share their excess with people in need are guilty of theft and even—if the poor die in their need—of murder, as the Hebrew prophets and early church fathers warn. Furthermore, the right to personal property must also be balanced with the greater right to work, through which people develop and express themselves, contribute to the good of the wider society, and support themselves and their families. Ultimately, labor should have priority over capital because people are more important than things (GS 64–72).

More recent social teachings have clarified that seeking communion in the context of inequality involves a "preferential option for the poor," the poor being those most easily discounted, marginalized, and excluded. God's special concern for the poor and the powerless is evident throughout the Bible, and the implications for Christian discipleship of this divine concern have been acknowledged throughout Christian history. However, the indispensability of the option for the poor, especially as requiring a priority of attention and inclusion that is more than charity, was articulated by

---

11. In addition to Curran, *Social Mission*, 57, see the succinct discussion of the development from preevangelization to evangelization in E. F. Sheridan, ed., *Do Justice: The Social Teaching of the Canadian Catholic Bishops* (Toronto: Jesuit Centre for Social Faith and Justice, 1987), 28–29. See also *Evangelii Gaudium*, chap. 4.

liberation theologians after Vatican II and further clarified by the Conference of Latin American Bishops (CELAM) in Medellín, Colombia, in 1968, and in Puebla, Mexico, in 1979.[12] Pope St. John Paul II introduced this option for the poor into papal writings, especially in his 1987 encyclical *Sollicitudo Rei Socialis*, and Pope Francis cites the writings of Pope Benedict XVI as well as of John Paul II in reiterating that the option for the poor is a well-established tenet of Catholic social thought.[13] Francis further contends that the option for the poor is a personal and not only a collective responsibility of Christians, maintaining that "no one must say that they cannot be close to the poor because their own lifestyle demands more attention to other areas" (*Evangelii Gaudium* [EG] 201). A life of genuine Christian discipleship cannot outsource the option for the poor.[14]

Pope Francis also develops Catholic social teaching with his trenchant criticism of the injustice and deformations of the now-dominant global capitalist system. Despite the good this global economy does, it has come to function as a potent force of counterevangelization, since the interests of the economy have become the central and often unquestioned value in much of public life. Francis astutely notes that the market has at times become the prevailing idol for society as well as for individuals; the economy, he contends, is then a false god who demands sacrifices of ourselves, our lives, and nature, while fostering divisions that oppose the reign of God (EG, esp. 55–59).

The Idolatry of the Market

There is nothing new, of course, in the recognition of the powerful temptation to make money and wealth one's greatest value, an idol that takes precedence over all else in one's life. The book of the

---

12. Gustavo Gutiérrez, *A Theology of Liberation: History, Politics, and Salvation* (Maryknoll, NY: Orbis, 1988); Gustavo Gutiérrez, "Option for the Poor," in *Mysterium Liberationis: Fundamental Concepts of Liberation Theology*, ed. Ignacio Ellacuría and Jon Sobrino (Maryknoll, NY: Orbis, 1993), 235–50.

13. John Paul II, On the Twentieth Anniversary of *Populorum Progressio* (*Sollicitudo Rei Socialis*), 42, http://w2.vatican.va/content/john-paul-ii/en/encyclicals/documents/hf_jp-ii_enc_30121987_sollicitudo-rei-socialis.html; EG 198.

14. I develop this point in my "Evangelizing in an Economy of Death," in Mannion, *Pope Francis*.

prophet Isaiah condemns the worship of gold and silver (2:20), Amos repudiates those who buy the poor for a pair of sandals (8:6), and the gospels tell us that Jesus warned his disciples they cannot serve both God and money (Luke 16:13; Matt 6:24). The inclination to make a false god of wealth, to worship the "almighty dollar," is a near constant in human life.

Nevertheless, Pope Francis recognizes there has been a change, in that global capitalism has begun to colonize society, functioning as the dominant concern in public—and in much of private—life. Since ensuring the vigor of the economy is frequently the central focus in public debate and indeed at times the only commonly shared value, amassing wealth is no longer merely a personal obsession of the greedy. Much of our politics is predicated on determining—and prioritizing—whatever the economy needs to avoid a recession that could wreak havoc in real lives through increased unemployment and poverty (EG 55, 53). There are, obviously, very good reasons in our competitive capitalist economy to fear economic stagnation. A vigorous economy is a valid goal; it is essential for keeping people employed and able to feed, clothe, and shelter their families.

This focus on the economy becomes problematic, however, when economic growth, at whatever cost, becomes the most important public interest. In this situation, market values so dominate public life that worth is increasingly based on exchange value, and everything (lives, bodies, even human organs) begins to be treated as a market commodity, as something to be bought and sold. As Pope Francis laments, "human beings are themselves considered consumer goods to be used and discarded" in an economy in which "the powerful feed upon the powerless" (EG 53). At the same time, whatever has no market or exchange value is considered worthless, and those who have nothing to offer the market are excluded from a society in which people appear less as citizens than as consumers. "Whatever is fragile, like the environment," Francis observes, "is defenseless before the interests of a deified market, which has become the only rule" (EG 56).

Pope Francis sees further evidence of market idolatry in the influence of neoliberal theories insisting that a minimally regulated economy will achieve the optimal good for all. The presumption that the profit motive will infallibly produce the best outcome is manifest in current tendencies in the United States to favor the privatization (or, more accurately, the monetization) of public goods and services, with little consideration of the pros and cons of subjecting to market forces the particular public needs in question. Although this privatization has begun to be challenged at least with regard to health insurance (largely due to the obvious failures of the market in this area), there is still considerable support in the United States for economic deregulation. The "free market" is often revered as a mythic force offering redemption from the hell of unemployment and poverty along with the possible reward of a consumer paradise to those who serve it well.[15]

Ignoring the role that governments necessarily play in constructing the rules by which the economy functions, neoliberalism emphasizes unfettered market forces as the solution for all economic problems, including poverty. The wealth produced by a robust economy will somehow "trickle down" so that all, including the poor, will be better off. As Francis argues, "this opinion, which has never been confirmed by the facts, expresses a crude and naïve trust . . . in the sacralized workings of the prevailing economic system. Meanwhile, the excluded are still waiting" (EG 54). Certainly in the United States, the economic revival after the 2008 recession benefitted the upper classes, but the middle and lower classes have not regained lost ground.[16]

Pope Francis also aptly notes that the deified market, this "dictatorship of an impersonal economy," undermines human freedom no less than the Marxist belief in the inevitability of the classless society (EG 55). Francis's predecessor, Pope Benedict XVI, rightly criticized the Marxist approach to history for denying the significance of human freedom in history.[17] Pope Francis similarly critiques

---

15. See the discussion of neoliberal economics in Angus Sibley, *Catholic Economics: Alternatives to the Jungle* (Collegeville, MN: Liturgical Press, 2015).

16. Fabrizio Perri, "Inequality, Recessions and Recoveries: 2013 Annual Report Essay," Federal Reserve Bank of Minneapolis publication *The Region*, April 30, 2014, https://www.minneapolisfed.org/publications/the-region/inequality-recessions-and-recoveries.

17. Benedict XVI, On Christian Hope (*Spe Salvi*), 21, http://w2.vatican.va/content/benedict-xvi/en/encyclicals/documents/hf_ben-xvi_enc_20071130_spe-salvi.html.

the refusal of freedom evident in the neoliberal insistence that the market will provide the best possible outcome as long as the economy is unhindered by government regulations. Instead of presuming that all will prosper if we only let the market do whatever it wants, Pope Francis insists that "the need to resolve the structural causes of poverty cannot be delayed . . . because society needs to be cured of a sickness which is weakening and frustrating it" (EG 202).

It is worth pointing out here that worry about government interference depressing the economy is not unreasonable. Overregulation can indeed stifle economic growth, and as yet no government has shown itself able to successfully plan and direct all aspects of the economy. However, the opposite extreme of too little regulation is equally damaging, leading, for example, to wasteful duplication or to monopolies that may finally cause economic stagnation, as Reinhold Niebuhr observed more than three-quarters of a century ago.[18] Recognizing the limits of human intelligence in directing the economy is wise, but to treat the market as a self-constituting and infallible force for prosperity ignores the role of government in setting the parameters that enable the market to function in the first place.[19] Furthermore, as Francis perceives, to treat economic processes as self-constituting denies human responsibility and puts us in the position of serving the idol we ourselves have created.

Sacrificing to the Idol of the Market

There is perhaps no clearer indication that the economy has become an idol than the fact that it demands sacrifices, which, as Orlando Espín has recently reminded us, is what all false gods do.[20] Thomas Friedman's description of the global economy as a life-and-death race clearly conveys the degree of pressure people are under

---

18. Reinhold Niebuhr, *The Children of Light and the Children of Darkness: A Vindication of Democracy and a Critique of Its Traditional Defense*, intro. Gary Dorrien (Chicago: University of Chicago Press, 2011), 98–118.

19. Robert Reich makes this point particularly well. See Robert B. Reich, *Saving Capitalism: For the Many, Not the Few* (New York: Penguin Random House, 2015), esp. 81–86.

20. Orlando O. Espín, *Idol and Grace: On Traditioning and Subversive Hope* (Maryknoll, NY: Orbis, 2014), 77–84. See also the earlier Gustavo Gutiérrez, *The God of Life* (Maryknoll, NY: Orbis, 1991).

to give their all in a desperate attempt to serve the market better than others. Fearful of taking time away from work, people sacrifice their health, time with their families, and the spiritual depth that makes life truly human, all in frantic pursuit of economic success. Even those with jobs in less competitive professions find work encroaching on evenings, weekends, and vacations in our 24/7 society. A common hope is that these years spent working will be rewarded with an "afterlife" of early retirement, in which one can finally experience the enjoyment of life deferred during the all-consuming years of employment. If this is the future they anticipate, it is no wonder that so many of our youth suffer elevated levels of anxiety.

In addition to the sacrifice of our lives, Francis warns, we risk sacrificing all that is without market value in a society focused on serving the goal of increasing profit above all else. This includes the beauty of the earth, its life-giving fertility, its careful ecological balance, and the many species that Pope Francis tells us praise God in inimitable ways but are being driven to extinction by an ever-expanding market and its throwaway culture (EG, esp. 56, 53). Communities are sacrificed when their sources of employment move to more profitable locations. People who have nothing of market value to offer are sacrificed, as evidenced by the many homeless who exist on the margins of society. As Pope Francis summarizes, "those excluded are no longer society's underside or its fringes or its disenfranchised—they are no longer even a part of it" (EG 53). It is not surprising then that so many become terrified, though devoted, acolytes of this pitiless economy: anyone who fails to serve well enough is in danger of being cast out of the economy and thus of losing their place in society.

Ultimately, of course, this deified economy kills, as Pope Francis clearly states (EG 53). The inequality of the economy kills the poor when they die for lack of adequate nutrition while others throw away food they do not need. It kills when people die unsheltered or for lack of access to medical care. It kills the many species going extinct today in what may be the sixth mass extinction event in the earth's history. Economic idolatry also kills spiritually, as when people despair of meaning or, perhaps more commonly, suffer the spiritual death of the "globalization of indifference" that has numbed so many to the unnecessary deaths of homeless people and of refugees (EG 54). Unless we oppose this economy of death, we cannot worship the God of life.

The Divisions and Exclusions of This False God

A final counterevangelical aspect of global capitalism is that it fosters division rather than unity. Economic inequality is dividing humanity, with the gap between the rich and everyone else in the world increasing to an alarming extent. According to Oxfam International, 1 percent of the world's population has more wealth than all the rest of the people on earth combined.[21]

On a global level, countries are experiencing vastly unequal economic realities, as some countries have great wealth while others are sunk into deep poverty. Quoting the New Zealand bishops, Pope Francis reminds us in his encyclical *Laudato Sí* of the scandal that "twenty percent of the world's population consumes resources at a rate that robs the poor and future generations of what they need to survive."[22] But there is also a good deal of division within societies. Many countries have considerable internal economic inequality, along with a deficit of good jobs—that is, jobs that pay a living wage and include reasonable benefits. When people see each other not as fellow community members but as competitors—lions and gazelles—in a desperate race for economic survival, the revival of ethnonationalist attacks on vulnerable minorities should come as no great surprise.

The American Baptist theologian Walter Rauschenbusch realized well over a century ago that economic inequality threatens the bonds that hold society together. He had the insight that this is not only because of the economic competition pitting people against each other but also because entrenched economic inequality eliminates the commonality necessary for mutual understanding.[23] Those

---

21. Hardoon, "Economy for the 1%."

22. Francis, On Care for Our Common Home (*Laudato Sí* [LS]), 95, http://w2.vatican.va/content/francesco/en/encyclicals/documents/papa-francesco_20150524_enciclica-laudato-si.html.

23. Walter Rauschenbusch, *Christianity and the Social Crisis in the 21st Century: The Classic That Woke Up the Church*, ed. Paul Rauschenbusch (New York: Macmillan, 1907; New York: HarperOne, 2008), 202–34. Citations refer to the HarperOne edition.

who inherit millions have little comprehension of the situation of people who live from paycheck to paycheck, and even those who struggle to balance their monthly budgets may not grasp what it is like to have no paycheck at all but to try to get by on less than 2 dollars per day per person, the situation of 1.5 million families in the United States according to one study![24] It is well worth asking how people can hope to follow Catholic social teaching's injunction to work for the common good when the conditions of our lives are so foreign to each other that we lack a basis for determining what our common good might be.

Rauschenbusch points to the further danger that such inequality will become habitual, leading to the acceptance of unequal treatment of persons as normal and even justified. The privileged come to assume they truly are more deserving than others, while the rest of society becomes accustomed to been treated as of less value. Class divisions become entrenched, and opportunities for interacting as equals in public spaces are scarce.[25] Inevitably, political inequality follows as well, corrupting any attempt at democracy because, as Rauschenbusch astutely observes (in 1907!), when 1 percent of the population own 50 percent of the national wealth, they will not be content with only 1 percent of the political power to protect that wealth. Those with great wealth will instead seek inordinate political influence, leading to the cycle in which government policies favor the wealthy, increasing their wealth.[26] The reality is that society more often embodies a preferential option for the rich, favoring the perspective and desires of the wealthy, rather than giving priority to the needs of the vulnerable and powerless.

Pope Francis further criticizes inequality as a source of violence, the antithesis of the loving communion the church seeks. Beyond the violence the poor might use in their desperation to attain what they need and can find no legitimate way to acquire, Francis sees a more subtle source: an obviously unequal society is evidently unjust,

---

24. Kathryn J. Edin and H. Luke Shaefer, *$2.00 a Day: Living on Almost Nothing in America* (Boston: Mariner Books, 2015), xvii. It should be noted that this statistic is based on studies in 2011.

25. Rauschenbusch, *Christianity and the Social Crisis*, esp. 205–6.

26. This process is described in detail in Reich, *Saving Capitalism*, esp. 11–80.

and this injustice undermines all members' respect for their society and its laws (EG 59–60). What Pope Francis calls the "evil crystallized in unjust social structures" weakens the social fabric and increases lawlessness and violence throughout society (EG 59).

As the writings of Pope Francis, his predecessors, and other bishops around the world thus clarify, a church that strives to be a sign and instrument of the unity of all in God cannot be indifferent to an economy that fosters inequality, division, and exclusion.[27] If the world, as Orthodox patriarch Bartholomew of Constantinople has said, should be "accepted as a sacrament of communion, a way of sharing with God and our neighbours on a global scale," then surely the economy is a primary way in which that global sharing occurs."[28] Pope Francis has been particularly incisive in his criticism of the current elevation of the free-market economy to the status of an unquestionable god to whom society sacrifices whatever this false god demands in hopes that it will save us from loss of wealth and power. Francis wants to make clear to all that this idol is a rival to the true God of life.

The point of these ecclesial documents is, of course, primarily to inspire and guide Christian life and work in the world. As Christine Firer Hinze astutely notes, no matter how eloquent and penetrating their analysis may be, Catholic social teachings risk becoming abstractions or pious platitudes unless they inspire people to action.[29] However, before turning to our discussion of what Christians might do to witness to and work for an alternative economy, we must address some key aspects of global capitalism that need further attention than they have thus far received from Catholic social teaching. These include the underdeveloped attention to women

---

27. See also United States Catholic Bishops, *Economic Justice for All: Pastoral Letter on Catholic Social Teaching and the US Economy* (Washington, DC: Confraternity of Christian Doctrine, 1986), http://www.usccb.org/upload/economic_justice_for_all.pdf; and Mark J. Allman, ed., *The Almighty and the Dollar: Reflections on Economic Justice for All* (Winona, MN: Anselm Academic, 2012).

28. Bartholomew, "Global Responsibility and Ecological Sustainability," Closing Remarks, Halki Summit I, Istanbul (June 20, 2012), as cited in *Laudato Si'* 9.

29. Christine Firer Hinze, *Glass Ceilings and Dirt Floors: Women, Work, and the Global Economy* (Mahwah, NJ: Paulist Press, 2015), 101.

and the challenges of a sustainable, grassroots, and local orientation within this increasingly global economy.

What about Women?

Women comprise nearly half of the world's population, yet much of our economic thought, including Catholic social teaching on the economy, pays little attention to the specific ways in which economic policies affect women. If there were no differences in how women and men experience economic pressures, this would be no problem. But in fact gender plays such a considerable role in one's economic prospects that a society's overall economic growth may not benefit the women in that society.[30] Ignoring gender in economic analysis or policy prescriptions reflects—and reinforces—the androcentric bias that increases economic inequality between men and women. For a church that strives to achieve greater unity-in-diversity and to honor the dignity of all people, this failure to attend to the economic situation and needs of women is not acceptable.

Two matters surface as especially problematic in considering women's economic realities. One issue is the inaccuracy of the assumption that a household's income and resources are distributed equally among its members.[31] This means that the economic status of women and girls cannot always be discerned based on the level of the household's income. Females may, in fact, experience considerably more economic deprivation and poverty than assessments of household income level suggest.

This inequality is especially likely when household resources are scarce and in societies where women lack status. A family with limited resources for food, medical care, or education may decide to deprive the females in the family in order to ensure that the males can be given what they need to thrive. As a Chinese official explained to reporters Sheryl WuDunn and Nicholas Kristof, among poor families, "if a boy gets sick, the parents may send him to the hospital at once. But if a girl gets sick, the parents may say to themselves,

---

30. Oxfam, "Economy That Works," 7.
31. Bureau of International Information Programs, "Women and Poverty."

'Well, let's see how she is tomorrow.' "[32] Scholars for the International Monetary Fund estimate that 3.9 million women and girls are "missing" from the world due to such unequal treatment from the womb forward, though Harvard economist Amartya Sen supports a much higher estimate of about 100 million missing women and girls.[33] In either case, the denial of resources to women and girls within families has real, and sometimes lethal, consequences.

However cruel and discriminatory this may seem, such decisions may be quite economically rational if a family's economic future depends on the earning power of its males. When the economic potential of women increases, as has happened when microloans, education, and other opportunities enable women to contribute significantly to their family's income, the status and treatment of women often improves as well.

A second issue that must be taken into account in order to understand women's economic situation is the reality of the care economy, the often unpaid but essential work of providing for the needs of embodied human beings. Global capitalism depends on these needs being met, yet too often the official economy makes no provision for this "extra" unremunerated labor that falls disproportionately on women around the world.[34] When women's paid and unpaid (or care) work are combined, women work over a month per year more than men.[35] As Christine Firer Hinze has aptly stated, "women are subsidizing the economy," through their unpaid care work, which contributes an estimated ten trillion dollars to the global economy every year.[36] Women, who overall experience more poverty and have

---

32. Nicholas D. Kristof and Sheryl WuDunn, *Half the Sky: Turning Oppression into Opportunity for Women Worldwide* (New York: Alfred A. Knopf, 2009), xiv.

33. Ana Revenga and Sudhir Shetty, "Empowering Women Is Smart Economics," *Finance and Development* 49, no. 1 (March 2012), International Monetary Fund, https://www.imf.org/external/pubs/ft/fandd/2012/03/revenga.htm; Amartya Sen, "More Than 100 Million Women Are Missing," *New York Review of Books*, December 20, 1990.

34. Oxfam, "Economy That Works," 3; Hinze, *Glass Ceilings*, 9–10, 88–92.

35. Will Dahlgreen, "Women Work 39 Days a Year More than Men, Report Says," *BBC News*, October 26, 2016, https://www.bbc.com/news/business-37767411.

36. Hinze, *Glass Ceilings*, 90; Oxfam, "Economy That Works," 3.

less access to education, are doing more than their share of the world's work while receiving less than their share of the benefits.

The demands of the care economy burden women economically in ways other than their longer hours of work. Women with responsibilities for the care of family members may not be able to accept jobs that require them to relocate, travel extensively, or spend longer hours at work.[37] This is not merely a matter of women having more handicaps that, along with straightforward sex discrimination, create the unjust "glass ceilings" that keep women from the most prestigious and lucrative employment. Poor women—and men—who cannot afford to pay others to do care work may be forced to make desperate choices between wage work and care work when both are necessary for their family members' health and well-being. Imagine the horrible risk of leaving a small child unattended in order to work for the money to provide food, or the heartbreak of leaving one's family behind to seek employment elsewhere.

Another result of the devaluation of the care economy is that when this work does involve paid labor, the jobs are held disproportionately by women and the wages are lower than jobs that involve equivalent levels of education and training but tend to be held by men.[38] Furthermore, because care work often necessarily involves a level of personal commitment and concern on the part of the caregiver, this dimension can be manipulated to make the demand for a more just wage seem mercenary or the refusal of unremunerated overtime an unconscionable abandonment of vulnerable people.[39]

The Oxfam International paper "An Economy That Works for Women" identifies three major steps toward an economy that fosters women's flourishing.[40] First, all paid labor should meet basic standards of decent work; that is, the labor should include a living wage for reasonable hours of work, a safe working environment, and secure contracts. This is especially important because too often women work in abusive and underpaid positions, whether in "sweat

---

37. Hinze, *Glass Ceilings*, 49; ix–xvi.
38. Hinze, *Glass Ceilings*, 49.
39. Hinze, *Glass Ceilings*, 84.
40. Oxfam, "Economy That Works," 4–5; cf. the six steps outlined in Hinze, *Glass Ceilings*, 104–17.

shop" factory conditions or in the informal sector doing poorly remunerated care work or performing piece work that is contracted out by manufacturers who take no responsibility for the excessive hours and low wages that enable their subcontractors to keep costs low. This subcontracting is especially ripe for abuse because highly lucrative fashion brands, owned by some of the wealthiest individuals in the world, can claim ignorance of the abusive conditions in which some of their products are produced. Moreover, the complicated layers of subcontracting common in the global economy make it extremely difficult for consumers to determine whether the goods they are purchasing are produced ethically, or at least without the use of child or slave labor.

Some argue against the idea that all labor should be paid a living wage on the grounds that in many cases women and young people are taking on extra work only to supplement an already adequate family income. Another argument is that requiring such work pay substantially more than it currently does could lead not only to higher costs for financially strapped consumers but also to the loss of many of these supposedly supplemental jobs when the economy will not support the price increases. In the United States, it is often alleged that raising the minimum wage to a living wage will lead to a reduction in available summer and part-time jobs for teenagers. The assumption, of course, is that those who do this work have someone in the household who makes a living "family" wage; unfortunately, this is often not the case. Too often women (and men) are trying to support themselves and their children on work that is structured to provide only supplemental wages. Such workers must then work multiple full-time jobs in order to pay their essential bills. When these working poor need government assistance, the economy and the extreme profits of the few are subsidized by taxpayers and by family members providing free care.

To be sure, the potential for unintended harm and counterproductive consequences of wage regulation is real and must be considered. Accurate economic data as well as labor unions and worker organizations should be consulted in determining the right minimum wage and which, if any, industries might be exempted.

The second step identified by the Oxfam paper is that unpaid care work needs to be recognized, redistributed, and reduced.

Acknowledging and remunerating care work reduces the pressure on women to shoulder this extra work in addition to their paid labor. Furthermore, valuing and paying a just wage for this work makes it more possible for those who find that such work fits their aptitudes and interests to pursue careers in these fields. Hinze is quite right that appropriate action on unpaid care work does not require a resolution to the debate about whether women are more inclined to care work and, if so, whether this is due to nature (such as the feminine "genius" lauded by Catholic teaching) or to nurture. Regardless of one's position on such gender issues, those who value women's lives and work can find common ground in a commitment to the recognition of the care economy as crucial work that ought to be appropriately remunerated by society, no matter whether that work is performed by women or by men.[41] Nor does this prevent women (and men) from voluntarily providing care work for free, whether to family members or in building up their local communities. After all, the fact that medical doctors generally receive good salaries enables—rather than prevents—the volunteer work some doctors provide to those without adequate medical care. The point is that care work should not be demanded of women in addition to their work in the paid economy. If wages are truly living wages, then there will be more possibilities for a family to reduce its paid labor hours so that it has sufficient time to do much of its own care work without undue stress or to pay fair wages to others who excel at this kind of work to do it for the family.

Thirdly, the Oxfam paper insists that women's voices must be heard and that women must be allowed to organize for their rights, including their right to have a say in the development of their work arrangements. If gender diversity is taken seriously, then policies will be based on what the women involved say their needs and concerns are, rather than on what men (or other women) assume them to be.

Overall, these three strategies outlined by the Oxfam paper fit well with the economic principles espoused in Catholic social teaching. As we have seen, papal and episcopal documents agree that

---

41. Hinze, *Glass Ceilings*, 108–9.

work ought to be secure and justly remunerated, that economic interests should not push aside concern for other aspects of social and personal life, and that all people should be involved in solving the societal problems that most affect them. Catholic social teaching defends a living wage sufficient to meet a family's economic needs with reasonable work hours that allow the time necessary for care work essential to the well-being of all members of the family, especially the children and elderly. While the rhetoric of a special feminine genius for care of persons suggests that women have a natural aptitude for this work, Catholic social teaching since the 1960s has nevertheless affirmed women's right to contribute to all sectors of society, including through work outside of the home.[42]

Still, Catholic social teaching remains underdeveloped with regard to the economic situation of women.[43] Little attention is given to the greater impoverishment of women, their lack of access to financial or educational resources, or the heavy burden of unpaid care work disproportionately borne by women. Perhaps the biggest problem is the general failure to recognize the need for the all-male ecclesial hierarchy to listen carefully to the many disparate voices of women, especially poor women. It is an unfortunate irony that Catholic social teaching documents uphold the principle of subsidiarity while usually modeling a top-down approach that gives no hint that women or others ought to be integrally involved in devising solutions to their economic struggles.

Other Unpaid Costs of Global Capitalism

Women's care work is not the only unpaid or underpaid economic cost. Global capitalism, seeking ever-greater market share and increased profits, is causing significant harm not only to people but also to the environment. The economy's impetus toward growth raises serious questions in a world of limited nonrenewable resources. If the global economy requires continual expansion, who will pay the costs of the resulting resource depletion? Does anyone assume responsibility for the real human and social costs to the

---

42. Hinze, *Glass Ceilings*, 22, 98.
43. Hinze, *Glass Ceilings*, 98–101.

peoples and areas left behind when industries move elsewhere in search of higher profits? Perhaps most troubling, what will happen if global capitalism is finally unsustainable in a finite world—and if so, how will the human race recover from the implosion of the global economy?

As Pope Francis realizes, the ecological sustainability of global capitalism is an economic as well as an environmental matter. While more attention will be given to this topic in the next chapter, we cannot prescind here from some mention of the problems entailed in the fact that the vigor of the economy is predicated on a continual growth that is driving species into extinction, polluting the world, and using up natural resources at an increasingly rapid rate. Underlying this situation is the reality that these costs are often not paid by those who profit most from the economic expansion. Instead, some of these costs are borne by taxpayers, for example through environmental cleanup funds or emergency assistance for areas hit by natural disasters, and by private citizens, including those who struggle with additional health costs or loss of property due to extreme weather events. Much of the impact of ecological destruction is experienced in the countries that benefit least from the global economy. And, of course, the most significant costs are being left to future generations, who will inherit a world with drastically diminished natural resources and ecological damage that may well affect every aspect of their lives.

In a just economy, surely the costs to the environment would be factored into the price of production. The low cost of consumer goods and the very high profits of successful businesses are being subsidized not only by the care economy but also by allowing producers to pollute and deplete without paying the full price. Some argue that future technological advances will find a way to make more with less so that the situation for coming generations will not be as dire as our current calculations indicate—presumably excepting the damage to the climate that is already reaching crisis levels. Of course, this argument depends on scientific discoveries not yet made, and in any case, it leaves a future population to pay for the benefits enjoyed in the present. There is also fear that requiring industries to pay for their use and abuse of natural resources will handicap these businesses in their competition with other companies whose countries do not require them to pay their environmental costs. Global capitalism thus tends toward a lowest common denominator in ethical responsibility, at least in the absence of sufficient enforcement of international standards.

Another area of significant concern is the human costs to the people and communities left behind when industries go bankrupt or leave for more profitable locations. As Friedman's *The World Is Flat* suggests, a ruthless search for lower costs and higher efficiency requires a great deal of flexibility, innovation, and frequent restructuring. What happens to the communities and the people remaining behind when their sources of employment move elsewhere? It may well be the case, as Friedman contends, that workers in the future will require frequent job retraining so that they can keep up with the demands of a highly innovative and changing economy. If so, much will have to be done to ensure that the necessary training is available and affordable. There will also have to be provisions for people who are unable to develop the requisite skills quickly enough, as well as for aging workers who find the latest need to retrain comes at a time when they are too close to retirement to be able to successfully retrain and be rehired.[44]

But economic shifts are already causing serious problems for the people and the communities left without adequate sources of employment, often quite suddenly when a factory closes or an industry moves its operations to another locale. Although there was some hope that telecommuting technologies would make it possible for rural populations to find jobs without relocating, large metropolitan areas continue, on the whole, to be more economically efficient sites for intellectual workers in the current economy. The result is that many small towns and rural areas are experiencing high unemployment and a dismal future, even while many large cities are doing well economically.[45] The increasing density may be a strain on infrastructure—and tempers—in large, overcrowded cities, but the loss of decent employment is devastating smaller communities. Those of us committed to strengthening human relationships should

---

44. Friedman, *The World Is Flat*, 358–80.
45. Paul Collier, *The Future of Capitalism: Facing the New Anxieties* (New York: HarperCollins, 2018).

be troubled by the fact that people forced to relocate to metropolitan areas must often sever long-standing ties with their home communities, losing relationships and bonds that they may not be able to replace easily in a large urban environment. We must also be concerned about the cost to workers who are unable or unwilling to abandon their homes, community support, and care responsibilities in hopes of employment elsewhere. Many of these people are left with poor economic prospects and in despair.

It is not surprising, then, that much of rural and small-town America feels left behind, resentful of urban areas and perhaps especially of the immigrants they fear are taking their jobs. There is no room for bigotry in Christian discipleship, of course, but it helps no one for economically successful urban people to dismiss the concerns of those living in hollowed-out communities. As Pope Francis has warned, one of the great costs of global capitalism is that it forces people to compete against each other, fraying solidarity and contributing to xenophobic rancor and even violence in the United States as well as around the world (EG 51, 59). Alas, there is no dearth of politicians willing to fan the flames of anger and resentment for their own gain.

It is possible that, as British economist Paul Collier contends, public policy can mitigate this economic devastation of small towns. He suggests taxing the economic advantage that comes from the concentration of talent in large cities, generating money that can be used to boost development in areas that have lost their industries.[46] It remains to be seen whether this is a viable policy. The assumptions motivating his proposal are nevertheless valid: Catholic social teaching agrees that we have a collective responsibility for those who suffer from the shifts of the economy, that communities matter, and that those who profit most ought to bear more of the costs of the harm to the people and communities discarded by this restless capitalism.

As Catholic social teachings have repeatedly pointed out, there are many structural injustices in the global economy. While all of these must be rectified, special attention must be given to the burden

---

46. Collier, *Future of Capitalism* 125–53.

of unpaid or underpaid care work, the pollution and depletion of national resources, and the destruction of the lives and communities of those who lose out in the global competition—whether through their own limitations or not. What is at stake here is whether the current economy can be sufficiently reformed so that it does not treat women, the environment, and much of the world's population as fuel for the engine driving greater profits for stockholders. An economy structured to benefit some at the expense of the many and of future generations is not consistent with responsible stewardship oriented toward the communion of all in God. Instead of pitting people against each other, the global economy should be the means through which we support ourselves, improve our communities, and cooperate for the good of the entire human race.

It is not clear whether global capitalism can be reformed to become a truly sustainable and just economic system that unites rather than divides the human community. As we will discuss in the next chapter, it is still possible that, if there is the political will to do so, the worst effects of the climate crisis can be averted using the technology currently available. Given its impetus for continual expansion, however, it remains to be seen to what extent global capitalism itself could be adapted to be consistent with the sustainable use of the world's limited natural resources.[47]

More work must be done to envision and explore economic reforms within and beyond the current global capitalist system. It seems clear that any viable economy will continue to include a role for market forces, at least for the foreseeable future, as no government has yet shown itself able to plan and direct the entire economy successfully within its own country, let alone in globally. Moreover, as the principle of subsidiarity maintains, economic solutions should not be devised and imposed by economic experts and politicians

---

47. As suggested by his title, Robert Reich makes the case in *Saving Capitalism* that appropriate governmental regulation has in the past and can in the future make this a workable system. On the other hand, Brent Waters's praise of capitalism, while rightly noting the good the global economy does, fails to analyze seriously capitalism's distortions and especially the climate crisis. See Brent Waters, *Just Capitalism: A Christian Ethic of Economic Globalization* (Louisville, KY: Westminster/John Knox, 2016).

without meaningful input from those most affected. Indeed, more support for the development of grassroots organizations and more cooperation with these groups in the process of reforming the economy will ensure that the economy better serves the flourishing of the human community and the care of the natural world, both now and in the future.[48]

Being Church in a Global Economy

A Prophetic Ecclesial Witness

The church, called to be sign and instrument of the union of all in God, is properly concerned with the economic relations that bind humanity together in ways that have improved some aspects of life but have also increased economic insecurity and inequality. A church that shares the hopes and fears of all people cannot be indifferent to their economic hopes and fears. As Pope Francis has further argued, the church must challenge the widespread idolatry of the market, which values profit over all else (EG, esp. 55, 202). Resistance to this idolatry requires a countercultural Christian discipleship that witnesses to faith in a God of life, a God who intends our common work to foster the communion of all rather than the profits of a few.

As should be evident, the church is not, in and of itself, an alternative economy. The vast majority of Christian people and their ecclesial institutions are inextricably involved in the global economy. Even the Amish, who supply a great deal of their economic essentials themselves as a cooperative community, are not entirely self-sufficient; they too satisfy some of their needs through trade with the broader economy. And, of course, few Christians live in sectarian communities that produce their own food, clothing, and shelter.

Participating in a common economy is not necessarily a bad thing: God intends the world's resources for the good of all, and a global economy can and should be a means of this mutual sharing and assistance. The challenge to the church is how to witness prophetically to an alternative and mutually supportive economy, even

---

48. John Sniegocki, *Catholic Social Teaching and Economic Globalization: The Quest for Alternatives* (Milwaukee, WI: Marquette University Press, 2009), 240–44.

while being very much involved in the distorted and abusive economy we currently have.

An obvious (but not easy!) first step in providing a countercultural witness is for Christians to commit themselves to living by the principles of a just economy personally, professionally, and in their ecclesial institutions. This includes paying living wages to workers and refusing to benefit from unjust wages paid by others. It follows that Christians personally and collectively—in the financial policies not only of churches but also of church-sponsored hospitals, nursing homes, social agencies, schools, and universities—should seek out fairly traded and sustainably produced items to the extent possible, while avoiding companies and products known to abuse workers and the environment. The witness of those churches that sponsor fair trade shops and sales is especially commendable.

Paying fair wages and buying goods produced according to the principles of Catholic social teaching will usually cost more, which may require reducing some higher salaries along with eliminating nonessentials to balance budgets. These changes are not likely to be minor and will take considerable commitment; many church institutions today contend that it is too expensive to pay a decent wage and work only with contractors and products that are "fair trade." For Christians to refuse to subsidize their institutions, ministries, and personal lifestyles through participating in the oppression of workers or the environment would be prophetic indeed. Yet how can we not do this, if we truly believe what we proclaim?

Such reorganizing of economic priorities in accordance with the principles of Catholic social teaching might seem less daunting to Christian communities that cultivate a spirituality centered on prayer and on an ecclesial and personal option for the poor.[49] These essential aspects of Christian life witness powerfully against the idolatry of the market, since neither prayer nor relationship with the poor has much market value. Indeed, when evaluated from the perspective of the capitalist economy, prayer and prioritizing the vulnerable can only appear to be a waste of time. Why interrupt busy careers in a 24/7 world to devote time instead to prayer, to worship on Sunday

---

49. EG 3, 201, 20, 187.

mornings, or to building outreach to powerless people? Such activities surely do not increase prestige or profit. Instead, they interrupt the hegemony of the market as well as the globalization of indifference that Francis critiques.[50] Even a small effort to respond to others' pain can be an expression of hope and love, a refusal to turn away from the overwhelming suffering of the world.

As argued above, this option for the poor further requires that women, who are often the poorest of the poor, receive particular attention. This is especially the case since women are so easily overlooked in androcentric societies and in male-dominated churches. It should go without saying that women and girls ought to receive a fair share of the family resources and equal opportunities to develop the full range of their abilities. At home and in church, women should not be expected to shoulder a larger share of unpaid care work than the men who work similar hours of paid labor.

An important question for the Catholic Church, which does not ordain women, is whether women's work in the church is fairly paid and appropriately valued compared to that of men with equivalent training and skill sets. What kind of witness do we proffer the world if the skills of laywomen and religious sisters are welcomed for pastoral work and parish administration when no priest is available, but then are dismissed when an ordained male shows up? Or when elderly religious women are left without sufficient means of subsistence by the church to which they have given so much? The actual treatment of women in the church and in ecclesial institutions speaks more clearly to society than any number of official statements praising women's gifts and affirming their theoretical equality.

---

50. Furthermore, as Pope Benedict XVI points out in his encyclical *Deus Caritas Est*, personal engagement with the poor is necessary to counteract an overly bureaucratic approach to poverty. Beyond the material assistance of food, shelter, or medical care provided (often) by an impersonal system, human flourishing requires affection, relationships, and a place in society. As Benedict explains, "Seeing with the eyes of Christ, I can give to others much more than their outward necessities; I can give them the look of love which they crave"—and, of course, be open to receiving love in return. See Benedict XVI, On Christian Love (*Deus Caritas Est*), 18, http://w2.vatican.va/content/benedict-xvi/en/encyclicals/documents/hf_ben-xvi_enc_20051225_deus-caritas-est.html.

As the example of women suggests, there are real challenges to developing a true option for the poor in the hierarchically organized Catholic Church. However, the Catholic Church's well-established national and international structures can also be valuable assets for building genuine, countercultural solidarity in a global economy. Catholic parishes are united at the diocesan level and, through the college of bishops, nationally and internationally as well. Given that one of the problems with a globally competitive economy is that smaller towns and rural areas can suddenly lose their major source of employment, the networks within and among dioceses might be deployed to assist such communities. Parishes could help to identify local leaders with firsthand knowledge of what their community needs and what it has to offer; bishops could facilitate relationships between these leaders and parishes elsewhere that have resources to help retrain people or to revitalize the economically depressed community. Properly developed, such cooperation would witness to subsidiarity and to a deeper solidarity than the more common collection and dispersal of charity funds, as important as those funds may be. A global church may be especially well positioned to model the solidarity necessary for a global economy that serves the good of all.

A Public Church

The distinction between prophetic witness and public agent is somewhat artificial, of course, and by no means absolute. The church's witness of economic justice, for example, is also transformative to the extent that the ecclesial use of economic resources can change lives, assisting those in need and inspiring others to live more simply or with more compassion. At the same time, a public church cooperating with the larger society is itself a witness to the church's commitment to the common good and its refusal of the growing tribalism of our time. Working with people of other religions and of no religion to transform society embodies a commitment to the ideal of a diverse communion that includes all.

Affirming that Christians have a responsibility to the broader society, much of Catholic social teaching focuses on the principles that should guide public policy. As Pope Francis reminds us, the Catholic Church holds that "participation in political life is a moral obligation," especially in societies where citizens have the opportunity to make their voices heard.[51] Furthermore, Christians are deeply involved in the global economy, many benefit greatly from it, and its systemic injustices can only be corrected to the extent that we work with others to change local, national, and international policies. Pope Francis rightly insists on the urgency of resolving the economic distortions that cause poverty and inequality, both for the good of the poor and for the health of society itself (EG 202). The extreme inequality of global capitalism causes suffering and death to the poor, while also increasing divisions and exclusions that are incompatible with the communion of all in which human beings truly flourish.

Catholic social teaching does not intend to dictate policy but rather to clarify the principles that ought to direct public life. As we saw above, these principles in themselves are quite countercultural in maintaining that the economy should be directed for the benefit of all but especially of the poor, that labor ought to have priority over capital, and that a dignified and truly human life is more important than the mindless pursuit of higher profits. Pope Francis is particularly insistent on the need to resist the current idolatry of the market and to acknowledge the political responsibility to direct the economy so that it serves humanity rather than humanity serving the economy. This chapter has argued for further consideration of gender inequalities and of the injustices of the unpaid care economy. Greater attention to the problems of communities left behind by economic shifts would also make Catholic social teaching more adequate to the current reality of contemporary global capitalism.

Focused on principles rather than policies, Catholic social teachings intentionally leave space for disagreement within the church about which policies will best realize these goals. It is never clear exactly how to ensure a just economy that serves the dignity of all rather than the profits of a few. Nevertheless, diverse views on the likely effect of economic policies should not be grounds for refusing

---

51. EG 220, quoting the United States Conference of Catholic Bishops' pastoral letter *Forming Consciences for Faithful Citizenship* (November 2007). This also echoes the obligation to political citizenship affirmed in *Gaudium et Spes* 75.

to discuss economic matters within or beyond the church. On the contrary, exploring different perspectives together not only reinforces the importance of these matters to Christian discipleship but also enables Christians to learn from one another so that their agency in the world is better informed. Moreover, in this climate of political polarization, any such dialogue is in itself a countercultural and deeply needed witness: neither church nor world will embody the unity-in-diversity of God's reign unless we learn to disagree without acrimonious division.

Efforts to transform the economy will often require that Christians act according to their own initiative and judgment in their personal, political, and professional activities. However, there is considerable room for the church to work not only to inform the judgment of individual Christians but also to support the common principles Christians espouse. As important as it is to avoid silencing legitimate diversity about solutions, the experience of the church in Latin America has shown that some policies are so contrary to Christian values that the church as a community must oppose them. It is also appropriate, and at times necessary, for church leaders publicly and clearly to proclaim the proper goals and values of economic policies, even while avoiding lobbying on behalf of specific political proposals.

There is, then, a role for explicitly religious beliefs and values in public life. The two previous popes, John Paul II and Benedict XVI, staunchly resisted the privatization of religion, especially as they argued against atheistic communism and the secularization of Europe. Pope Francis similarly defends the public role of religion, arguing that a religiously pluralistic society must include all beliefs in the public conversation. The point, of course, is not to legislate religious matters but to allow religious values to inform public policies.[52]

Francis further supports a Catholic emphasis on the accessibility of a religious tradition's wisdom even to those outside of the tradition. Religious classics, he contends, embody perceptions about the

---

52. EG 255, 257. See also the discussion of secularity without secularism in chapter 1 of this volume.

human condition that all might learn from.[53] Instead of downplaying or suppressing religious disagreements, then, Francis encourages public dialogue that engages differing religious perspectives as a means not only to mutual understanding but also to greater insight into our common humanity (EG 238–58, esp. 250).

A triumphalist Christianity that has all the answers and nothing to learn from others is obviously not conducive to public discourse. If Christians expect their religious views to be given respectful consideration in public debate, then they have to be open to considering others' positions as well. Such openness is not a denial of Christian truth but rather an embrace of the divine mystery that can never be fully encompassed in any human perspective.

A willingness to learn from others is also essential to the project of overcoming Christian supersessionism. Mindful of the church's failure to maintain unity-in-diversity with regard to its Jewish other, Christians must actively resist the assumption that Judaism has nothing to contribute to public life that has not already been subsumed into and perfected by Christianity. In fact, Christians have much to learn from Jews and from Judaism (as from other religions). Judaism has continued to attend to aspects of the Hebrew Bible that have been marginalized in the Christian tradition, including God's desire for the liberation of the poor in this world and the limitation of debts. Moreover, the ongoing Jewish tradition has developed no less than has Christianity in the two thousand years since the two faiths diverged, and there may be much we can learn from the path each other has taken.

Conclusion

A church that witnesses to and works for greater unity-in-diversity cannot ignore the manner in which the global economy is uniting the world. Indeed, according to Pope Francis, efforts to create more just political and economic structures are "the social dimension of evangelization" (EG 178–84). The church as sign and instrument is

---

53. EG 256. Cf. the similar defense of the public role of religious classics in David Tracy, *The Analogical Imagination: Christian Theology and the Culture of Pluralism* (New York: Crossroad, 1981).

called to spread God's reign not only by preaching about it but by embodying harmonious unity-in-diversity as an ecclesial community while also working to increase that harmony in the world. Efforts to make the world more just are not "preevangelization," but rather are constitutive of the communion the church is called to serve.

Christian churches have erred by considering economics religiously irrelevant or at best marginal to the religious concerns of the church. There is much to be done to ensure that the basic principles of human dignity and inclusion are more fully embodied in the economic practices of ecclesial communities and institutions as well as of individual Christians. The church's concern for justice extends to the whole world, and the Catholic tradition joins other Christian communities in maintaining that Christians cannot be indifferent to the injustices of our (now global) common life. Yet the ideals of a just economy must also transform the church in its relations to all within the church and all those outside the church; this includes especially women and Jews, whom the church has long marginalized and even maligned.

The church must prophetically and publicly refuse to accept a global economy construed as a lethal competition between lions and gazelles. Instead of seeing us as pitted against one another, Christians are challenged to imagine and act as though the world is united around a single table. The Eucharist, the memorial of Jesus' Last Supper and crucifixion for the salvation of the world, is also a proleptic celebration of the eschatological banquet in God's reign. All—not just Christians—are ultimately to be gathered into what Mercy Amba Oduyoye aptly terms "the hearth-hold of God," fed by the divine abundance that is intended for all but currently monopolized by the few.[54]

---

54. Mercy Amba Oduyoye, *Introducing African Women's Theology* (Cleveland: Pilgrim Press, 2001), 78–89.

Chapter 5

A Prophetic, Public Church in a Climate Crisis

Two very different environmental incidents captured the world's attention in August 2019. The first was a memorial erected to Okjökull, or Ok glacier, the first major Icelandic glacier lost to climate change.[1] The second was the large number of fires burning in the Amazon rain forest, contributing to the deforestation of what has been called "the lungs of the planet" for its role in sequestering carbon dioxide and releasing oxygen. The glacier was lost because of the warming of the planet; the fires in the Amazon were evidently set by farmers emboldened by Brazilian president Jair Bolsonaro's dismissal of concern for global warming.[2]

These two events remind us that the global capitalist economy is wreaking havoc on the environment. Natural resources are being depleted at a rate far surpassing their renewability while the market continues to expand to meet the needs and desires of the growing human population. The strain on this finite planet, limited in its supply of resources and in its ability to absorb the discarded waste, is evidence that human production and consumption must be drastically

---

1. Brandon Specktor, "The First Glacier Killed by Climate Change Is Getting a Haunting Memorial in Iceland," *Live Science*, July 22, 2019, https://www.livescience.com/65996-iceland-ok-glacier-memorial-plaque.html.

2. Alexandria Symonds, "Amazon Rainforest Fires: Here's What's Really Happening," *New York Times*, August 23, 2019, https://www.nytimes.com/2019/08/23/world/americas/amazon-fire-brazil-bolsonaro.html.

changed. Plastic garbage is choking the ocean and, as Pope Francis has pointed out, the world is filling up with trash piles and garbage dumps since everything thrown "away" must in fact go somewhere (*Laudato Sí* [LS] 21, 22, 50).

Most critically, we face a global climate emergency that is threatening the life and health of the planet. The average atmospheric level of carbon dioxide for the 800,000 years before the Industrial Revolution never surpassed 300 parts per million, but the level of carbon dioxide has now reached 415 parts per million and is still rising as fossil fuels continue to be burned.[3] Carbon dioxide holds heat in the earth's atmosphere, raising the planet's overall temperature, which has already increased by 1 degree Celsius, with significant effects on many ecosystems. Glaciers are melting, the ocean is acidifying, and extreme weather events such as storms, droughts, and hurricanes are becoming common.[4] Even more frightening is the possibility of a feedback loop in which the climate change already underway brings about further warming. Melting glaciers and sea ice may cause even higher global temperatures as oceans absorb the heat that ice would have deflected, thus speeding up the rate of global warming. Since a great deal of polar ice has already melted and since carbon dioxide remains in the atmosphere and continues to trap heat for decades after its release, the earth may be approaching—or have already reached—a tipping point that triggers an irreversible sequence of climate reactions.[5] According

---

3. Rebecca Lindsey, "Climate Change: Atmospheric Carbon Dioxide," *ClimateWatch*, September 19, 2019, https://www.climate.gov/news-features/understanding-climate/climate-change-atmospheric-carbon-dioxide.

4. For current climate information, see especially "Climate Change: How Do We Know," NASA Global Climate Change: Vital Signs of the Planet, http://climate.nasa.gov/evidence/. See also Jeffrey Bennett, *A Global Warming Primer: Answering Your Questions about the Science, the Consequences, and the Solutions* (Boulder, CO: Big Kid Science, 2016).

5. See "Another Climate Milestone Falls at Mauna Loa Observatory," Scripps Institution of Oceanography: The Keeling Curve, June 7, 2018, https://scripps.ucsd.edu/programs/keelingcurve/2018/06/07/another-climate-milestone-falls-at-mauna-loa-observatory/. See also James Hansen et al., "Target Atmospheric CO_2: Where Should Humanity Aim?," *Open Atmospheric Science Journal* 2 (2008), 217–31, http://www-users.math.umn.edu/~mcgehee/Seminars/ClimateChange/references/Hansen2008OpenAtmosSciJp217-TargetCO2.pdf.

to the 2018 Intergovernmental Panel on Climate Change (IPCC), we must dramatically reduce the human race's carbon dioxide and other greenhouse gas emissions by 2030 to escape the most extreme upheavals that total global climate change will bring if humanity continues on its current path. Although the exact time line is disputable, the overwhelming scientific consensus is that humanity must act quickly to reduce atmospheric greenhouse gases.[6]

The situation is dire, but there is good news as well. Renewable energy sources, such as wind and sun, that do not produce greenhouse gases are plentiful, and the technology needed to harness and store this energy is improving and becoming more affordable. According to a 2014 report of the IPCC, the technology already exists to transition to fossil-free energy without damaging the economy.[7] The more serious economic cost is likely to be the expense of extreme weather events, crop failure, disease, and violent conflicts over limited resources if action to abate climate change is not taken. Of course, stopping global warming will not solve all of the ecological problems of a human population nearing eight billion, but it would be a crucial first step.

Unfortunately, there is not yet sufficient political will to substantially reduce greenhouse gas emissions, especially in the United States, which is one of the top three nations contributing to climate change.[8] To be sure, the concerted efforts of climate scientists and environmental activists to alert people to the dangers and to increase support

6. Intergovernmental Panel on Climate Change, *Global Warming of 1.5°C* (October 2018), https://www.ipcc.ch/sr15/. In addition to Bennett, *Global Warming Primer*, see also James Hansen et al., "Assessing 'Dangerous Climate Change': Required Reduction of Carbon Emissions to Protect Young People, Future Generations and Nature," *PLoS ONE* 8, no. 12 (December 2013), https://doi.org/10.1371/journal.pone.0081648.

7. Intergovernmental Panel on Climate Change, *Climate Change 2014: Mitigation of Climate Change* (New York: Cambridge University Press, 2014), https://www.ipcc.ch/site/assets/uploads/2018/02/ipcc_wg3_ar5_frontmatter.pdf. See also Levi Tillemann et al., "Revolution Now: The Future Arrives for Four Clean Energy Technologies" (United States Department of Energy, September 7, 2013), https://www.energy.gov/sites/prod/files/2013/09/f2/200130917-revolution-now.pdf.

8. Johannes Friedrich, Mengpin Ge, and Andrew Pickens, "This Interactive Chart Explains World's Top 10 Emitters, and How They've Changed," World Resources Institute, April 11, 2017, https://www.wri.org/blog/2017/04/interactive-chart-explains-worlds-top-10-emitters-and-how-theyve-changed.

for political action have had some positive effects. According to recent polls, a majority of Americans now accept that human-caused climate change is occurring, notwithstanding the misinformation of climate change deniers, who insist that this is a huge (presumably global) scientific hoax.[9] Nevertheless, climate change has come to be treated as a partisan issue in the United States' deeply polarized political landscape. At the time of this writing, the Republican Party officially opposes government action to decrease greenhouse gas emissions,[10] and centrist Democrats worry that environmental legislation will cause them to lose votes in Republican-leaning districts. Rightly or wrongly, people fear being outcompeted in the global economy if other nations do not accept equally rigorous emissions standards, and it is no simple matter to implement an international plan that distributes the burdens of climate action fairly. Furthermore, those who own fossil fuel reserves have considerable incentive to resist these reserves' becoming "stranded assets" that lose their value if fossil fuels are no longer used.

Many religious groups have identified environmental degradation, and especially the climate emergency, as profoundly religious concerns. The danger to human life and health, as well as to international peace when resources become scarce, cannot be ignored by any religious tradition valuing human well-being. Moreover, the climate crisis is inspiring reconsideration of Christian neglect of environmental ethics, including discussion of whether nature has intrinsic worth. The Orthodox patriarch Bartholomew of Constantinople has been a pioneer, campaigning publicly for Christian attention to the care of nature since the early 1990s, and Vatican City has been carbon-neutral since 2007. In recent years, many churches have issued statements calling for action on climate change, and in 2015 Pope Francis released the first Catholic encyclical devoted entirely to the environment, On Care for Our Common Home (*Laudato Si*).

---

9. See, for example, the Associated Press-NORC Center for Public Affairs Research, "Public Opinion on Energy Policy under the Trump Administration," accessed May 20, 2019, http://www.apnorc.org/projects/Pages/Public-Opinion-on-Energy-Policy-under-the-Trump-Administration.aspx.

10. See "Republican Platform 2016," accessed May 20, 2019, https://prod-cdn-static.gop.com/media/documents/DRAFT_12_FINAL[1]-ben_1468872234.pdf.

Religious faith can be a powerful motivator of personal and even political action, and the church could play an important role here. Particularly in those areas where Christians are a significant percentage of the population, Christian engagement with environmental and climate ethics might be sufficient to create the political will needed to reduce greenhouse gases and other forms of ecological damage before it is too late. Unfortunately, this possibility is complicated by the fact that, at least in the United States, Christians are more bitterly divided by politics than by denomination. Reminiscent of the pre–Civil War period, in which denominations in the United States split into those that supported and those that opposed slavery, Christians today often differ among themselves less over doctrinal issues than over political worldview. In a context in which climate change is (mistakenly) treated as a matter of political worldview rather than scientific study, there is reason to fear that Christians choose their religious ethics on the basis of their political commitments instead of the reverse.[11] Moreover, an individualistic and otherworldly understanding of Christianity is still widespread enough that the conditions of life on earth strike many as—at best—secondary issues that ought not distract the church from its supposedly primary focus on the salvation of souls. This reductive but common view of Christianity is a significant obstacle to concerted Christian action to avert a climate disaster.

These divisions and misunderstandings among Christians are further evidence that the church must engage the serious problem of ecological degradation for the good of the church and of the world. The reduction of Christianity to a concern for the afterlife of immaterial, individual souls is a bastardization of Christian hope and an impediment to the church's call to be a sign and instrument of communion. The church's mission is integrally involved with the conditions of life on this planet, not only because human life develops on earth and depends on natural resources but also because, as recent

---

11. Alas, one study suggests that young people in the United States do indeed consider their political affiliation first and only secondarily adopt the religious beliefs consistent with their political identity. See Michele Margolis, "When Politicians Determine Your Religious Beliefs," *New York Times*, July 11, 2018, https://www.nytimes.com/2018/07/11/opinion/religion-republican-democrat.html.

papal teachings have clarified, all of creation has a destiny in the God who created it. Furthermore, the history of changing Christian positions on the morality of slavery and religious freedom gives reason for hope that the sources of Christian faith, the prayerful experiences of Christian communities, and the teachings of Christian leaders may be powerful enough to break through the scleroses of status quo versions of Christianity to inform a Christian discipleship that recognizes the centrality of care for the natural world.

The task of this chapter is to investigate what it means to be a prophetic, public church in the midst of the unprecedented contemporary challenges posed by the abuse of the environment and specifically by anthropogenic global climate change. While official Catholic social teachings have focused overall on socioeconomic structures and governmental policies, more recent documents, including Pope Francis's encyclical *Laudato Sí*, address the treatment of nature as itself a moral and religious matter. After examining Pope Francis's contribution to Catholic social teaching on the environment, this chapter will explore the connections between the oppression of women and the exploitation of nature because an understanding of this link contributes both to the analysis of ecological issues and to a better Christian witness. We will then turn to a brief discussion of recent developments in the scientific consensus on the impending dangers of climate change before concluding with a reflection on the demands of being a prophetic, public church in the face of this global climate emergency. It is imperative that Christians have a clear grasp both of where the defense of nature fits into the church's mission to be a sign and instrument of the union of all in God and of what resources the Christian tradition has for sustaining a countercultural witness appropriate to the serious ecological problems that confront us all.

Overcoming Tyrannical Anthropocentrism: Catholic Social Teaching and *Laudato Sí*

As early as 1967, Christian anthropocentrism was identified as a major factor in the modern devastation of the environment. In his classic article "The Historical Roots of Our Ecological Crisis," Lynn White Jr. contends that the creation stories in Genesis portray the world as created for the benefit of humans, leading Christians to claim a God-given right to use nature however they wish.[12] Along with many scholars, Pope Francis rejects this interpretation of Genesis, arguing in *Laudato Si* that the dominion humanity is given in Genesis 1 is more accurately interpreted as stewardship than as absolute rule. Instead of being allowed to do whatever they like to the rest of creation, humans are commanded to "'till and keep' the garden of the world," serving God by caring for the earth on God's behalf (LS 67). As Pope Francis further notes, the laws in the Hebrew Bible set limits on human use of nature, including—among other examples—the requirement that one's ox and donkey be allowed to rest on the Sabbath and the prohibition against the permanent sale of land on the grounds that the land finally belongs ultimately to God (LS 67–69).

However, White's charge is not baseless. Though Genesis 1 may not support the position as well as is widely believed, Christians have cited this passage as authorization for humanity to use the earth in whatever manner they please. In my own undergraduate study, a Catholic theology professor asserted—as though it were obvious and uncontroversial—that the Bible supports the belief that God gave humans the privilege of using nature as they wish.

This anthropocentrism is reinforced by the common Christian focus on salvation as a divine-human drama in which the rest of creation has little role. Moral obligations then center on what is owed to God or to other people, and the final goal of history is often envisioned as the destruction of the world rather than as the restoration of harmony on earth and among all creatures, as described in the book of Isaiah (11:6-9), for example. In fact, the claim that the human being is the "only creature on earth that God willed for itself" (GS 24) appears in official Catholic documents through the late twentieth century, further suggesting that only humans have intrinsic value and that the rest of creation exists for the sake of humanity.[13]

---

12. Lynn White Jr., "The Historical Roots of Our Ecological Crisis," *Science* 155, no 3767 (March 1967), 1203–7.

13. See also John Paul II, *Redemptor Hominis*, 13, http://w2.vatican.va/content/john-paul-ii/en/encyclicals/documents/hf_jp-ii_enc_04031979_redemptor-hominis.html.

Such anthropocentrism is also reinforced by statements of the church's mission to be a sign and instrument of union with God and of the unity of all humanity. Throughout the Second Vatican Council's *Gaudium et Spes*, communion involves human hearts and minds, such that the church's mission to contribute to the union of all in God clearly focuses on building up unity among people (GS 42). The document could be read as hinting that something of the nonhuman world might be included in the eschaton when it discusses human achievements being included and perfected in the reign of God: "When we have spread on earth the fruits of our . . . enterprise . . . we will find them once again, cleansed this time from the stain of sin, illuminated and transfigured" (GS 39). There is, however, little elaboration on this point. For the most part, those who suppose that only human beings have souls and thus are alone among earthly creatures in being destined for eternal life with God will find little in official Catholic teaching to challenge their belief. They can then assign the rest of creation only temporary and instrumental value: the world, it seems, is here for the sake of humanity and serves no other purpose.

In recent decades, this Christian anthropocentrism has come into serious question. Recognition of the horrifying damage humans are now able to inflict on ecosystems has increased attention to environmental ethics. As mentioned above, the Orthodox patriarch Bartholomew is a leading advocate of Christian obligations to nature, and the work of ecological and ecofeminist theologians has informed various denominational statements on humanity's moral responsibility to care for the earth.[14] In the Catholic Church, several recent popes have denounced environmental degradation, and various regional conferences of Catholic bishops have addressed the topic and taken positions such as that of the United States Conference of Catholic Bishops, who insist that "if we harm the atmosphere, we dishonor our Creator and the gift of creation."[15]

---

14. See, for example, Bartholomew, *On Earth as in Heaven*, ed. John Chryssavgis (New York: Fordham University Press, 2011); and Lynn Whitney and Ellie Whitney, *Faith Based Statements on Climate Change* (CreateSpace, 2012).

15. United States Conference of Catholic Bishops, "Global Climate Change: A Plea for Dialogue, Prudence, and the Common Good," June 15, 2001, http://www

Drawing on this work by bishops, past popes, and theologians, Pope Francis's encyclical *Laudato Sí* reiterates key ideas found in these and other recent Catholic social teachings. The encyclical engages science with appreciation and respect, as is consistent with the long-standing Catholic tradition of embracing both faith and reason as gifts from God to lead humanity to the truth. The central Catholic social principles of the common good, of solidarity, and of the option for the poor are also prevalent. Pope Francis emphasizes that God intends the earth's resources for the good of all humanity, that Christians owe solidarity to future generations as well as to all humans alive today, and that the poor, who suffer most from the ravages and disasters of climate change, ought to be at the center of Christian concern. For all of these reasons, careful stewardship of the environment is a moral obligation.[16]

Pope Francis also repeats the criticism from his 2013 apostolic exhortation *Evangelii Gaudium* of a global economy that encourages consumerist waste in its relentless drive for greater profits. While many people struggle to live without adequate food and shelter, others suffer the spiritual emptiness brought on by a consumerism devoted to the pursuit of financial gain and seeking fulfillment in the distractions of superfluous experiences and objects. These are manifestations of a distorted and unhealthy culture, Francis observes. Moreover, he includes again in *Laudato Sí* his earlier critique that, in the current economy, "whatever is fragile, like the environment, is defenceless before the interests of a deified market, which becomes the only rule" (LS 56, quoting from EG 56).

Interestingly, one key principle of Catholic social teaching that is not included in *Laudato Sí* is the need for prudential reasoning, a topic that figures prominently in the United States Conference of

---

.usccb.org/issues-and-action/human-life-and-dignity/environment/global-climate-change-a-plea-for-dialogue-prudence-and-the-common-good.cfm. See also John Paul II, Message for the Celebration of the World Day of Peace, January 1, 1990, 48–51, http://w2.vatican.va/content/john-paul-ii/en/messages/peace/documents/hf_jp-ii_mes_19891208_xxiii-world-day-for-peace.html; and Benedict XVI, On Integral Human Development in Charity and Truth (*Caritas in Veritate*), 48–51, http://w2.vatican.va/content/benedict-xvi/en/encyclicals/documents/hf_ben-xvi_enc_20090629_caritas-in-veritate.html.

16. LS, esp. 93–95, 158–159.

Catholic Bishops' 2001 document on the environment, *Global Climate Change: A Plea for Dialogue, Prudence, and the Common Good*. There is, of course, no reason to assume that Pope Francis generally disregards the virtue of prudence. His neglect of prudence here seems to stem from the fact that the scientific data on climate change has increased so that global warming is no longer merely a possible risk to be weighed prudentially against other factors in deciding what action is appropriate. By 2015, the pope finds the science conclusive. In addition to his discussions of the degree of pollution, the depletion of essential resources (including water), and the loss of biodiversity, Pope Francis unambiguously states, "A very solid scientific consensus indicates that we are presently witnessing a disturbing warming of the climate system. . . . [A] number of scientific studies indicate that most global warming in recent decades is due to the great concentration of greenhouse gases (carbon dioxide, methane, nitrogen oxides and others) released mainly as a result of human activity" (LS 23).

The major contribution of *Laudato Sí* is not, of course, its reiteration of contemporary scientific findings (helpful as this may be in the current context of climate denial) but rather its development of doctrine regarding humanity's relationship to nature as well as nature's intrinsic value and destiny in God. Despite the scriptural and traditional grounds that Pope Francis cites for his rethinking of the meaning of nature, past Catholic social teaching has tended to be human-centered, defending care of the environment for the good of humanity now and in the future. Pope St. John Paul II, for example, acknowledges the Christian obligation to ethical interactions with the natural world, and he considered abuse of the environment to be part of a "profound moral crisis" devaluing both humanity and nature.[17] Nevertheless, John Paul II's approach to environment issues remains largely anthropocentric, focusing on care for nature because the environment is essential to human life and flourishing.[18]

---

17. John Paul II, Message for the World Day of Peace 5.
18. See the discussion of John Paul II's environmental statements in LS 5. It should be noted that Pope St. John Paul II's growing concern for the environment focuses on healthy human attitudes rather than on the intrinsic value of nature itself.

The USCCB's 2001 statement on climate change is similarly human-centered, emphasizing the proper treatment of nature for the common good of humanity and as an act of solidarity with the poor and with future generations, since these are the people who will suffer the most from the destruction of the environment. Taking care of the earth is thus presented primarily as a dimension of the moral responsibility to act for the good of other human beings, who depend on the earth's resources.[19]

Pope Francis, however, contends in *Laudato Sí* that to be human is to be fundamentally oriented to communion with nature as well as with God and with the rest of humanity. Returning to the stories of creation and of the fall of humanity in the beginning of Genesis, Francis notes that these three central relationships—with God, with all human beings, and with nature—are depicted as being so thoroughly intertwined as to be inseparable.[20] Hence, disruption or disharmony in any one of these three relationships affects the other two. This is evident in the biblical description of the threefold separation (from God, each other, and nature) that follows both Adam and Eve's disobedience and Cain's murder of his brother Abel. Pope Francis draws this important conclusion: those who abuse the natural world, acting as though nature has no value beyond its role in the economy, are likely to apply this same attitude to their fellow human beings, just as those who exploit people are more inclined to mistreat animals and nature (LS 82).

If Pope Francis is right that human beings are constituted in and through their relationships with nature as well as those with other people and with God, then it is a mistake to set a concern for nature and a concern for humanity against each other, as though this is a zero-sum game. Rather than choosing between the good of human beings and that of the environment, Pope Francis insists, we must recognize that humanity and the rest of creation are interconnected to such an extent that they flourish or decline together. In fact, he

---

19. In addition to USCCB, "Global Climate Change," see also United States Conference of Catholic Bishops, *Forming Consciences for Faithful Citizenship* (November 2007) 86, http://www.usccb.org/issues-and-action/faithful-citizenship/forming-consciences-for-faithful-citizenship-title.cfm.

20. For Pope Francis's treatment of communion, see especially LS 89–92.

believes that as humans we are so intimately bound up with the rest of the natural world that "we can feel the desertification of the soil almost as a physical ailment, and the extinction of a species as a painful disfigurement" (LS 89, quoting EG 215). Pope Francis would not be surprised to hear that experts are beginning to talk of a "nature deficit disorder" affecting children who spend too much time indoors, or that evidence suggests that people need to spend time in nature, surrounded by fresh air and healthy vegetation, for optimal physical and mental health. As Pope Francis observes, "we were not meant to be inundated by cement, asphalt, glass and metal, and deprived of physical contact with nature" (LS 44).

Developing further the implications of the interrelationality of a creation made in the image of the triune God, Pope Francis comes to a conclusion that some have found unsettling. He declares that all of creation, and not just humanity, has an eternal destiny in God. Furthermore, it is not only humans who are restored to God in the salvific event of Jesus Christ, the central mystery of the Christian faith. Instead, Pope Francis contends, nature is also assumed in the incarnation through which Jesus joined all of creation to God's self by becoming human, taking on the physical flesh composed of the elements of the cosmos (LS 99).[21] Pope Francis concludes that all of creation is willed by God, is given a specific place in God's plan, and is intended for the final communion of all in God. "The ultimate destiny of the universe is in the fullness of God," he proclaims (LS 83; see also 99–100).

It follows, then, that nature has intrinsic and not merely instrumental value. Where earlier documents assume that humans are "the only creature God wills for itself," Francis maintains that each aspect of creation is "willed in its own being" by God, so that no part of nature should be reduced to its value to human beings (LS 69).[22] Moreover, a consistent option for the poor requires that priority be given not only to the needs of impoverished and vulnerable

---

21. See also the development of this concept of incarnation in Denis Edwards, *Partaking of God: Trinity, Evolution, and Ecology* (Collegeville, MN: Liturgical Press, 2014).

22. See especially *Gaudium et Spes* 24 and *Redemptor Hominis* 13, for the earlier, more human-centered teaching.

human beings but also to the care of creation because "the earth herself, burdened and laid waste, is among the most abandoned and maltreated of our poor" (LS 2).

Pope Francis thus rejects the "tyrannical anthropocentrism" in which nature is seen as existing solely to serve human beings (LS 68). Such anthropocentrism is incompatible with the deeper Christian vision in which humanity has a vocation to care for creation, a care that involves much more than simply preserving the environment. The human race has a further responsibility to "lead all creatures back to their Creator," Francis insists (LS 83).[23] Indeed, God intends that all creatures, human and nonhuman, support each other as they move toward their common goal of communion in the divine. As Pope Francis declares, "creatures exist only in dependence on each other, to complete each other, in service of each other" (LS 86).

Pope Francis's understanding of environmental stewardship is, then, a bit more nuanced than the usual concept of stewardship critiqued by Elizabeth Johnson. Too often, as Johnson observes, stewardship is envisioned as a one-way relationship in which humans care for a natural world they are presumed to be distinct from. Johnson argues for a relationship of "kindom" rather than "stewardship" on the grounds that the word *kindom* better reflects the reality that humans are integrally a part of nature and depend on the world they are stewards of.[24] Although Pope Francis continues to use the term *stewardship*, his account of the interconnectedness of humans with the rest of creation emphasizes that humanity is sustained by the environment we are directed to care for.

Pope Francis further develops his description of interrelationality to include a sacramental encounter with God through all of creation. Drawing on the spirituality of St. Francis of Assisi, Pope Francis maintains that each and every created being reflects the glory of God in its own way and uniquely praises God through its being, as St. Francis was so keenly aware. Every part of nature also communicates a distinct message from God and is in fact a means of contact with the divine. As he asserts: "The entire material universe speaks of

---

23. See also LS 107, 118–122.
24. Elizabeth A. Johnson, *Women, Earth, and Creator Spirit* (Mahwah, NJ: Paulist Press, 1993), 30.

God's love, his boundless affection for us. Soil, water, mountains: everything is, as it were, a caress of God" (LS 84). God is not separate from the world, then, but is found in and experienced through creation; all of nature is a sacrament of the divine presence.

This leads Pope Francis to lament the loss of biodiversity through species extinction. "It is not enough," he declares, "to think of different species merely as potential 'resources' to be exploited, while overlooking the fact that they have value in themselves. . . . Because of us, thousands of species will no longer give glory to God by their very existence, nor convey their message to us. We have no such right" (LS 33, 69).

Given his account of the thoroughly intertwined network of relations between God, humanity, and nature, the only appropriate response to the challenges of our time is one that Pope Francis calls an "integral ecology" (LS 137–62, esp. 138). Although global warming may well be the most important issue today, climate change cannot be addressed apart from the rapaciousness of the economy, the disintegration of public institutions and political culture, and the lack of balance so many of us experience between the demands of work and other aspects of a good and fully human life. These are all manifestations of the same moral and cultural distortion that is causing the climate emergency by focusing on short-term economic gain above all else (LS 137–162, esp. 142). When the rest of nature is treated solely as a means for increasing profits, other human beings will be similarly reduced to instruments of economic gain, as will our own lives and even God, as the current popularity of the prosperity gospel confirms.

Pope Francis's emphasis on integral ecology thus interrupts conservative efforts to concentrate Catholic political activism on sexual matters while sidelining climate change, racism, economic inequality, and other Catholic social teachings as of minor importance.[25] Instead, integral ecology requires resistance to all threats to the web of relationality, including—but by no means limited to—the meaning of our bodies as part of the intrinsic value of all of creation (LS 155). Integral ecology also then opposes the individualistic, "me-n-Jesus"

---

25. See, for example, the discussion in USCCB, *Faithful Citizenship*, 34–37.

focus of much of American Christianity. Francis consistently maintains that the Christian tradition espouses a relational, community-centered concept of the person that is incompatible with any form of individualism.

This is all obviously relevant to the proper understanding of the church's mission. Recognizing that people are constituted in and through their relationships with nature as well as with God and others in society, Pope Francis explicitly includes nature in the final communion with God toward which humanity is oriented. The pope leaves no doubt that the church is called to be a sign and instrument of unity with nature as well as with the rest of humanity. As he reminds us, "Jesus lived in full harmony with creation, and others were amazed" (LS 98). The church as the Body of Christ in the world must strive to emulate the comprehensive redemption Jesus exemplified in this still-fallen world.

An anthropocentric interpretation of the church's task in history, concerned exclusively with uniting humanity with and within God, thus fails to be adequate either to the deepest meanings of the Christian tradition or to the challenges of the climate crisis of our day. The life of Christian discipleship requires what Pope Francis describes as an "ecological conversion," in which one's relationship with Jesus is manifest in care for a natural world that not only is necessary for human flourishing but also has intrinsic and sacramental value. As the pope declares, "living our vocation to be protectors of God's handiwork is essential to a life of virtue; it is not an optional or a secondary aspect of our Christian experience" (LS 217).

Power, Gender, and the Effects of Environmental Degradation

Ecological degradation and climate change impact all people, but they do not impact all equally. In the United States, toxic waste and pollution are found at higher levels in the neighborhoods of poor people and people of color, endangering their lives and health disproportionately in comparison to wealthy and white people.[26] It is scarcely

---

26. A 2018 report of scientists of the National Center for Environmental Assessment, a branch of the Environmental Protection Agency found that there are higher levels of particulate matter in neighborhoods of poorer people but also even

imaginable that the high levels of lead and other life-threatening pollutants in the drinking water of the predominantly poor and black city of Flint, Michigan, from 2014 to at least 2017 would have been officially ignored for so long in largely white and affluent communities, to mention just one recent and particularly egregious example. Moreover, as Pope Francis notes, unequal distribution of pollution exists on a global scale. Waste from economically powerful countries is exported to underdeveloped countries while at the same time multinational companies operating in these underdeveloped countries pollute in ways they do not in their home countries (LS 51).

In 1991, when Lawrence Summers was vice president of the World Bank, he set off a public uproar by signing a memo that set forth an economic justification for concentrating toxic pollutions in less-developed countries. Perhaps, as Summers later claimed, the argument that it is most cost-effective for pollution to shorten the life spans of lower (rather than higher) wage earners was intended to be satire.[27] Nevertheless, the reality remains that the global economy does indeed function as though the poor have less worth, and the dumping of waste and toxins where they will most affect the health of poor and nonwhite people is one example of this systemic devaluation of the lives of the majority of human beings. The anger over Summers's memo has unfortunately not been matched by a similar degree of public outcry at the actual practices that secure the comforts of the rich and powerful at the expense of others' lives and health. Alas, the principle that some lives are more valuable than others meets greater resistance when it is expressed than when it is enacted.

Moreover, different geographical areas and the various populations within those areas are affected by climate change in distinct ways. Although global warming is altering the entire planet, those with the least resources to adapt are likely to face the most extreme effects. As Pope Francis observes, "the warming caused by huge

---

more in areas where black people live. See Ihab Mikati et al., "Disparities in Distribution of Particulate Matter Emission Sources by Race and Poverty Status," in *American Journal of Public Health* 108, no. 4 (April 2018), 480–85, https://doi.org/10.2105/AJPH.2017.304297.

27. "Toxic Memo," *Harvard Magazine*, May 1, 2001, https://www.harvardmagazine.com/2001/05/toxic-memo.html.

consumption on the part of some rich countries has repercussions on the poorest areas of the world, especially Africa, where a rise in temperature, together with drought, has proved devastating for farming" (LS 51). He further notes that the poor, who are more often dependent on nature for their livelihood, have the least capacity to cope when climate change and the accompanying natural disasters wipe out their homes or their means of subsistence, increase disease, or threaten the supply of potable water. The number of environmental refugees is growing; like economic refugees, they suffer the consequences of global systems and others' decisions, yet lack the legal recognition officially accorded to political refugees (LS 25).

Notwithstanding Pope Francis's concern for the impact of environmental degradation on the poor, he does not explore the influence that gender, race, or minority culture has on one's experience of ecological hazards. The one exception is indigenous peoples, whose cultural and historical ties to the land Francis recognizes as grounds for prioritizing their perspectives in decisions about environmental policy (LS 146). Yet all of these factors—gender, race, and minority status, in addition to economic class—clearly influence how people are affected by ecological devastation. An adequate vision of environmental justice requires attention to all of these categories in their intersectionality. However, given the limitations of this book and its particular concern with ecclesial exclusions of women, our attention here will focus primarily on the significance of gender in relation to the environment.

That an unhealthy environment hurts women in specific ways is widely recognized. It is well established that environmental toxins are especially hazardous for pregnant and lactating women and their babies, for example. Another reality among the poor is that women are usually responsible for cooking and are therefore more exposed to the hazards of smoke inhalation due to insufficient ventilation. Interestingly, while Pope Francis notes the dangers to the poor of inhaling smoke from cooking and heating fuels, he does not mention that it is women who are most affected (LS 20).[28] Furthermore, as was discussed in chapter 3, women and girls sometimes receive less

---

28. For statistics on women and girls exposed to indoor pollutants, see UN Women, "Fact Sheet—Global," in *Turning Promises into Action: Gender Equality in the 2030 Agenda for Sustainable Development* (2018), https://www.unwomen

of poor family's limited resources for food and medicine, so they suffer graver harm when climate change contributes to the spread of disease or threatens the food supply.[29]

Drought and desertification due to climate change may also intensify the labor demands on women and girls. The task of supplying the family's daily water and cooking fuel tends to be assigned to females among the world's poorest populations, and the scarcity of these vital resources requires that they walk more and work longer each day to gather what is needed. In addition, traveling greater distances may increase the likelihood of sexual violence as women and girls venture farther from home, often alone.[30]

Another gendered effect of climate change is that women and girls are at significantly higher risk during extreme weather events. Studies indicate that women are considerably more likely than men to die in natural disasters, probably because more women than men choose to remain in their homes rather than to move to public shelters where they face the threat of sexual violence or simply the cultural impropriety of sleeping in proximity to men from outside their family.[31] An additional factor may be that girls and women are less likely to have been taught to swim or to be adept at other survival skills that men and boys are encouraged to learn.[32]

The economic impact of climate change can also affect poor women differently than it affects men. Loss of family income due

---

.org/-/media/headquarters/attachments/sections/library/publications/2018/sdg-report-fact-sheet-global-en.pdf.

29. Nicholas D. Kristof and Sheryl WuDunn, *Half the Sky: Turning Oppression into Opportunity for Women Worldwide* (New York: Alfred A. Knopf, 2009), xiv.

30. See Mayesha Alam, Rukmani Bhatia, and Briana Mawby, *Women and Climate Change: Impact and Agency in Human Rights, Security, and Economic Development* (Georgetown Institute for Women, Peace and Security, 2015), https://issuu.com/georgetownsfs/docs/women_and_climate_change.

31. Mary Halton, "Climate Change 'Impacts Women More than Men,'" *BBC News*, March 8, 2018, https://www.bbc.com/news/science-environment-43294221; see also "Fact Sheet—Global."

32. Taylor Evensen, "Typhoon Haiyan: Women in the Wake of Natural Disasters," *Penn Political Review*, March 18, 2014, https://pennpoliticalreview.org/2014/03/typhoon-haiyan-women-in-the-wake-of-natural-disasters/. See also "Gender and Health in Disasters," World Health Organization website, July 2002, https://www.who.int/gender/other_health/genderdisasters.pdf.

to the effects of climate change on farming, logging, or fishing may force more women into the wage labor market to supplement the family income, even while they continue their responsibilities in the home. If there is not enough work to sustain the family and it becomes necessary to seek work elsewhere, men may migrate while women remain behind due to their obligations to care for family members. In those cases where women are able to migrate, they face the added dangers of sexual violence and the greater chance of being trafficked.[33]

The point here is that the differential effect of climate change on women should be taken into account in the prioritizing of abatement strategies and other policies responding to climate disasters. Pope Francis rightly protests that the poor are an afterthought and that their specific needs are overlooked because experts in climate policy are generally from the privileged classes. However, he fails to notice that women too are underrepresented among those involved in climate and environmental decision-making, so their concerns are also frequently ignored. Androcentric policy debates, like an androcentric church, neglect the experiences of women, who are often the poorest of the poor.

Another lacuna in *Laudato Sí* is that even while Pope Francis calls attention to the interrelationship between the abuse of the poor and the abuse of the environment, he does not explore the well-established connection between the devaluation of nature and the devaluation of women. At least since Sherry Ortner's classic 1974 article "Is Female to Male as Nature Is to Culture?" identified the parallels between the denigration of nature and of women, feminist thinkers have analyzed this connection, giving rise to ecofeminist thought and practice.[34] Pope Francis's neglect of the relationship

---

33. Alam et al., *Women and Climate Change*.

34. Sherry B. Ortner, "Is Female to Male as Nature Is to Culture?," in *Women, Culture, and Society*, ed. Michelle Zimbalist Rosaldo and Louise Lamphere, (Stanford, CA: Stanford University Press, 1974), 68–87. See also Rosemary Radford Ruether, *New Woman, New Earth: Sexist Ideologies and Human Liberation* (New York: Seabury Press, 1975); Yvonne Gebarra, *Longing for Running Water: Ecofeminism and Liberation* (Minneapolis: Augsburg Fortress, 1999); and Johnson, *Women, Earth, Creator Spirit*.

between the oppression of women and that of nature undermines his integral approach to ecology, which intends to address all of the interrelated distortions that lead to the abuse of the human and nonhuman natural world.

As discussed in chapter 3, feminist theorists argue that the structure of Western thought involves hierarchical binaries that assign phenomena to opposite categories such that man is opposed to woman, culture to nature, reason to emotion, "white" people to people of color, and finally God to the world. Not only are these categories simplistic and rigid in their division of complex reality into binary options, but the binaries also function so that the first term in each pair listed here is more highly valued than the second term. Moreover, the supposedly superior categories of male, culture, reason, white, and God are mutually associated, as are the putatively inferior ones of women, nature, emotion, people of color, and the world. These binaries suggest that ("white") men more appropriately represent God, are rational creators of culture, and naturally rule over women, nature, and the rest of the world.[35] As Ellen Armour has argued, the modern Man is constructed in opposition to his raced, sexed, and animal other.[36] It should not be surprising, then, that just as women's unpaid and underpaid care work subsidizes the global economy, so also do the unpaid and underpaid costs of the depletion of natural resources and destruction of the environment subsidize the global economy.

Ecofeminism understands that women cannot be liberated without the dismantling of the entire system of interwoven oppressions that devalue women, people of color, and nature. In the Catholic Church, it is women religious who have most clearly perceived this connection and embraced the challenge of responding to climate change as an essential Christian ministry and an option for the poor. Well before Pope Francis's encyclical or even the regional bishops' documents on climate change, Catholic sisters had developed active green ministries seeking to reduce greenhouse gases, remove carbon

---

35. See Johnson, *Women, Earth, Creator Spirit*, 10–22.
36. Ellen T. Armour, *Signs and Wonders: Theology after Modernity* (New York: Columbia University, 2016).

from the atmosphere, and foster a spirituality of care and mutuality in relation to nature.[37]

Given the ecclesial mission to be a sign and instrument of the communion of all creation in God, the entire church should join these religious women not only in their ecological practices but also in resisting—and replacing—the hierarchical binaries that reinforce inequality and oppression. Instead, as Elizabeth Johnson has observed, even in the church, our three fundamental relationships—to God, to others, and to nature—have been constructed according to patriarchal binaries contrary to the harmonious reciprocity willed by God.[38] Certainly in the practices of the Catholic Church, God is predominantly construed as male and as represented by a male-only priesthood; the dominance of "white" males continues to be taken for granted within and beyond the Euro-American church; and the nonhuman natural world is still often treated as inert material of no value other than for human purposes, despite Pope Francis's efforts to overcome this attitude toward nature. As evidenced by the failure of Pope Francis's integral ecology to address the recognized connections between environmental degradation and the devaluation of women, ecclesial thought and practice remain patriarchal.

There are, of course, traditions in Christianity that resist the hierarchical binaries that devalue women, people of color, and nature. Pope Francis highlights the rich sacramental tradition celebrating the presence of God in nature rather than opposing God to nature (LS 235). The church also has a long history of honoring those who opt for the vulnerable and the oppressed, of maintaining women's baptismal equality (at least in principle), and of allowing women options for agency that frequently surpassed what was otherwise available to them in society. These key strands of the Christian tradition are valuable resources for critiquing and correcting the patriarchal distortions that support the rule of powerful males over women and nature.

---

37. Angela Evancie, "Nuns with a New Creed: Environmentalism," *The Atlantic*, October 16, 2013, https://www.theatlantic.com/national/archive/2013/10/nuns-with-a-new-creed-environmentalism/280608/.

38. Johnson, *Women, Earth, Creator Spirit*, 3, 17–22.

It must be noted that identification of gender as a significant difference is not in itself problematic. After all, there is no real unity without diversity. Nevertheless, the insistence on strict division into an essentialist gender binary denies the very real plurality of biological and cultural differences in gender and sexuality. In fact, the supposed distinction underlying most binaries is an illusion masking the sameness inherent in defining the other in terms of its opposition to the dominant category.

Moreover, the hierarchical character of these binaries impedes the equality in mutuality that the Catholic Church and most other churches officially affirm as integral to true unity-in-diversity. Binary thinking that sets some humans over others and all humanity over nature is the antithesis of the sacramental and harmonious communion the church exists to promote. An integral ecology that seeks to overcome the human/nature dichotomy along with colonial, racist, and class hierarchies cannot succeed while leaving in place the fundamental gender binary that divides the world into important, governing males and insignificant, governed females.

Recent Developments in Climate Studies

The climate situation has not improved in the few years since Pope Francis published *Laudato Sí*. The levels of carbon dioxide in the atmosphere have continued to rise from around 400 parts per million in 2015 to 415 parts per million in 2019. Glaciers are melting, animal and plant ranges have shifted, hurricanes have become more deadly, and new record high temperatures continue to be set.[39]

The October 2018 IPCC report *Global Warming of 1.5°C* received a great deal of media attention for warning that humanity must lower its carbon output 45 percent by 2030 and reduce the carbon output to zero by 2050 in order to prevent earth's average temperature from rising more than 1.5 degrees Celsius above the preindustrial average. According to this report, if carbon emissions are lowered only 20 percent by 2030 (which would still require

---

39. See especially "Another Climate Milestone," Scripps Institution; and "Climate Change," NASA.

significant societal change!) and are not zeroed out until 2075, the temperature will likely rise by 2 degrees Celsius.⁴⁰

This 0.5 degree Celsius difference may not seem like much, especially since the planet's average temperature is already 1 degree Celsius over the average before industrialization increased the burning of fossil fuels. Yet the IPCC's 2018 report, reviewing the extant scientific literature involving some 6,000 scientific studies, concludes that the difference is dramatic. If the temperature rises to 2 degrees rather than 1.5 degrees Celsius above the preindustrial average, a 50 percent increase in people experiencing water scarcity is likely, and hundreds of millions more people will be at risk of poverty due to climate change. The impact on nonhuman species is even greater: for example, 99 percent of the coral will be gone, and insects necessary for pollination are twice as likely to lose their habitats than if the temperature rises only another 0.5 degrees Celsius.⁴¹

Of course, even if humanity begins to act now, there will still be drought and famine and extreme weather events, as these have already begun and will continue as the world warms. The increase to 1.5 degrees Celsius is probably inevitable due to the greenhouse gases already in the atmosphere and the time needed to make the substantial transformations required to reduce emissions significantly.⁴² In addition to the "unprecedented transitions in all aspects of society, including energy, land and ecosystems, urban and infrastructure as well as industry," there will also have to be ongoing efforts to enable society to adapt to the climate changes already underway.⁴³ Yet the more we delay decreasing greenhouse gas emissions, the less effective our adaptations will be.

---

40. IPCC, *Global Warming of 1.5°C*. See also Jonathan Watts, "We Have 12 Years to Limit Climate Change Catastrophe, Warns UN," *The Guardian*, October 8, 2018, https://www.theguardian.com/environment/2018/oct/08/global-warming-must-not-exceed-15c-warns-landmark-un-report.

41. IPCC, *Global Warming of 1.5°C*; and Watts, "We Have 12 Years."

42. IPCC, "Executive Summary," in *Global Warming of 1.5°C*.

43. Debra Roberts, co-chair of IPCC Working Group II, as quoted in Intergovernmental Panel on Climate Change, "Choices Made Now Are Critical for the Future of Our Ocean and Cryosphere," press release, September 25, 2019, https://www.ipcc.ch/2019/09/25/srocc-press-release/.

The IPCC has recently released reports reviewing extant scientific studies of climate change's effects on food and agriculture (August 2019) and on the oceans and cryosphere (September 2019).[44] While climate change does increase agricultural productivity in some areas, scientific studies have determined that, overall, climate change decreases food supplies, especially due to land lost through erosion, desertification, extreme weather events, and rising seas. The August 2019 report concludes that climate change is threatening humanity's ability to feed itself, placing us at risk of "multi-breadbasket failure," according to Cynthia Rosenzweig, senior researcher at the NASA Goddard Institute for Space Studies and one of the report's lead authors.[45] The September 2019 report adds further evidence of damage already underway, as fish populations have decreased and marine ecosystems are being disrupted by climate change. Oceans, which have been absorbing 90 percent of the earth's excess heat, are "hotter, more acidic, less oxygen rich," with increasing marine "heat waves" that kill fish, coral reefs, and plants while spreading pathogens that harm sea life as well as humans.[46]

Obviously, the time to act is now, since it is already too late to have acted earlier. The science is clear: ecosystems are being damaged, and the effects are significant for all forms of life on this planet, including human beings. While all people will be affected to some extent, it is, unfortunately, the poor whose lives and health are most at risk.[47] Millions of the world's most vulnerable people

---

44. Intergovernmental Panel on Climate Change, *Climate Change and Land*, August 2019, https://www.ipcc.ch/report/srccl/; Intergovernmental Panel on Climate Change, *Special Report on the Ocean and Cryosphere in a Changing Climate*, September 2019, https://www.ipcc.ch/srocc/home/.

45. Christopher Flavelle, "Climate Change Threatens the World's Food Supply, United Nations Warns," *New York Times*, August 8, 2019, https://www.nytimes.com/2019/08/08/climate/climate-change-food-supply.html.

46. In addition to IPCC, *Special Report on Ocean and Cryosphere*, see also Brad Plumer, "The World's Oceans Are in Danger, Major Climate Change Report Warns," *New York Times*, September 25, 2019, https://www.nytimes.com/2019/09/25/climate/climate-change-oceans-united-nations.html; and IPCC, "Choices Made Now."

47. Flavelle, "Climate Change Threatens." See also IPCC, "Executive Summary," in *Global Warming of 1.5°C*.

will suffer food scarcity and greater impoverishment if the world fails to decrease greenhouse gas emissions substantially. Increased famine, disease, natural disasters, mass migrations, and war are among the likely results of failure to mitigate and adapt to climate change. These results would be failures of harmony that strike at the heart of the communion the church is called to serve.

While it is still possible to avert at least the worst effects of global warming, significant reductions in greenhouse gases and actions to sequester some of the carbon already in the atmosphere are imperative. Radical transitions are needed in transportation and energy infrastructures, in production, in dietary habits, and in consumption patterns, as outlined in the IPCC 2018 and 2019 reports. The necessary change in infrastructures will happen only if there is broad support for governmental policies informed by the best scientific evidence. But people, especially those of us who are among the overconsuming populations that most contribute to greenhouse gas emissions, will also have to alter their daily habits of consumption. This requires shifts in diet to include much less beef and dairy than most people in the United States currently eat, rapid changes away from fossil fuels to renewable energy sources, and efforts to consume less and more sustainably in all aspects of life.[48] "Reduce, reuse, recycle, and bicycle" remains good advice for individuals, but the degree of change the world needs requires the coordination of governments at local, national, and international levels.

Among the many obstacles to action on climate change, the power of mass marketing, of the distractions of social media, and of the entertainment approach to politics should not be underestimated. Mass marketing continually bombards people with messages to increase unnecessary consumption, while social media shortens attention spans and leaves little time for the serious public discussions our situation demands. It is easier to make political decisions based on feelings about images or the desire for diversion than to make them based on careful consideration of the issues at stake, especially as people become accustomed to the dominance of entertainment in their lives. Much work must be done to revitalize responsible

---

48. J. Poore and T. Nemecek, "Reducing Food's Environmental Impacts through Producers and Consumers," *Science* 360, no. 6392 (June 1, 2018): 987–92.

citizenship, especially through the hard work of reconstructing serious and nuanced public conversations about issues rather than through appeal to image as the basis of political affiliation.

Can the church make a difference here? Christianity (like other religions) has a long history of training people to resist shallow temptations in order to live more truly satisfying lives. Today, a church faithful to this tradition would emphasize forming Christians to live less distracted and more thoughtful lives and to look for meaning in deep relationships with others, with God, and with nature rather than in the consumption of ephemeral products and images. Such a church might also discover, as a community, new ways to live the serious, but also joyful, responsibility of care for our communities, our public life, and our world.

Being Church in a Climate Crisis

A Prophetic Witness to Harmony with Nature

Pope Francis's retrieval of nature as part of the goal of full communion puts concern for the environment at the heart of the mission of the church. Of course, the good of humanity is ample reason to protect the climate and the delicate balance of the earth's ecosystems. Loving one's neighbor as another self is clearly incompatible with so abusing natural resources that the lives of others and of future generations are diminished. Already the effects of climate change are manifest in wars over scarce resources, increases in disease, and climate refugees who have lost homes and livelihood due to sea level rise, extreme drought, and more frequent and powerful hurricanes. The poor and vulnerable are paying the cost of global capitalism's disregard for long-term sustainability, and the 2018 IPCC report makes it clear that continuing to burn fossil fuels at current rates for even a few more decades will jeopardize the lives of millions more people.

Nevertheless, care of the environment becomes even more pressing when nature is recognized as having intrinsic value, as mattering in itself and not merely for sustaining humans. Instead of waiting to be sure that the abuse of the natural world will impact humans negatively, Christians should act immediately, out of loving concern for the well-being of God's creation, to minimize the suffering of animals and to preserve the biodiversity that witnesses to the glory of God. Harmony with nature is an integral aspect of the communion of all creation that God intends and that the church is called to serve.

There is much that Christians can do, individually and as church, to witness to caring for nature and especially to decreasing the greenhouse gas emissions that are causing the climate crisis. Climate scientists indicate that the most important ways to shrink one's "carbon footprint" are through changes in transportation and diet. Solar-powered, all-electric cars are great ways to lower the use of fossil fuels, but so are less costly options like bicycles, walking, avoiding unnecessary travel, and using public transportation. Eating much less meat and dairy would not only decrease carbon emissions but would allow for more humane farming methods and better human health. These and other steps toward a more sustainable lifestyle should be an integral part of Christian discipleship today, modeled and encouraged by church communities. A mindful gratitude in all consumption, including attention to "reduce, reuse, and recycle," is a nonnegotiable element of the Christian witness to harmony in the current global economy.

To be sure, there is nothing particularly countercultural in espousing environmentalism or even in making some "green" gestures toward reducing one's personal or institutional carbon footprint. People around the world are aware of the severity of the climate crisis, and many are taking steps to be less wasteful. Nevertheless, the kind of large-scale transformation that would dramatically reduce carbon emissions is not happening; instead, levels of carbon dioxide in the atmosphere continue to rise. A revolutionary change is needed in the consumption patterns of daily life among the privileged, along with governmental action to restructure transportation and economic systems. If Christians began to approximate a sustainable lifestyle in their personal lives and in their institutions, that would indeed be countercultural—and that is why it is so seldom done. The amount of change, including restructuring current habits and social expectations, requires a degree of motivation that is far from common.

This is where religious faith and institutions could make a real difference. The world knows what has to be done, but there is not yet sufficient commitment to undertake the radical transformation needed, especially when people fear that others will not sacrifice equally. Religion has been a powerful force in human history, changing lives and even cultures. Religious views insisting that a sustainable lifestyle is essential to living a truly human life in the twenty-first century might make all the difference, empowering people to make significant changes in their own lives while also working to transform society.

A Christian people committed to harmony with all of creation as integral to their own greatest good certainly ought to have sufficient motivation to live a more sustainable, less consumerist lifestyle. As Pope Francis observes, hearts open to communion are open to all (LS 92). This includes opening one's heart to the natural world, to the poor who suffer from climate change, and to the future generations who will be deprived of the natural beauty and resources today's excessive consumption is destroying.

As Pope Francis further contends, it is only through cultivating a contemplative attention to the intrinsic goodness, beauty, and unity of creation that we will be able to sustain the witness of a truly prophetic life focused on appreciative enjoyment rather than ever more consumption (LS 222, 215–16). We cannot simply argue ourselves into this necessary change of attitude, particularly in the context of what Pope Francis aptly calls a "throw away culture" (EG 53). Instead, a harmonious way of life flows from a contemplative spirituality that restores inner peace, issuing in "a balanced lifestyle together with a capacity for wonder which takes us to a deeper understanding of life" (LS 225). As Pope Francis sees it, the Christian countercultural call to cooperate with God's grace in healing and reconciling the world is based on a deep sense of gratitude to God for all the blessings of life as well as an acute awareness that our lives are so fully interconnected that the flourishing of each one of us is tied to the well-being of all others and of the natural world.

A prophetic and thoroughly countercultural witness of sustainable living is not, then, a matter of dour self-denial, which in any case is not a very compelling witness. The joyful harmony envisioned in the Hebrew Bible and celebrated in the Jewish tradition is evident in the Good News of Jesus and the joy of the great saints, like St. Francis of Assisi. Throughout the history of Christianity, people have been inspired to live more simply in order to live more deeply, making room for loving communion with God and others by abstaining from the distractions of inordinate consumption.

This emphasis on joy does not neglect the seriousness of sin. Along with the other monotheistic religions, Christianity has a long tradition of developing practices that strengthen resistance to the immediate pleasures that conflict with what is truly good for oneself and for society. Certainly much spiritual discipline is needed today to overcome the powerful (but finally empty and depressing) temptations of modern marketing and the distracting addictions of social media. If the church seems irrelevant to so many people of good will, it may be because the church has obscured rather than clarified how much we need salvation from the compulsions of our narrow, self-centered, and overly consuming lifestyles.

The contemplative spirituality that Pope Francis advocates also sustains the integral ecology necessary to heal the interwoven distortions of modern life. As discussed in the previous chapter, Pope Francis astutely critiques the idolatry of the market that is trapping people in a competitive struggle to maximize short-term economic profits. Putting profit above all else is destructive of the environment, of the poor, and of the health of society, including its political institutions.

As Pope Francis maintains, attitudes toward other people and attitudes toward nature are interconnected. It follows, then, that a Christian witness of integral ecology must include an ecofeminist stance that rejects the hierarchical binary structures that place women, people of color, and nature at the disposal of white male power. A contemplative spirituality oriented to harmony with all cannot exclude women, nor can it consider of secondary importance the equality of women, or of any people.

A Public Church: Agent of Global Harmony

As important as the witness of joyful communion with nature, humanity, and God is, changing Christians' consumption patterns will not alone solve the climate crisis the world is experiencing, not even if all Christians in the world personally embrace sustainable living. Substantial changes in the economy, and especially in energy and transportation systems, are needed, and soon. There is much that local and national governments must do, yet this is ultimately a global project—people everywhere must cooperate in dramatically reducing carbon emissions over the coming decades.

Of course, the change of hearts and the changing of structures are inseparable. Sufficient change in public policies is unlikely if people are unwilling to change their own use and abuse of natural resources. At the same time, governmental resources are essential for the infrastructural changes needed to provide sustainable energy and less-carbon-intensive transportation options so that people can live and work without continuing to inflict irreparable damage on the earth and its ecosystems. And without international cooperation, the good some countries do can easily be undone by other countries' burning even more fossil fuels. Significant and binding international agreements are thus indispensable to the effective reduction of global greenhouse gas emissions. With global warming already underway and the levels of carbon dioxide in the atmosphere increasing, the world cannot wait for an ecclesial witness to slowly change hearts and minds. A church that cares about communion with nature, with the poor, and with future generations must be not only a witness to communion but also a very active agent in the construction of local, national, and international policies to reduce carbon emissions and mitigate climate change.

There will, of course, be differences among Christians about which policies are likely to be most effective and just in decreasing levels of greenhouse gases. Christians may well favor diverse policies and strategies, though the seriousness of the issue ought to keep such disagreements in perspective. In this climate emergency, we need carefully designed and thoughtful political action, but we cannot wait for a perfect option. Reasonable, though not paralyzing, disagreement is an important step toward effective climate action, but Christians—along with others of good will—must prioritize taking steps (even imperfect ones) to preserve the ecosystems that sustain all life on earth.

Since political change is necessary at local, national, and international levels, church communities and their leaders are especially well positioned to be effective advocates for climate action and care for the environment. Committed ecclesial voices in support of political efforts to curb greenhouse gas emissions can be quite effective, whether at the local level, where church members may be personally known, or at the national and international levels, where networks of larger churches have been able to lobby effectively. Church lobbying is consistent with the separation of religious and political authorities in the United States insofar as church leaders advocate for action to abate climate change without specifying the particular legislation. The Catholic Church has shown itself quite capable of affecting national and international policies on issues involving human reproduction; it could do at least as much for the reproductive health of the planet if it were similarly committed to lobbying on that issue. Of course, the laity need not wait for their leaders to act or leave all efforts to them; it is proper to the lay vocation to work with others in and beyond the church to achieve the needed transformation in energy, transportation, and other economic policies.

This kind of extensive sociopolitical change requires not only coordinated action but also, of course, extensive dialogue. This includes dialogue with other religions about their resources for overcoming anthropocentrism. Eastern religions have deep insights into the unity of all that is; indigenous peoples have traditions emphasizing their relations to land and nature. The Jewish tradition's honoring of the ongoing relevance of the Torah has led to further rabbinic reflection on obligations to care for nature and to avoid needless harm to God's creation.

The church will also want to ensure that women and the poor, who are often most affected by climate change, are included in the conversation. Women have much at stake and much wisdom to share about how to adapt to the climate change that is already happening so as to mitigate suffering and strengthen threatened communities.

Ecclesial witness and agency also come together in discussion of the scientific consensus on the climate crisis. This is an important place to demonstrate the Catholic Church's very long tradition of embracing the mutual coherence of faith and reason. Within and beyond the church, Christians working to curb climate change should strive to base their arguments on an honest look at current data. Too many people today feel free to reject unpleasant truths and instead assert their own "facts." This is lethal to healthy political discourse and disastrous for public life; democracy and political accountability cannot survive without acknowledgment of a shared reality. Within and beyond the church, Christians who are honest and reasonable in striving for the truth could do much to revive public discourse based on a common reality.

There is deep wisdom in Pope Francis's inclusion in his discussion of integral ecology of an emphasis on habits of mutual respect and relationship, without which there can be no genuine dialogue and no public discourse (LS 181). If we can learn to recognize and nurture our interrelatedness, acknowledging that each of us is a part of all others, then we might yet be able to heal not only our distorted and abusive relationship to nature but also the divisions, antipathy, and distortions of our public life.

Conclusion

In January 2011, I had the privilege of joining with other University of San Diego faculty on a "faculty immersion" trip to the Dominican Republic. We were welcomed by a local faith community willing to share with us its efforts to combat both their extreme poverty and the threatening environmental degradation through sustainable farming practices. The community was deeply aware that care for the environment, not its abuse, was key to their economic progress, and they were particularly committed to preventing deforestation in order to preserve the balance of rainfall the land's fertility depended on. Their project also showcased the centrality of local wisdom, especially that of women, in developing practices appropriate to their needs and rooted in a commitment to prayerful community at many levels. While initiatives were based in the small community and often women-led, resources of support came from the bishop as well as from a Catholic parish in New York City. The farming collective sought to work respectfully with nature, to prevent and reverse deforestation, to provide nutritional supplements for infants and children, and to produce organic vegetables for the international market. It might well be described as an example of integral ecology in action.

Pope Francis has since made it clear that the church's mission to be a sign and instrument of unity includes communion with nature as well as with other humans and with God. The call to communion embraces all of creation. If the church now fails to act decisively to counter the unsustainable consumption that is destroying so many species and ecosystems, that would be more than irresponsible. For Christians, it would be a failure in their mission.

The seriousness of the climate challenges we face is unprecedented. Never before has humanity had the capacity to have such an impact on the conditions of the planet that sustains us. In the face of this crisis, the church must be prophetic, embodying a thoroughly countercultural (but traditionally Christian) lifestyle of simplicity and of grateful use of natural resources. At the same time, the church must also be thoroughly public in working for structural transformation on local, national, and international levels. But as with the injustices of the global economy, the issue of climate change cannot be solved through an alternative witness alone. Humanity will have to act together and quickly for the good of all the planet, a concern at the heart of the church's mission.

Chapter 6

A Prophetic, Public Church amid Global Migration

> These least ones are abandoned and cheated into dying in the desert; these least ones are tortured, abused and violated in detention camps; these least ones face the waves of an unforgiving sea; these least ones are left in reception camps too long for them to be called temporary.
>
> Pope Francis, Homily on July 8, 2019,
> the sixth anniversary of his visit to Lampedusa, Italy[1]

The story of humanity is in many respects a story of migration. The movement of human populations as they dissolved established communities and formed new ones elsewhere is recorded in our DNA as well as in human religions, languages, and cultures. The vast majority of people, of course, live in their home countries. Even with today's global economy, communication systems, and relative ease of transportation, only about 3 percent of the world's population lives outside their country of birth. Yet at least three times that many have migrated within national boundaries, so that approximately

---

1. Francis, papal mass on July 8, 2019, as cited by Elise Harris, "On Lampedusa Anniversary, Pope Prays for Suffering Migrants," *Crux*, July 8, 2019, https://cruxnow.com/vatican/2019/07/08/on-lampedusa-anniversary-pope-prays-for-suffering-migrants/.

1 in 7 people on the planet are living away from the area and community in which they were raised.[2] Humanity, it seems, is fairly adept at maintaining flexible societies, able to sustain significant changes in membership while preserving continuity.

This human adaptability is an important resource, since, as the UNHCR 2018 *Global Trends* report determined, global levels of displacement of persons are at the highest levels recorded.[3] Recent statistics indicate that approximately 70.8 million people are forcibly displaced due to conflict or persecution: 41.3 million of these are internally displaced, while 29.4 million are international refugees or asylum seekers. The scope of the humanitarian crisis comes into clearer focus when one considers that another 37,000 people are forcibly displaced each day, and some refugees have remained for 25 years in what were intended as temporary camps.[4]

Even more concerning is that this number of "forced migrants" comprises only those fleeing war, violence, or persecution. Not included in these numbers are the many more who migrate due to extreme poverty or to seek refuge from natural disasters, though surely having to move from one's home to obtain the essentials of food and shelter is a form of forced rather than voluntary migration.[5] The predominant reason for migration is the desire (or critical need) for a higher wage, but the situation of those who move to

---

2. World Health Organization, "Refugee and Migrant Health," https://www.who.int/migrants/en/. See also World Bank Group, "Policy Research Project Overview," *Moving for Prosperity: Global Migration and Labor Markets* (Washington, DC: World Bank Group, 2018), 4–6, https://openknowledge.worldbank.org/bitstream/handle/10986/29806/211281ov.pdf.

3. United Nations High Commissioner for Refugees, *Global Trends: Forced Displacement in 2018*, June 20, 2019, 4, https://www.unhcr.org/5d08d7ee7.pdf.

4. UNHCR, *Global Trends*, 2–3; Elizabeth W. Collier and Charles R. Strain, *Global Migration: What's Happening, Why, and a Just Response* (Winona, MN: Anselm Academic, 2017), 23.

5. Often, of course, growing impoverishment or increasing ecological threats to livelihood are gradual so that there is no single moment when the situation transitions from a choice to a forced decision. See especially the nuanced discussion in Dina Ionesco, "Let's Talk about Climate Migrants, Not Climate Refugees," June 6, 2019, United Nations Sustainable Development Goals website, https://www.un.org/sustainabledevelopment/blog/2019/06/lets-talk-about-climate-migrants-not-climate-refugees/.

advance already successful careers is not comparable to that of those who migrate in desperate hope of a wage sufficient to sustain their lives. For the poor, whose only asset may be their capacity to work, migration to secure a good job can be a matter of life or death.[6] Furthermore, according to the International Organization for Migration's *World Migration Report 2018*, "each year, new displacements associated with rapid-onset hazards far outnumber those due to conflict and violence."[7] With weather severity increased by climate and other environmental changes, natural disasters have forced an additional 22.5 million people to migrate during each of the past several years.[8]

The global economy and the related environmental crisis of global warming thus have a great deal to do with current migration pressures. Some migrants are clearly climate refugees, forced to move because their homes have been submerged due to sea level rise.[9] Others are escaping famine and poverty, which may be exacerbated by climate-related factors such as drought and desertification; when their crops fail or a fish population is exhausted, farmers and fishermen must often move in search of food or work.[10] Still others are fleeing violence and political upheaval, though economic and climate shifts may well have contributed to the civil unrest. The greatest number of refugees in 2018 came from Syria,[11] with people seeking refuge from the violence of a brutal civil war that many contend was partly caused by governmental failure to manage water scarcity due to climate change. This forced many young farmers into crowded

---

6. For discussion of wage migration, see especially World Bank Group, *Moving for Prosperity*, esp. 1–37.

7. International Organization for Migration, "Migration and Migrants: A Global Overview," chap. 2 of *World Migration Report 2018* (Geneva: IOM, 2018), 29, https://publications.iom.int/system/files/pdf/wmr_2018_en_chapter2.pdf.

8. Collier and Strain, *Global Migration*, 9. It should be noted that these statistics apply specifically to the eight years preceding 2017, when the book was published.

9. See especially Collier and Strain, *Global Migration*, 28–35; and Emily Buder, Lisa Hornak, and Erin Stone, "The Next Wave of Climate Refugees, *The Atlantic*, June 17, 2019, https://www.theatlantic.com/video/index/591832/climate-refugees/.

10. See Collier and Strain, *Global Migration*, 28–35.

11. For statistics on the countries from which most refugees come, see UNHCR, *Global Trends*, 3.

cities where they were unable to find jobs, thus increasing economic and political instability.[12] Another major source of refugees is South Sudan, which has experienced severe droughts and floods in recent years and is described as one of the East African nations most affected by climate change.[13] The cycle of violence is hard to break, since political conflict further impedes the sustainable management of resources, and this leads to even more tension and conflict.

In the United States, there has been much recent attention to the caravans of immigrants coming from Central America. Many of these people are requesting asylum from persecution and violence due to governmental corruption and drug gangs seeking to compel children to aid in their illicit activity. Others of these migrants are predominantly economic refugees desperately seeking work to support their families. Yet here too climate change may be a factor, as the wave of increased migration from Central America coincides with severe and unusual droughts that may be caused by global warming.[14]

As these cases suggest, violence, poverty, and climate change can be so interconnected that it is impossible at times to distinguish political refugees from economic and climate refugees.[15] Moreover, even

---

12. See especially Peter H. Gleick, "Water, Drought, Climate Change, and Conflict in Syria," *Weather, Climate and Society* 6, no. 3 (July 2014), 331–40, https://doi.org/10.1175/WCAS-D-13-00059.1.

13. See especially UN Environment, "South Sudan: First State of Environment and Outlook Report 2018," (Nairobi: United Nations Environment Programme, 2018), https://wedocs.unep.org/bitstream/handle/20.500.11822/25528/SouthSudan_SoE2018.pdf. See also UN Environment, "Resource Competition and Climate Change Hampering South Sudan Peace and Development," press release, June 7, 2018, https://www.unenvironment.org/news-and-stories/press-release/resource-competition-and-climate-change-hampering-south-sudan-peace.

14. Rebecca Gordon, "How the U.S. Created the Central American Immigration Crisis, *Common Dreams*, August 15, 2019, https://www.commondreams.org/views/2019/08/15/how-us-created-central-american-immigration-crisis#. See also Christopher Flavelle, "Climate Change Threatens the World's Food Supply, United Nations Warns," *New York Times*, August 8, 2019, https://www.nytimes.com/2019/08/08/climate/climate-change-food-supply.html.

15. This point is explored further in John Wihbey, "Nuancing 'Climate Refugee' Language and Images," Yale Climate Connections, December 14, 2015, https://www.yaleclimateconnections.org/2015/12/nuancing-climate-refugee-narratives-and-images/.

in the absence of war or violent persecution, people fleeing extreme poverty or natural disasters are surely more appropriately described as forced refugees than as voluntary migrants. As Pope Francis reminds us, these are among the most vulnerable people on earth, whether they are escaping war, poverty, or climate disasters.[16] They have few possessions; they have left their communities and often many or even all of their family members; and they are in grave need of secure homes and adequate employment. Forced migrants are especially at risk as they travel through treacherous terrain and are subject to the whims of smugglers who may demand additional money en route, force them into dangerous and inhumane transportation conditions, or traffic them into slave labor.[17]

The suffering of these migrants is one of the most devastating aspects of the global economy. Globalization enables some of the world to enjoy a consumer abundance that previous generations could scarcely have imagined; this same globalization is also causing the economic inequality and climate change that are increasing pressures on the most vulnerable populations on the planet. Yet when people are forced to migrate in search of jobs or secure living conditions, they do so with much less protection than is accorded the movement of capital and of jobs in and out of countries.

In fact, the reality of migration for many is an experience of violence and the threat of violence throughout. Forced from their homes, often by brutal political or natural forces, migrants are at risk of attack during their travels, may be assaulted in shelters, and frequently meet with hostility in the countries they travel to. A virulent nationalist populism is on the rise in the United States and Europe, with political groups protesting against immigrants and sometimes physically attacking them. Migrants continue to drown crossing the Mediterranean Sea in their desperation to escape the

---

16. Francis, papal mass, July 8 2019.
17. See especially Daniel G. Groody, *Border of Death, Valley of Life: An Immigrant Journey of Heart and Spirit* (Lanham, MD: Rowman and Littlefield, 2007). See also United Nations Office on Drugs and Crime, "Statement by the United Nations Network on Migration," press release, July 30, 2019, https://www.unodc.org/unodc/en/press/releases/2019/Juli/statement-by-the-united-nations-network-on-migration_30-july-2019.html.

life-threatening violence and poverty in their homelands of Syria, Sudan, and Nigeria (among other places). Despite the heartbreaking image of three-year-old Alan Kurdi, a Syrian refugee who drowned with other family members and refugees attempting to cross the Mediterranean Sea in 2015, ships that rescue drowning migrants have been criminalized for entering Italian territorial waters and refused safe docking in Italy.[18] In the United States, immigrant children are taken from their parents and held in brutal conditions that are expressly intended to discourage other families from seeking asylum. Amid the indifference to such suffering, Pope Francis rightly wonders if we have forgotten how to cry.[19]

Moreover, women experience additional risks and specific forms of abuse, which are often neglected in discussions of migration. In some cases, when the men from their families and communities migrate, women remain at home due to family duties or because their labor is worth less on the global market. They are left to manage the household and hope for remittances to support themselves and their children.[20] In other cases, it is the men who stay behind while women and children seek refuge from the violence. This is the situation with Syrian refugees, four out of five of whom are women and children. Some of these women have never before been the head of a household and must now shoulder the entire responsibility for securing financial support as well as finding shelter and providing care for dependent family members in a foreign country.[21]

Women migrants also face particular dangers due to gender-related violence. In one week of August 2019, the *New York Times*

---

18. Elisabetta Povoledo, "Ship Captain Who Landed Migrants in Italy Sails into Political Storm," *New York Times*, July 5, 2019, https://www.nytimes.com/2019/07/05/world/europe/carola-rackete-italy-migrants.html.

19. Francis, Homily during visit to Lampedusa, July 8, 2013, http://w2.vatican.va/content/francesco/en/homilies/2013/documents/papa-francesco_20130708_omelia-lampedusa.html.

20. "Practicing an Ancient Craft in a Village without Men," *Economist*, August 23, 2018, https://www.economist.com/the-americas/2018/08/23/practising-an-ancient-craft-in-a-village-without-men.

21. United Nations High Commissioner for Refugees, *Woman Alone: The Fight for Survival by Syria's Refugee Women*, July 2014, https://www.refworld.org/pdfid/53be84aa4.pdf.

reported two separate stories about the relationship between migration and violence against women. The first account relates the experiences of two girls in their mid-teens who were recruited with the offer of better-paying waitressing jobs by a neighbor in their impoverished town in Myanmar.[22] Believing they were being taken to a larger town in their home state of Shan, Nyo and Phyu were in fact trafficked across the border into China. There they, like thousands of other Myanmar girls, were sold to Chinese men desperate for "brides" in a country with a large gender gap due to the one-child policy enforced by the Chinese government.

The second *New York Times* story focuses on the gender violence seldom recognized as one of the causes of refugees escaping Central America, which has some of the highest rates of murder of women in the world. In this particular case, a Guatemalan father, Romeo de Jesus Sasvin Dominguez, was wounded and his wife killed by the abusive boyfriend of their (then) sixteen-year-old daughter. With the boyfriend due to be released from jail after only four years, Mr. Sasvin Dominguez sold his simple house to fund the long trek to the United States for himself and his youngest daughter in hopes of receiving asylum and getting a job that would enable him to bring his other daughters to safety.[23]

Unfortunately, these are not isolated cases. The horrifying level of sexual violence against Sudanese women has been well documented, as has the sexual violence against Philippine women who sought refuge during Typhoon Haiyan.[24] A brothel of seventy-five

---

22. Hannah Beech, "Teenage Brides Trafficked to China Reveal Ordeal: 'Ma, I've Been Sold,'" *New York Times*, August 17, 2019, https://www.nytimes.com/2019/08/17/world/asia/china-bride-trafficking.html.

23. Azam Ahmed, "Women Are Fleeing Death at Home. The U.S. Wants to Keep Them Out," *New York Times*, August 18, 2019, https://www.nytimes.com/2019/08/18/world/americas/guatemala-violence-women-asylum.html.

24. Amnesty International, "Sudan Human Rights," Amnesty International website, accessed September 20, 2019, https://www.amnestyusa.org/countries/sudan/; Taylor Evensen, "Typhoon Haiyan: Women in the Wake of Natural Disasters" *Penn Political Review*, March 18, 2014, https://pennpoliticalreview.org/2014/03/typhoon-haiyan-women-in-the-wake-of-natural-disasters/. See also "Gender and Health in Disasters," World Health Organization website, July 2002, https://www.who.int/gender/other_health/genderdisasters.pdf.

enslaved Syrian refugee women was discovered in Lebanon in 2016, and there is little reason to presume that this was the only one of its kind.[25] Nadia Murad, a Yazidi refugee who escaped sexual captivity by the Islamic State, received the 2018 Nobel Peace Prize for her work drawing attention to the widespread use of sexual violence against women as a tactic of war in the Middle East.[26]

The task of this chapter is to explore how the church should respond to the reality of these desperate migrants—vulnerable women, men, and children—who are ignored or exploited as though they are disposable. What does it mean to be a sign and instrument of the communion of all in God when refugees are risking their lives—and dying at the rate of well over four thousand per year—to obtain the basic levels of food, shelter, and security that many of us take for granted?[27] Surely the church today fails its mission if it does not commit itself to integrating these immigrants into new communities, to healing them from the traumas they've suffered, and to strengthening their home communities so that fewer people are forced to migrate. Furthermore, a church that truly exercises an option for the poor must attend to the particular difficulties of migrant women and children, who are often the poorest of these poor.

This chapter's exploration of what it means to be a prophetic, public church in the context of global migration begins with Catholic social teachings on migration. We will focus primarily on the joint pastoral letter issued in 2003 by the Catholic bishops of Mexico and of the United States: *Strangers No Longer: Together on the Journey of Hope.* This episcopal document provides a clear foundational statement of Catholic social principles as applied to the challenges of migration and an insightful discussion of the com-

---

25. Kareem Shaheen, "Dozens of Syrians Forced into Sexual Slavery in Derelict Lebanese House," *The Guardian*, April 30, 2016, https://www.theguardian.com/world/2016/apr/30/syrians-forced-sexual-slavery-lebanon.

26. "Nadia Murad: Facts," Nobel Prize website, accessed August 20, 2019, https://www.nobelprize.org/prizes/peace/2018/murad/facts/.

27. "Migrant Deaths and Disappearances," Migrant Data Portal website, accessed September 15, 2019, https://migrationdataportal.org/themes/migrant-deaths-and-disappearances. According to the data on this site, more than four thousand deaths of migrants have been recorded each year since 2014, and one can safely assume that the numbers are actually much higher, as many deaths would be unreported.

plexities that church communities as well as public policy must confront in responding to immigrants with both justice and mercy. However, as is frequently the case with Catholic social teaching, the specific struggles of women are not adequately addressed in what remains a largely androcentric approach. After further exploration of the situations that women migrants face, this chapter will then consider how the Christian church, as a religious community and in cooperation with other religious traditions and communities, might fulfill its public and prophetic obligations to foster communion in the current context of global migration and large-scale population displacement.

Strangers No Longer: Catholic Social Teaching on Migration

Migration is, of course, integral to the sources of Christianity, as it is to many other religions. The stranger and the alien are particular concerns in the Hebrew Bible, in part because of their vulnerability traveling through a harsh desert climate and without the protection of their tribes, but also because of the significance of migration to the identity of the people of Israel. Migration is pivotal in the story of Abraham, the father (or father in faith) of Jews, Christians, and Muslims. Furthermore, the account of the Exodus migration is central to the Torah as well as to Judaism. The story of the Exodus is repeatedly invoked in other biblical texts to remind the faithful of the experience of their ancestors, who migrated to Egypt during a climate-induced famine and then were enslaved until liberated by God. Again and again, the legal codes direct the people of Israel to remember that they were once aliens and so to refrain from oppressing the alien as they were once oppressed.[28]

In the New Testament, the Gospel of Matthew recounts a story of the Holy Family as political refugees forced to seek asylum in Egypt from Herod's murderous wrath (see 2:13-15). Furthermore, the canonical gospels describe Jesus during his ministry as a homeless migrant within the land of Israel: "Foxes have holes, and birds

---

28. See, for example, Exod 22:21 and 23:9, among other passages.

of the air have nests; but the Son of Man has nowhere to lay his head" (Matt 8:20; Luke 9:58). Finally, Jesus sends his followers out as migrants to spread the Good News, and the New Testament accounts of the early church focus on the extensive travels of church leaders, especially St. Paul.

Attentive readers (and hearers) of the Bible are thus taught to see their heroes—if not themselves—as vulnerable migrants. Indeed, Jesus is depicted as having made just such a connection between himself and migrants when he describes a Final Judgment in which the Son of Man will give either a positive verdict because "I was a stranger and you welcomed me" or a negative one on the grounds that "I was a stranger and you did not welcome me" (Matt 25:35, 43). Indeed, it has been argued that the Christian doctrine of the Incarnation represents a cosmic migration in which the Second Person of the Trinity relinquishes the perquisites of divinity to migrate to the human condition, where (like many migrants) he is more rejected than welcomed.[29]

The 2003 joint pastoral letter of the United States Conference of Catholic Bishops and the Conferencia del Episcopado Mexicano, *Strangers No Longer: Together on the Journey of Hope*, is rooted in this biblical tradition of special concern for the migrant or alien. Drawing on these biblical themes along with the relevant principles of Catholic social teaching, *Strangers No Longer* articulates five basic principles that the bishops contend govern a just approach to migration. These principles are: (1) persons have the right to find opportunities in their homeland; (2) persons have the right to migrate to support themselves and their families; (3) sovereign nations have the right to control their borders; (4) refugees and asylum seekers should be afforded protection; and (5) the human dignity and human rights of undocumented migrants should be respected.[30]

---

29. See John 1; Phil 2:6; and Daniel G. Groody, "A Theology of Migration: A New Method for Understanding a God on the Move," *America: The Jesuit Review*, February 7, 2011, https://www.americamagazine.org/issue/763/article/theology-migration.

30. United States Conference of Catholic Bishops and Conferencia del Episcopado Mexicano, *Strangers No Longer: Together on the Journey of Hope*. A Pastoral Letter Concerning Migration from the Catholic Bishops of Mexico and the

The challenge, of course, is to apply these principles in practice, particularly when they conflict with each other, as the right to migrate and the right to control national borders certainly seem to do. However, justice frequently requires finding the appropriate balance between competing rights. Affirming these five principles together does not, as I will argue below, result in irresolvable contradictions but rather provides the basis for a nuanced balance that is scarce in the too-often absolutist and one-sided political debates on immigration policy today.

The bishops' decision to begin with the principle that people have the right to opportunity in their own homeland may seem to be odd, a bit beside the point in this discussion of migration. After all, forced migration (including migration compelled by dire poverty or natural disasters) occurs precisely because a decent life is not possible in the homeland. One may well wonder what the point is of specifying a right that cannot be exercised under existing conditions, especially when there is no single party guilty of denying the right, as is the case when natural disasters or economic distress caused by complex global forces make life in a certain locale unlivable.

I believe the bishops' intent here is to frame the conversation about migration with a reminder that coerced migration is not the way things ought to be. Ideally, no one should have to leave their home country, community, and culture to obtain a life with dignity. The urgent situation of those who have already been compelled to migrate should not eclipse the need to solve the underlying issues so that others will be able to remain in their home countries. In the context of globalization, it may be fair to say that all share (though differently) in the collective responsibility to strengthen community resources and political structures so that no one is forced by violence, poverty, or natural disaster to emigrate from their home country.

The second principle, that everyone has the right to migrate to attain a life with dignity when such a life is not possible in his or her home country, is more obviously relevant to contemporary debates about immigration policy and especially about how to respond to

---

United States (Washington, DC: USCCB, 2003), 33–38, http://www.usccb.org/issues-and-action/human-life-and-dignity/immigration/strangers-no-longer-together-on-the-journey-of-hope.cfm.

undocumented immigrants. In the current public discourse in the United States, the idea that people have a right to migrate to save their lives is seldom highlighted. Yet this principle follows from basic Christian beliefs that the earth belongs ultimately to God, that the goods of the earth are intended for all, and that human life takes precedence over property.[31] It follows, then, that people do not have to wait to be invited but instead have the right to migrate to obtain sufficient food, water, shelter, and security to sustain their lives. This right holds whether their lives are imperiled due to war, violence, unjust governments, natural disasters, hunger, famine, or drought.

But this is where a potentially significant conflict between these principles emerges. What if there are not enough resources to provide for both the home population and the immigrant population? Consider that the right to find opportunity in one's homeland requires not only adequate supplies of food and shelter but also political stability and a viable economic system. Many people fear that excessive immigration will degrade these necessities. Could exercising the right to migrate to support oneself and one's family jeopardize others' right to find opportunities in their own homeland? Or, conversely, does the right to opportunities in one's homeland negate the right of others to migrate there? These questions present a version of the classic ethical quandary of the lifeboat: if a lifeboat is already completely filled to capacity, it cannot save any more drowning people without swamping the boat and drowning them all. In such a case, is it not more ethical to save the few already aboard than to take on more people and lose them all?[32]

At this time, it is not likely that the United States, Canada, or the countries of Western Europe will run out of sufficient supplies of adequate food if they admit immigrants. With 40 percent of food regularly wasted in the United States and high levels of obesity in the population, there are clearly enough resources to supply the

---

31. *Laudato Sí* 67–69; *Gaudium et Spes* 64–72.

32. Garrett Hardin, "Lifeboat Ethics: The Case against Helping the Poor," 1974, Garrett Hardin Society website, https://www.garretthardinsociety.org/articles/art_lifeboat_ethics_case_against_helping_poor.html. See also the discussion in Elizabeth W. Collier and Charles R. Strain, *Global Migration: What's Happening, Why, and a Just Response* (Winona, MN: Anselm Academic, 2017), 30–31.

nutritional needs of the current population and of a good many more immigrants than are seeking admission.[33] Still, many fear economic displacement by immigrants, wondering how many low-wage workers can be absorbed without increasing unemployment among US citizens. Others worry that an influx of needy immigrants will bring with them the political chaos and crime they are fleeing or will overwhelm an already stressed network of publicly funded education and social services. Just as there are a variety of causes of forced migration, so too are there many ways that the socioeconomic and political systems within apparently stable countries might be disrupted. This raises valid questions about whether a country can make opportunities available to immigrants without significantly diminishing the economic prospects of its current population or, in a worst-case scenario, altogether losing its ability to guarantee political and social stability for anyone.

There is a further, and probably more common, concern that must be acknowledged as well. Catholic social teaching affirms that people have a right to culture, especially since it is through culture that one becomes fully human, as Pope St. John Paul II notably insisted.[34] The significance of this right to culture is frequently cited in Catholic discussions of migration, particularly in emphasizing that immigrants should be received in a manner supportive of their distinct cultures.[35] The importance of culture is also at least implicitly recognized in the assertion of the right to find opportunities in one's homeland. Yet it is just this desire to protect one's culture that is invoked in much

---

33. Dana Gunders, "Wasted: How America Is Losing up to 40 percent of Its Food from Farm to Fork to Landfill," National Resources Defense Council, August 16, 2017, https://www.nrdc.org/resources/wasted-how-america-losing-40-percent-its-food-farm-fork-landfill.

34. See especially John Paul II, Address to UNESCO: June 2, 1980, 6–7, *Interdisciplinary Encyclopedia of Religion and Science* online, http://inters.org/John-Paul-II-UNESCO-Culture. See also *Gaudium et Spes* 53.

35. See especially National Conference of Catholic Bishops, "A Call to Communion," in *Welcoming the Stranger among Us: Unity in Diversity* (Washington, DC: United States Catholic Conference, 2000), http://www.usccb.org/issues-and-action/cultural-diversity/pastoral-care-of-migrants-refugees-and-travelers/resources/welcoming-the-stranger-among-us-unity-in-diversity.cfm. See also USCCB and CEM, *Strangers No Longer*, 42.

resistance to immigration. To be sure, the rejection of the cultures of immigrants is often bigoted, based on distorted views of foreign cultures, and even at times hateful. Nevertheless, Catholic teaching about culture as integral to one's humanity supports maintaining and nurturing one's culture as a human good and even a right. Might citizens not then appropriately resist being overwhelmed by the cultures of immigrants, especially those with such different values that some have warned of an epoch-defining clash of civilizations?

These issues lead to the third principle, the right of sovereign nations to secure their borders. In Catholic thought, politics is a good that is necessary for the coordination of human activity, and each level of government has its proper subsidiary responsibility along with the rights necessary to fulfill these duties.[36] In the absence of an effective world government (which has not yet been envisioned in a manner consistent with human freedom in a world of more than seven billion people), sovereign nations remain at this point an effective way of organizing political authority. To satisfy their obligation to protect the common good and the public order, these states retain the right to control the boundaries of the people and territory they govern.

It must be acknowledged, however, that the right of sovereign states to secure their borders is not an absolute or unlimited right. As the bishops elaborate, "the Church recognizes the right of sovereign nations to control their territories but rejects such control when it is exerted merely for the purpose of acquiring additional wealth."[37] The right to regulate borders extends as far as necessary for the state to fulfill its duties to maintain its own public order, but this right is not properly invoked merely to avoid assisting people in distress. It is certainly not appropriately wielded to justify increasing political power through rhetoric that creates a demonized and threatening other. As Collier and Strain explain, "human dignity and human flourishing are ultimate realities that precede the current human-created political structures and rules."[38]

---

36. *Gaudium et Spes* 74.
37. USCCB and CEM, *Strangers No Longer*, 36.
38. Collier and Strain, *Global Migration*, 76.

The right to secure borders could be compared, then, to the right of a family to secure its home and to provide for the members of the household before sharing with those in need beyond the family circle. Nations, according to this third principle, have a similar responsibility to ensure the well-being of their own people before serving the broader common good of humanity. This priority of care is not inherently selfish in either case, since human experience has confirmed the wisdom of such differentiated levels of obligation. Even Catholic Worker houses find they have to moderate how many guests they can take in and under what conditions, lest there be no more house left to extend hospitality.

It is not easy, however, to determine when one has made sufficient provisions, whether for the family or for the nation, so that one's responsibility to the wider community begins.[39] Who defines what is essential and what is excess, particularly when it is impossible to store enough to provide for all future contingencies? It is also unclear how far the government's role in fostering culture and protecting the economic opportunities of citizens extends and when the needs of immigrants seeking the means to survive supersede the priority accorded to citizens of the nation. Resolving the tension between these various rights and responsibilities requires much practical wisdom. Nevertheless, recognizing that the right to secure borders is a valid but limited right is a significant preliminary step in the discernment of the appropriate governmental response to immigration.

The fourth principle, affirming that refugees and asylum seekers should be afforded protection, is a further qualification of the right of the state to control its borders. Nevertheless, this principle should be uncontroversial, at least among the nations who are parties to the United Nations' *Convention Relating to the Status of Refugees* or the related "1967 Protocol."[40] Given the value of human life, these nations have agreed that refugees may not be returned to a country where their lives are in danger, though it is quite reasonable

---

39. For strong statements on the principle that should govern any such discernment, see *Gaudium et Spes* (GS) 69; *Evangelii Gaudium* (EG) 57.

40. United Nations, *Convention and Protocol Relating to the Status of Refugees* (1951, 1967), https://www.unhcr.org/en-us/protection/basic/3b66c2aa10/convention-protocol-relating-status-refugees.html.

to expect governments to cooperate in sharing responsibilities for refugees according to each country's ability to absorb them without undue hardship. One difficulty with this fourth principle, however, is that it is often not a simple matter to determine whether an asylum seeker's life would truly be in danger if he or she were repatriated. Those fleeing for their lives, after all, often have no chance to secure the documentation needed to support their application for asylum. At the same time, government officials may have reason to suspect that claims of persecution are invented or exaggerated as a way to "game the system" and gain admission to a country. In cases of legitimate doubt, it seems preferable to err on the side of preserving life, but in any case people ought to be able to agree to condemn procedures that refuse asylum on legalistic grounds (such as by eliminating qualifying categories of persecuted groups) rather than because the refugees truly face no danger.[41]

It is important to note too that, according to the US and Mexican bishops, this fourth principle "requires, at a minimum, that migrants have a right to claim refugee status without incarceration and to have their claims fully considered by a competent authority."[42] There can be no doubt that the current US government's practices of discouraging applications for asylum by incarcerating refugees in dehumanizing conditions and through the unconscionable policy of separating children from their parents violates this fourth principle and is by these standards an unjustifiable denial of the rights of refugees.[43]

The final principle, respecting the human dignity and human rights of undocumented immigrants, is fundamental to all aspects of immigration policy and debate. Regardless of whether immigrants lack the requisite documentation (which may have been impossible to obtain), they remain human beings and should be treated as such.

---

41. See *inter alia* Ahmed, "Women Are Fleeing."
42. USCCB and CEM, *Strangers No Longer*, 37.
43. Michael Crowley, "Pence's Border Trip Illustrates Conflicting Messages about Detained Migrants," *New York Times*, July 15, 2019, https://www.nytimes.com/2019/07/15/us/politics/mike-pence-border-visit.html; Ron Nixon, "Trump Officials Urge End of Time Limits on Detaining Migrant Children," *New York Times,* September 18, 2018, https://www.nytimes.com/2018/09/18/us/politics/migrant-children-detention-trump.html.

The widespread criminalization and even demonization of undocumented immigrants in the United States today is an assault on our shared humanity and gives rise to a violent brutality that unravels the bonds of society. No matter what position people take on issues of immigration policy, we should agree to treat all people, including undocumented immigrants, with the respect human beings deserve.

As suggested above, the application of these five principles in actual immigration policies is neither simple nor straightforward. Legitimate, indeed essential, rights compete, and people will weigh the claims differently. Still, the public debate—and justice—would be advanced if all of these principles were widely recognized as having validity. We might then be able to talk to each other about our different evaluations of the competing rights rather than talking (or shouting) past each other because each side believes it alone has a principled position.

It is, moreover, generally accepted that certain values take precedence when rights conflict, and that is clearly the case here. For most people, the right to life has at least a prima facie claim to priority, a point implicit in the bishops' insistence that the right to secure borders is not unlimited and that endangered refugees should be given protection. The issue for debate should not be whether the state has a right to secure its borders, then, but rather whether immigrants' right to life outweighs this right. Many will also want to join the bishops in emphasizing care for the most vulnerable and the obligation to share our excess with those in need as among the highest of considerations, though obviously not all people give the weight to these values that Christianity and other religions do. Moreover, respecting immigrants' humanity, whether they are welcomed or deported, ought to be asserted as an inviolable principle.

In addition to acknowledging that some rights are more important than others, the appropriate application of these five principles requires accurate knowledge of the situation, including the gravity of immigrants' circumstances as well as the likely effects of their immigration on the host country. Unfortunately, honest attempts to ascertain such facts are in short supply in contemporary public discourse, as political movements gain traction by appealing to fear and nationalist fervor while evidence is frequently disregarded, distorted, or simply fabricated. Anyone interested in the just adjudication of the competing rights at stake in immigration debates must insist on truthful and honest investigation of evidence, regardless of which side the evidence supports.

Citizens, then, must attend carefully to the real facts of the situation as well as engage in nuanced reasoning about the competing values and rights at stake in order to determine which immigration policies to support. This is a great deal to require. Moreover, as Victor Carmona has argued, a country's inhabitants must risk the often-disconcerting experience of strangeness in welcoming immigrants with their linguistic and cultural diversity.[44] It is not easy for those who benefit from the taken-for-grantedness of their own, majority culture to find that culture called into question, perhaps even in daily life. Nevertheless, as the bishops remind us, cultures are never stagnant but are constantly changing. One's culture is best fostered not by rejecting or marginalizing others' cultures but rather by intentional discernment that is willing to benefit from the strengths of other cultures, even while defending what is best in one's own.[45] Immigrants thus bring a challenge but also a gift that, when appropriately received, contributes to a greater unity-in-diversity that strengthens society.[46]

As the bishops' five principles indicate, just immigration policies require a strong commitment to the common good of all humanity. Not only in personal charity but in public policy as well, concern for others must not stop at national borders. This universal common good is central to the church's social teaching and fundamental to the church's mission to promote the communion of all. As Pope Francis says, he is the pastor of a church without borders (EG 210). But national policies must also consider the common good of humanity. Even though the government is primarily responsible for

---

44. Victor Carmona, "Bridge-Building with Virtue Ethics in Times of Strangeness," in *Bridge Building in Sarajevo: The Plenary Papers from CTEWC 2018*, ed. Kristin E. Heyer, James F. Keenan, and Andrea Vicini (Maryknoll, NY: Orbis, 2019), 91–99.

45. See especially "Cultural Fears," in NCCB, *Welcoming the Stranger*.

46. See especially Francis, Message of His Holiness Pope Francis for the World Day of Migrants and Refugees, August 5, 2013, http://w2.vatican.va/content/francesco/en/messages/migration/documents/papa-francesco_20130805_world-migrants-day.html.

the well-being of those within its national boundaries, policies that pursue the country's good without regard for its effects on the rest of the planet are not just. This is not only a matter of justice, however; in our globalized world, it is the simple truth that we are all in this together, affecting and being affected by one another. The national common good and the global common good have become inseparable.[47]

Women, Migration, and Trafficking

That women experience migration distinctly from men is well established, yet neither *Strangers No Longer* (2003) nor the earlier US bishops' statement, *Welcoming the Stranger among Us* (2000), mentions the specific hardships women migrants contend with. These documents do not acknowledge the fact that displacement encourages the conditions for gender-based violence.[48] They briefly note the vulnerability and particular needs of children[49] but not the greater dangers of violence and exploitation that women confront, the higher likelihood that they won't have the requisite identification documents to receive aid, or the common failure of shelters to provide adequately for women's hygiene and privacy needs. Perhaps most disturbing is that, while the vast majority—72 percent—of trafficking victims are women and girls, the bishops discuss trafficking as though it is a gender-neutral reality, condemning the "trafficking in persons, in which men, women, and children from all over the globe are transported to other countries for the purposes of forced prostitution or labor."[50]

The same androcentric bias is evident in Pope Francis's July 2015 statement to the Pontifical Academy of Social Sciences workshop

---

47. See especially Thomas L. Friedman, *The World Is Flat: A Brief History of the Twenty-First Century*, rev. ed. (New York: Farrar, Straus and Giroux, 2006).

48. Sierra Club, *Women on the Move in a Changing Climate: A Discussion Paper on Gender, Climate and Mobility*, December 2018, https://www.sierraclub.org/sites/www.sierraclub.org/files/uploads-wysiwig/Women%20On%20The%20Move%20In%20A%20Changing%20Climate%20report.pdf. See also UNHCR, *Woman Alone*.

49. NCCB, "The Special Needs of Youth," in *Welcoming the Stranger*.

50. USCCB and CEM, *Strangers No Longer*, 90.

"Modern Slavery and Climate Change." He is astute in his brief analysis of the connections between disregard of the environment and the poverty that increases the risk of being trafficked, and he rightly calls attention to the dangers migrants face of being exploited, trafficked, and enslaved.[51] Traveling away from their communities, often covertly and without the protection of any government, migrants and refugees can easily disappear into the forced-labor economy. Indeed, studies confirm that trafficking increases when people are displaced from their homes by conflict or natural disaster.[52] Pope Francis expresses specific concern about slave labor in mines and about the sexual exploitation of children, and he mentions human trafficking for purposes of prostitution (which can and does include the prostitution of men and boys).[53] Yet, like the US and Mexican bishops, Pope Francis does not indicate that women are by far the most likely to be trafficked. He too treats migration and trafficking as largely gender-neutral, ignoring the particular problems that women confront as well as their particular insights into how best to improve their situations.[54]

Of course, women and children experience migration differently from men in many ways. As noted above, in some instances the gendering of work results in women having less-marketable skills, although in other cases women's labor is more easily sold, though frequently for lower wages. At times, women migrate with their children; at other times, they are more likely to remain behind. Nevertheless, throughout the process, women face greater danger of sexual violence, including the danger of being trafficked for prostitution.[55]

While all forms of migrant abuse deserve attention, I would like to focus here on the global trafficking in women and children for

---

51. Francis, "Statement of His Holiness Pope Francis to the Workshop 'Modern Slavery and Climate Change: The Commitment of the Cities,'" July 21, 2015, http://w2.vatican.va/content/francesco/en/speeches/2015/july/documents/papa-francesco_20150721_sindaci-grandi-citta.html.

52. Sierra Club, *Women on the Move*.

53. Francis, "Statement to the Workshop."

54. Sierra Club, *Women on the Move*.

55. In addition to above-cited references, see Justine Calma, "Climate Change Has Created a New Generation of Sex-Trafficking Victims," *Quartz*, May 2, 2017, https://qz.com/970394/climate-change-has-created-a-new-generation-of-sex-trafficking-victims/.

sexual exploitation, as this trafficking has in recent years reached its highest recorded levels.⁵⁶ The vagaries of the global economy leave impoverished young women and girls around the world at risk of being trafficked into the sex trade, sometimes when they accept deceptive offers of paid labor in a distant place and sometimes when they are sold by their desperate families.⁵⁷ Climate change may also play a role: Wudan Yan reports that Rohingya women and girls were being trafficked into brothels as early monsoons threatened their refugee camps in Bangladesh.⁵⁸

Regardless of whether they are trafficked across or within borders, these young women and girls are often truly slaves, objects in market exchanges between others—between their family and traffickers, between traffickers and brothel owners, between pimps and johns. Most of these women and children are forced, as all slaves are, to accept their condition by violence and the threat of violence.⁵⁹ Beaten and mutilated, drugged, isolated, and closely monitored (when not literally locked up), prostituted women and children learn to act willing and eager to sell sexual services in order to make the quotas imposed on them so they will not have to go without food for the day or face another brutal beating. Not surprisingly, studies have found that prostituted women experience posttraumatic stress disorder at levels equivalent to combat veterans and survivors of state-sponsored torture.⁶⁰

The horrific details of enormous brothels buying young girls from their families in Kolkata, or the torture chambers for girls who resist

---

56. UN News, "Human Trafficking Cases Hit a 13-Year Record High, New UN Report Shows," *UN News*, January 29, 2019, https://news.un.org/en/story/2019/01/1031552.

57. In addition to Beech, "Teenage Brides," and Shaheen, "Dozens of Syrians," see also Nicholas D. Kristof and Sheryl WuDunn, *Half the Sky: Turning Oppression into Opportunity for Women Worldwide* (New York: Alfred A. Knopf, 2009).

58. Wudan Yan, "The Surprising Link between Climate Change and Human Trafficking," *The Revelator*, May 7, 2018, https://therevelator.org/climate-change-human-trafficking/.

59. See Kristof and WuDunn, *Half the Sky;* Rachel Lloyd, *Girls Like Us* (New York: HarperCollins, 2011).

60. Melissa Farley and Emily Butler, "Prostitution and Trafficking—Quick Facts" (San Francisco: Prostitution Research & Education, 2012), http://www.prostitutionresearch.com/Prostitution%20Quick%20Facts%2012-21-12.pdf.

sex work in Cambodia, should not lead us to assume that trafficking for sexual exploitation is primarily a third-world problem.[61] Many sex tourists are American and European males, and the United States has played a prominent role in the development of the international sex industry, including (for example) fostering sex tourism in Thailand during the Vietnam War. Furthermore, young women and girls are regularly trafficked into and within Europe and the United States. My own city of San Diego is a major site of sex trafficking because it is a border city, a military town, a vacation destination, and a popular location for conventions.[62] Each of these characteristics has been found to increase the likelihood of sex trafficking, and each involves a fluid population. Sex trafficking is highly correlated with transience, including the transience of international and intranational migration.

It may be that the sex industry will never be totally eradicated, but the extent to which it flourishes depends on many factors. Harvard professor Siddharth Kara's study of the economics of sex slavery has led him to conclude that sex trafficking can be successfully combatted by raising the cost to the madams and pimps through higher prosecution rates and stiffer penalties for sex traffickers. Increasing the costs associated with sex trafficking raises the price for sex acts, thereby lowering demand and eroding the profit margin to the point that trafficking becomes unprofitable.[63] As Kristof and WuDunn have documented, brothels have gone out of business and sex slaves have been released when governmental and intergovernmental action—and the resultant fines, necessary bribes, and other legal hassles—have made prostituting women and children unprofitable.[64]

Prosecution of traffickers, rather than of trafficked victims, is thus a key strategy in combatting sex slavery. However, protection and

---

61. See Kristof and WuDunn, *Half the Sky*.
62. Karla Peterson, "Human Traffickers Target San Diego County Girls," *San Diego Union-Tribune*, January 11, 2019, https://www.sandiegouniontribune.com/news/columnists/karla-peterson/sd-me-karla-trafficking-girlsinc-20190111-story.html.
63. Siddharth Kara, *Sex Trafficking: Inside the Business of Modern Slavery* (New York: Columbia University Press, 2009), esp. 16–37, 83–94.
64. Kristof and WuDunn, *Half the Sky*, 26–27.

prevention are also important. One major form of protection of victims is to regularize the trafficked victims' immigration status. Trafficked people are likely to be reluctant to seek assistance from or cooperate with law enforcement agents if they fear being deported to the unlivable situations from which they fled. This fact is recognized by the United States' Trafficking Victims Protection Act, which authorizes visas for victims of sex trafficking and their families.[65]

Hostility to migrants is another major impediment to the protection and healing of victims from foreign countries. People trafficked from abroad are not likely to reach out for help in a context of widespread hostility toward immigrants, so that, as Maria Grazia Giammarinaro, UN special rapporteur on trafficking in persons, pointed out, "xenophobic migration policies and the criminalisation of migrants . . . are incompatible with effective action against human trafficking."[66] Furthermore, the social integration that is indispensable to the healing of trafficked victims is difficult to provide in countries where immigrants are treated as social pariahs.[67]

Strategies for the prevention of sex trafficking, which is the best option when successful, include strengthening economic opportunities, especially for women and girls. Studies have demonstrated that lack of educational opportunities and job possibilities for young women contributes to the probability they will be sold, coerced, or enticed into the sex trade.[68] A more equal distribution of the benefits and opportunities of our global economy would help to ensure that

---

65. U.S. Citizenship and Immigration Services, "Victims of Human Trafficking: T Nonimmigrant Status," May 10, 2018, https://www.uscis.gov/humanitarian/victims-human-trafficking-other-crimes/victims-human-trafficking-t-nonimmigrant-status.

66. UN News, "Conflict, Climate Change among Factors that Increase 'Desperation that Enables Human Trafficking to Flourish,' Says UN Chief," July 30, 2019, https://news.un.org/en/story/2019/07/1043391.

67. UN News, "Conflict, Climate Change."

68. Michelle Bachelet, "Fighting Human Trafficking: Partnership and Innovation to End Violence against Women and Children" (speech delivered at UN General Assembly Interactive Dialogue, April 3, 2012), https://www.unwomen.org/en/news/stories/2012/4/fighting-human-trafficking-partnership-and-innovation-to-end-violence-against-women-and-children.

the daughters of the poor around the world have options other than to become objects for consumption in the growing world market.

Another important prevention strategy is to decrease the conflicts and environmental devastation that cause so many to become refugees. When international diplomacy or peacekeeping forces can prevent violent conflicts, people are spared from becoming refugees and are at less risk of being trafficked.[69] Action to mitigate climate change, along with work to increase communities' ability to adapt to the environmental changes already underway, can also contribute to keeping communities together so that there are fewer desperate migrants at risk of being trafficked. However, since even the best international efforts cannot prevent all political conflict and natural disasters, early assistance to refugees in these crisis situations is key to preventing these vulnerable people from being trafficked.

Increasing awareness of the modern slavery that is prevalent in the sex industry as well as in the production of many goods is another valuable strategy for decreasing trafficking. It is very difficult to end trafficking as long as there is demand as well as money to be made in meeting that demand. For this reason, alongside efforts to increase the costs to suppliers by prosecuting traffickers, campaigns drawing attention to the reality of global trafficking are an important strategy to interrupt the supply-and-demand cycle of the modern slave trade.

Normalizing the sex industry as though it involves freely chosen work is not helpful here, especially since this claim to choice is belied by the reality of much of the industry. Even if many of the young women and children trafficked in the sex industry in the United States are not kidnapped but rather are originally enticed by a pimp feigning love and offering a home, the coercion is no less real for many of these "sex workers," who are constantly monitored, receive violent beatings if they fail to earn as much as expected, and are threatened with worse violence if they try to leave. A study of the sex industry in Portland, Oregon, found that 84 percent of prosti-

---

69. Unfortunately, recent history suggests that better supervision of and more accountability for peacekeepers is necessary to ensure that they do not themselves engage in the abuse and trafficking of vulnerable populations. See UN News, "UN Receives 70 New Allegations of Sexual Exploitation and Abuse in Three Months," July 30, 2018, https://news.un.org/en/story/2018/07/1015912.

tuted women had been violently assaulted—many to the point of requiring hospitalization, 53 percent had experienced sexual assault and torture, and 27 percent had been mutilated.[70] There is no reason to believe this is anomalous, given the accounts of many who have been involved in the sex industry.

Living with violence and threats of violence, faced with social rejection and low self-esteem for having been involved in prostitution, and often lacking a stable home to return to, these girls and young women may be as imprisoned in the sex industry as those who are literally locked in a cage in Thailand or in a trailer in Florida. To be sure, there are some women who more or less freely choose to enter the sex industry, and I do not wish to deny or to undermine any woman's capacity for agency. Nevertheless, as Kathleen Mitchell, a former sex worker and madam who is currently an activist working on behalf of prostituted girls in Arizona, has rightly noted, "in order to have a choice, you need to have two viable options to choose from."[71] However much some of these girls and young women affirm that they choose to work in the sex industry, many have very few options. They often experience prostitution as a choice for life and for a more stable (and, sadly, more caring) environment than they otherwise had available.

Furthermore, girls who begin sex work before they are legally allowed to drive a car (or to consent to sex!) do not have sufficient age, maturity, or awareness of the reality of prostitution to be capable of making a responsible choice in this matter. All prostituted minors are thus appropriately recognized in US law as victims of sex trafficking, even though society—and too often the police and the courts—still see and treat these girls as criminal delinquents rather than as victims of abuse.[72]

---

70. These statistics are based on a study conducted by the Council for Prostitution Alternative in Portland, Oregon, as cited by Janice G. Roberts, "Health Effects of Prostitution," in *Making the Harm Visible: Global Sexual Exploitation of Women and Girls, Speaking Out and Providing Services*, ed. Donna M. Hughes and Claire M. Roche (New York: Coalition against Trafficking in Women, 1999).

71. As quoted in Julian Sher, *Somebody's Daughter: The Hidden Story of America's Prostituted Children and the Battle to Save Them* (Chicago: Chicago Review Press, 2011), 53.

72. Victims of Trafficking and Violence Protection Act of 2000, Pub. L. No. 106–386, 114 Stat. 1464, https://www.govinfo.gov/content/pkg/PLAW-106publ386

While the Christian tradition resists the normalization of purchasing sex, Christianity has contributed to distortions about the real conditions of these women's and girls' lives through its descriptions of "sex workers" as women with insatiable lusts and/or greed for money and luxury. Consider, for example, the Christian tradition of depicting Mary Magdalene as a deeply repentant prostitute who is forgiven much. Of course, close readers of the gospels know that Mary Magdalene is never described in Scripture as having engaged in prostitution, and the repentant public woman is not identified as Mary Magdalene. Nevertheless, the traditional identification of Mary Magdalene as a penitent prostitute has functioned to create a powerful virgin/whore binary in which women are defined by their sexuality—as either chaste virgins or sexually voracious women available to all. Mary Magdalene is no longer remembered primarily as the courageous disciple of Jesus who first witnessed the resurrection and was sent as "apostle to the apostles" to tell the others. Instead, the focus is on her repentance for her sexual sins, so that she stands in as the polar opposite of the purity of the other great Mary, the Virgin mother of Jesus.

This binary approach to female sexuality emerged very early and has profoundly influenced Christian perceptions of women and especially of women involved in prostitution. In the early church story of yet another Mary, Mary of Egypt, this concept of the hypersexuality of women in the sex industry is even more clearly emphasized: at least one version explicitly states that this Mary works as a prostitute because of her insatiable lust. On encountering an icon of the chaste Virgin Mary, Mary of Egypt has a change of heart and spends the rest of her life in the desert in a penance of deep deprivation, another model of female repentance for unbridled sexuality.[73]

/pdf/PLAW-106publ386.pdf. See also "Summary of the Trafficking Victims Protection Act (TVPA) and Reauthorizations FY 2017," Alliance to End Slavery and Trafficking website, January 11, 2017, https://endslaveryandtrafficking.org/summary-trafficking-victims-protection-act-tvpa-reauthorizations-fy-2017-2/.

73. Joseph MacRory, "St. Mary of Egypt," in *Catholic Encyclopedia* (New York: Robert Appleton, 1910), http://www.newadvent.org/cathen/09763a.htm. See also Peter Anthony Mena, *Place and Identity in the Lives of Antony, Paul, and Mary of Egypt: Desert as Borderland* (New York: Palgrave Macmillan, 2019).

Although the virgin/whore binary approach to women's sexuality has much less traction in today's world than in the past, this tradition has contributed to the tendency to ignore the circumstances of women's lives and the context in which sex for sale takes place. Christians are thus formed to take at face value the marketing of young women as highly sexed and/or enjoying the supposedly easy money, rather than considering that they may have been forced—as have women throughout history—to accept prostitution to keep themselves or their families alive. Similarly little thought is given to the fact that these women may be abused, traumatized, and scarred by the sexual abuse that commonly predates their involvement in the sex industry as well as by their experiences within it. Having been conditioned first by a tradition of moralizing tales that condemn prostituted women for their wantonness and now perhaps by a societal emphasis on the nonjudgmental acceptance of selling sex as a consensual economic transaction, Christians may find it easy to overlook the complex reality and lives of trafficked women, who do not fit into a simplistic virgin/whore binary any more than does the biblical Mary Magdalene.

This trafficking of women, children, and men in the modern slave trade, whether for sexual exploitation or for any other form of forced labor, is one of the horrors of our time. The connections between trafficking and the vulnerability of migrants, especially when displaced by war or natural disaster, are widely recognized by those who work on the issues of migration in general or of trafficking in particular. However, migration itself is often a gendered experience, and the role of gender in increasing the risk of being trafficked is especially clear. Any appropriate response to migration generally, or to trafficking specifically, begins with the recognition that women and men are impacted differently by these realities.

Being Church in a World on the Move

A Prophetic Ecclesial Witness

In *Strangers No Longer*, the US and Mexican bishops rightly emphasize the ideal of unity-in-diversity in their discussions of migration.[74] Harmony enriched by difference is presented not only as

---

74. USCCB and CEM, *Strangers No Longer*, esp. 17, 20. See also NCCB, *Welcoming the Stranger*.

a human good but as integral to the communion the church serves. The bishops succeed in combining perspectives on migration as both an opportunity for the church to witness inclusive communion and a demand for morally informed public policy. These recent episcopal documents on migration thus serve in many respects as models for the integration of the prophetic (sign) and the public (instrument) dimensions of the church's mission. If the statements have had less effect in transforming Catholic parish life and political activity than might be hoped, that may be because they overestimate Catholic awareness of how integral communion is to the life of Christian faith. Even among the minority of Catholics who occasionally read such official teachings, many assume that the church serves primarily to bring individuals into an otherworldly salvation. Much work remains to be done to increase awareness that the mission of the church is to be a sign and instrument of communion, so that all the faithful grasp more clearly the inherent unity of God's salvific activity in history, the command to love one's neighbor, and Christian practices of care for the vulnerable in society.

Of course, faith is not primarily an intellectual activity but rather a practice and habit that itself is the basis for greater conceptual clarity. As liberation theologians have emphasized, understanding of Christianity grows and deepens through an ongoing hermeneutical spiral of lived discipleship and reflection.[75] The practice of welcoming migrants enables Christians not only to engage with the most significant issues of our time—including global economic inequality and the effects of climate change—but also to learn better what it means to be a disciple of Christ, serving as a sign and instrument of communion in the twenty-first century.

Christians and many others motivated by religious and humanitarian concerns are already doing much to respond to the pressing needs of migrants. In the United States, people are providing water in the desert where migrants cross, legal aid to assist in applications for asylum, help to recover children held in detention centers, counseling for trauma, and shelters for asylum seekers discharged in the middle of the night with no place to go. All of this is a countercul-

---

75. See *inter alia* Juan Luis Segundo, *Liberation of Theology* (Maryknoll, NY: Orbis, 1976).

tural witness that chooses solidarity with vulnerable human beings over the economic advantage that contributes to human and environmental abuse.

For several decades now, an ecumenical movement of sanctuary churches housing undocumented immigrants and refugees on church premises has been an ongoing prophetic witness against US policies of ruthless deportations.[76] Although law enforcement in the United States is legally allowed to enter church premises to arrest people for deportation, they refrain from doing so. Families have been kept together, and in some cases people have avoided being repatriated to life-threatening situations. In August of 2019, the Evangelical Lutheran Church in America declared itself a "sanctuary church body" committed to providing hospitality to immigrants and working for more just immigration policies.[77]

Pope Francis, himself the son of immigrants, has advocated a similarly direct yet less politically confrontational approach to the refugee crisis in Europe: he has asked each parish in Europe to take responsibility for one family of refugees in order to abate the refugee crisis there. Under Francis's direction, the Vatican itself has taken in several immigrant families, freeing them from refugee camps and helping to resettle them in Italy.[78] That is a truly transformative prophetic witness!

The US and Mexican Catholic bishops ask their congregations to carry out what may be an even more demanding and prophetic ministry of inclusion: modeling the unity-in-diversity the church preaches by integrating immigrants—with their different cultures—

---

76. Bill Rodgers, "More Undocumented Immigrants Are Living in US Sanctuary Churches," *VOA News*, January 29, 2019, https://www.voanews.com/usa/more-undocumented-immigrants-are-living-us-sanctuary-churches.

77. Zachary Halaschak, "Protestant Denomination Becomes First 'Sanctuary Church Body,'" *Washington Examiner*, August 9, 2019, https://www.washingtonexaminer.com/news/protestant-denomination-becomes-first-sanctuary-church-body.

78. Stephanie Kirchgaessner, "Vatican to Take in Two Refugee Families as Pope Calls for 'Every Religion' to Help," *The Guardian*, September 6, 2015, https://www.theguardian.com/world/2015/sep/06/pope-francis-calls-on-catholics-to-take-in-refugee-families.

into the life of the parish.[79] The goal is neither to establish separate communities that worship in the same building at different times nor to absorb immigrants into the ways of the dominant cultural group. Instead, the different ethnic and linguistic groups should be encouraged to retain their distinctness while becoming one community of mutual care and support.

This is not easy, as the bishops recognize, since making room for new cultures suggests that there may be less room for the established culture. Decisions about how to allot worship times to different language groups and determine which devotions to highlight in festivals or church décor may seem petty, but they have a powerful impact on how much people feel at home, or no longer at home, within their faith community. Moreover, if parish communities are to form real relationships amid the different cultures, each group will have to experience the uncomfortable strangeness of encountering the other and be willing to be changed through this encounter. Catholic social teaching calls for a discernment through which cultures are enriched while their strengths are retained.[80]

It is easier, of course, for the distinct groups to remain separate, as has been the dominant tendency in US Christian life. It is often pointed out that eleven o'clock on Sunday morning is the most segregated time in America. New immigrant groups moving into neighborhoods, especially at a time when the Catholic Church lacks enough priests to serve the populations separately, provide an opportunity to break down some of the established patterns of everyday segregation. This cultural intermingling is a chance to witness to—and experience the joy of—a deeper, more genuine unity-in-diversity.[81]

Local churches have much to offer immigrants in need of welcome, community, and healing, even while the immigrants themselves have a great deal to contribute. Restored dignity, social

---

79. USCCB and CEM, *Strangers No Longer*, 42; NCCB, "A Call to Communion," in *Welcoming the Stranger*.

80. *Gaudium et Spes* 56; NCCB, "Call to Communion," in *Welcoming the Stranger*.

81. Virgilio Elizondo, *The Future Is Mestizo: Life Where Cultures Meet* (Boulder, CO: University Press of Colorado, 2000); Virgilio P. Elizondo, *Guadalupe: Mother of the New Creation* (Maryknoll, NY: Orbis, 1997).

inclusion, and spiritual healing may be essential to migrants who have left home and often family to find themselves in a strange place where they are vilified and demonized. In one case studied by Daniel Groody, already-settled immigrants drew on their own experiences to organize church resources and provide retreats of spiritual healing for newer immigrants.[82]

There is considerable work to be done within parishes to manifest unity-in-diversity more fully, yet our churches must also reach out to immigrants beyond the church walls. Since US congregations frequently mirror the class, race, and ethnic divisions of the larger society, many parishes will not experience an influx of immigrant members. Besides, not all immigrants are Christian. An integral part of the church's witness to unity-in-diversity thus involves reaching out to immigrants in the community who are not fellow parishioners. The bishops direct parishes to welcome all immigrants, provide assistance with the many challenges they face, and even make space available for their different forms of religious worship and other spiritual needs as appropriate to their religious traditions.[83] This would more closely resemble the church that Pope Francis envisions as "bruised, hurting and dirty because it has been out on the streets, rather than . . . unhealthy from being confined and from clinging to its own security" (EG 49).

A church thus witnessing to solidarity with all migrants could do much to overcome prejudices against non-Christian religions, especially against Islam, which have become widespread recently. Not only would Church members demonstrate respect for the religious traditions of non-Christians, but they could also learn more themselves about the power and beauty of these religions. Interreligious understanding might be further increased if parishes follow the bishops' direction and help to organize cooperative efforts among the various religious groups involved in outreach to newly arrived immigrants.

But what about women? Central to my argument here has been that perspectives on migration are often androcentric in their neglect of sexual and gender differences. Unless churches are intentional

---

82. Groody, *Border of Death*.
83. NCCB, *Welcoming the Stranger*.

about including women's voices, concerns, and experiences, male church leaders risk a male-centered outreach to migrants that neglects women, their specific needs, and their perspectives. Women often emerge as leaders within their immigrant families and communities and have important insights into their community's needs and strengths. However, sometimes cultural gender expectations along with family care responsibilities may keep women more isolated in the home, with less chance to become adept in the language and culture of their new community. In either situation, women church members can be especially valuable in reaching out to these women, and churches should be attentive to fostering this work.

Trafficking victims, however, have particular needs and pose special challenges. Given that Jesus was especially remembered for seeking out the company of prostituted women, a church that strives to follow Jesus cannot ignore this most vulnerable, yet often hidden segment of the population. Unfortunately, those who have been trafficked in the sex industry often (and for good reason) associate church with a judgmentalism that reinforces their sense of pollution and lack of self-worth. They may feel least welcome in church, even while they are in great need of spiritual healing as well as social inclusion.

Much of the important work being done to heal survivors of trafficking is currently undertaken by religious women, including Catholic sisters.[84] The love, compassion, and respect they communicate does wonders for the psychic, spiritual, and physical healing of trafficked girls. Church communities, especially churches in areas where trafficking abounds, should do all they can to support these ministries. There is a great need for resources to set up and staff safe houses and for (especially) women who are able to teach skills and extend community to these survivors. They can use a lot of help, but women experienced in this work must determine and direct the assistance given.

There is, then, great need for prophetic, countercultural Christian responses to migration as the processes of globalization reshuffle populations. Along with ease of transportation, shifts of the global

---

84. Beth Griffin, "Religious Sisters at Forefront of Fight against Human Trafficking, Slavery," *Crux*, July 31, 2019, https://cruxnow.com/church-in-the-usa/2019/07/31/religious-sisters-at-forefront-of-fight-against-human-trafficking-slavery/.

economy, climate change, and the perennial challenges of war and violence continue to increase the number of displaced and trafficked persons. These vulnerable migrants often meet with hostility, are considered threats, and are otherwise treated as disposable people. By extending welcome, inclusion, and mutual care to vulnerable and too-often rejected immigrants, the church provides a countercultural witness that interrupts social trends toward fearful selfishness, affirms the dignity of all human persons, and fulfills its task to be a sign of communion in this time.

A Public Church

As noted repeatedly above, the prophetic witness of the church has public effects that make it impossible to neatly demarcate public and prophetic aspects of the church's mission. This is certainly true with regard to ecclesial responses to immigration. Building bonds with immigrants in and through parish communities, for example, may strengthen the integration of immigrants into the broader society. Such church action may well transform the public perception of, and openness to, immigrants within the community, thus increasing communion in the world beyond the church.

However, we cannot neglect the church's responsibility to work for more just and humane public policies. We cannot claim to be an instrument for communion in the world and say nothing when our governments jeopardize the lives of desperate migrants by forcing them into more dangerous desert areas or perilous sea crossings. We cannot acquiesce in the growing attitude that national governments have no proper concern with the common good of humanity but are properly concerned only with increasing the prosperity of their own citizens. Most importantly, we cannot sit by while outrages against humanity, including the most vulnerable children, are occurring at our borders and in our communities.

These are most certainly issues that cannot be resolved apart from engagement in politics. To be an instrument in the world of ending slavery, of stopping trafficking of women and girls, of resettling refugees and restoring them to a place in the human community—all of this requires political action. There is political work to be done at the local level to ensure that trafficked or otherwise enslaved people are not treated by the legal system as criminals and pushed further into the shadows, for example. There is political work to be done at the national level to ensure just and humane border policies that respect immigrants' and refugees' humanity and family bonds, for example. And there is much political and diplomatic work to be done internationally, to coordinate the care of refugees, to end hidden slavery, to stop the trafficking of women and girls—and to address the global inequality and climate change that force people to emigrate.

A Christian ecclesial witness of forming deeper communion with immigrants can do a great deal to help migrants and to change social attitudes, but finally these issues require the organized community response that government exists to coordinate. This is especially the case with human trafficking: the church can facilitate the healing of trafficked victims, but decreasing or even ending the trafficking itself requires the enforcement of well-designed and well-enforced laws and international policies.

While official Catholic teachings rightly recognize the role of personal conscience in determining how each Christian evaluates the political issues and policy decisions involving migration (or any matter of politics), there is room for more ecclesial attention to the communal formation of Christian consciences. As with the global economy and climate change, the reality of mass migration and the plight of migrants is a challenge to the church's call to be a sign and instrument of greater unity-in-diversity in the world. Migration is thus a proper concern of the church as church. This fact should inspire Christian congregations and parishes to meet together to form deeper understandings of the political issues in the light of faith and with careful attention to the complex realities of the current situation. The model of the Sunday sermon discussing general Christian values, after which each Christian goes home to make up his or her mind is overly individualistic and inadequate to the needs of our fractured and distracted age. Especially in societies sorely lacking thoughtful, substantive public discourse, and with nuanced Christian perspectives rare in the media, there is a need for congregations to come together, not to achieve a uniform opinion but to learn from each other's wisdom and insight.

There is, of course, also an appropriate, and even necessary, role for church leaders to address policy issues. Again, church leaders should avoid indicating that any one particular policy is *the* Christian answer, whether in addressing the government or in speaking to their congregants. Nevertheless, given the human life and dignity at stake, as well as the opportunity to form greater unity among peoples, church leaders do well to speak publicly about the moral values at stake in immigration and trafficking policies. Indeed, the May 17, 2019, statement of the president and the chairman of migration of the United States Conference of Catholic Bishops on President Trump's proposed immigration policy is exemplary in providing a moral assessment of the strengths and weaknesses of the policy without seeking to infringe on Catholics' freedom of conscience or on the lay vocation to judge the best of available options.[85] Additionally, given the weakness of international coordination with regard to resettling refugees, international church bodies along with other nongovernmental organizations can do much to facilitate the coordination of national resources and responses to the pressing needs of the large numbers of migrants and refugees.

Conclusion

Massive human migration is an opportunity and a challenge to the church's mission to be a sign and instrument of the unity of all humanity. The ideal of unity-in-diversity is demanding enough when populations are stable. Amid large-scale shifts in population, however, the church's sacramental mission of unity is truly challenging, requiring that all engage in the decentering process of engaging otherness and welcoming people of different languages, cultures, and religions, with all of the change this requires of everyone in the community. At the same time, the church can and must play a public role in resisting the xenophobic attitudes and policies that safeguard the comfort of established populations over the lives and right to dignity of migrants.

---

85. United States Conference of Catholic Bishops, "President of U.S. Bishops and Chairman of Migration Issue Statement on President's Proposed Immigration Reform Plan," press release, May 17, 2019, http://www.usccb.org/news/2019/19-090.cfm.

The Christian tradition has long recognized a responsibility to the stranger, the poor, and the vulnerable. With the articulation of the option for the poor in Catholic social thought of the latter twentieth century, this obligation has become explicitly part of ecclesial self-understanding. Living this option for the poor in the early twenty-first century requires not only welcoming vulnerable immigrants and refugees but also being attentive to the hidden victims of the global economy: the enslaved and trafficked, especially women and girls. These discounted people, who are treated as property and objects to be used and abused by others, are so devalued that it is often only those deeply formed with a heart for the most socially insignificant who even notice their existence.

A church called to increase communion among humanity must overcome the androcentric bias that overlooks these and other sufferings of women. It is often, and rightly, said that the church is itself on pilgrimage, and certainly the church (as an institution and as a community) is continually called to emigrate from positions of power and privilege, to follow Jesus in migrating to be among the poor and powerless. Today, this migration requires that the church surrender the androcentrism that marginalizes women's perspectives and is blind to their experiences. Migrating from power and privilege does not, however, mean abandoning public life. The church has a responsibility to bring Christian views (including those of women) into the public discourse, though without the triumphalism that seeks to impose its perspective or refuses to learn from others. To the contrary, as a sign and instrument of the unity of all, the church is called to share its insights while also seeking to learn from the wisdom of other religions about migration, including the many religious perspectives on the transmigration of souls, Islamic reverence for Muhammad's flight to Medina, and the Jewish experience of diasporic migration for the past two thousand years.

Conclusion

The challenges of our time can seem overwhelming. The problems of the global economy, climate change, and human migration are of unprecedented magnitude in their impact on humanity and on the planet itself. The church has always been concerned with inequality, with the plight of refugees and migrants, and to some extent even with humanity's relationship to nature. But neither the church nor the human race has ever had to deal with a global economy that is uniting more than seven billion people, with over seventy million displaced persons, and with anthropogenic climate change affecting the conditions of all life on this planet.[1] Each of these is a problem of enormous magnitude requiring a response from the church, and each is not quite like anything the church has dealt with before.

Yet these are not finally separate problems, as Pope Francis has noted. Instead, they are distinct manifestations of an economy structured to seek profits for a few rather than a sustainable life for all. One aspect of what is required for the resolution of this complex set of problems, then, is that we understand their interconnectedness so that we can undertake the degree of systemic change demanded. To respond to these interwoven issues is not to disperse our energy among competing problems but to deal with different effects of the one underlying problem of a global socioeconomic system based on the dysfunctional division and competitive selfishness against which the church at its best has always recognized it was called to witness and to work.

---

1. United Nations High Commissioner on Refugees, "Figures at a Glance," June 20, 2019, https://www.unhcr.org/en-us/figures-at-a-glance.html.

To be sure, there are many complicated problems involved in setting this situation aright. The many, many people working to develop technological, economic, political, and diplomatic solutions to make the global economy more just, to mitigate climate change, and to resolve the refugee crisis are all to be commended for doing important, even holy, work. But as has been noted repeatedly with the climate crisis, the biggest obstacle is the lack of motivation to undertake the degree of change needed. We have long had the food to feed the world; we now have the capacity to sharply reduce carbon emissions. Yet we have not done so.

We can give many reasons, of course. As Pope Francis has argued, an idolatry of the market has taken over that insists the economy functions best when it is undirected, so people believe themselves to be justified in profiting from oppressive wages and working conditions.[2] Even as this false god of the economy demands the sacrifice of the ecosystems that sustain life on this planet, many are reluctant to deny global capitalism what it needs to keep producing the plethora of amusing and distracting goods. To give up economic privilege in a globally competitive economy is to risk becoming one of those left out or left behind. To welcome migrants and make room for others is to risk being pushed out by those welcomed in. Most pressing, of course, is the climate crisis, but to develop a sustainable life is to risk a life without the comfort, conveniences, and distractions of consumerism.

Though most people prefer to justify their actions as somehow for the greater good, the deeper truth is that many of us are reluctant to make sacrifices that will make a difference only if others do the same. Why should I bike if everyone else is going to keep driving? Why should my country devote the enormous resources (and possibly tax money) necessary to transition to a carbon-free economy if other countries will use the cheaper oil, burn more fossil fuels, and outcompete us in the global economy? Additionally in the United States, of course, there has been an industry of climate deniers fostering doubts about the scientific consensus on climate change and suggesting that there is no need to change anything.

---

2. *Evangelii Gaudium* 54–56.

The denial of climate change is no longer persuasive to many, though much time has been lost due to the confusion sown. The climate science consensus has become clear, and the situation is widely recognized as dire. The financial interests at stake in the fossil fuel industry are formidable, but they can be overcome just as the slave economy once was. The biggest problem is the unwillingness to make sacrificial change—to give up the ease of driving cheap cars by ourselves, of eating unhealthy quantities of meat and dairy, of having lots of cheap goods and conveniences, and of being able to avoid the decentering strangeness of negotiating other languages and unfamiliar customs.

Christian faith, rightly understood, provides powerful motivation to undertake the systemic change needed. For two millennia, Christianity has taught that true joy is found in love, not selfishness; in community, not competition; and in harmony, not division. The moral demands of our time (and of all times) are not arbitrary tests we must pass to gain entrance into an utterly other heaven but rather are themselves occasions to strive to live now, as best we can, the genuine fulfillment in communion that will be perfected only in the eschaton. The church has rich resources to draw on in forming people in a spirituality of communion with God that is inseparable from communion with others and, indeed, with all of God's creation. To love God is to love the world God has created.

The church is also a great source of hope because this overwhelming task does not depend on us alone. God is with us and will never abandon us. There may be good reason to doubt that we, including the church, are up to handling issues of the magnitude we face. Alone we have good reason to despair. With God, we have great reason to hope.

The sacramental mission of the church to build communion with all in God, in hope of the realization of full communion at the end of history, has not changed. However, the church of today must discover what it means to be a sign and instrument, prophetic and public, of harmony in a dysfunctional, divisive, and global economy. I have argued here that because God intends the goods of creation for all people, the church must prioritize a prophetic witness, communally and in the personal lives of Christians, to economic practices that are just and that secure dignified work and wages for all.

I have argued further for a prophetic ecclesial witness to the intrinsic value of nature as integral to the mission of the church, because nature shares with humanity the ultimate destiny of all in God. Christians must act immediately in their personal lives and institutions to decrease carbon emissions, not only for the sake of the poor and for future generations but because the earth itself has a right not to be abused. Finally, I have argued that Christians must welcome migrants into their congregations and communities. All will be changed through this encounter, but that is how God intends it to be. There is no unity in sameness; unity is only possible when there are differences to bring together.

In each of these aspects of our contemporary global reality, the church is called to live a prophetically countercultural witness in resistance to the selfish competitive consumerism of modern life. Such a witness, when lived as joyful love, is compelling and transformative and may do more than now seems possible to motivate others to undertake the necessary changes as well.

Yet none of the above problems can be solved through a countercultural church alone. Government policies and international agreements are necessary to make the global economy more just, to mitigate climate change, and to respond to migrants in need of asylum. The church is called to be an instrument as well as a sign and, as argued above, these two dimensions of the church's mission are inseparable. The church will fail in its mission if it does not act publicly, working with others to increase communion in the world.

It is also the case that the world needs all the help it can get to tackle these problems and especially to undertake the systemic transformations necessary to stop global warming from getting any worse than it already is. The situation is urgent, and the challenge is daunting. Humanity needs all hands on deck to respond to this climate crisis, including the hands of the church (and other religious bodies). The world needs the church here, and the church will have failed its mission if it does not respond fully to this most pressing grief and anxiety of our day.

And yet, notwithstanding the global crises of our time, I have also argued here that the church must look within at its own deepest failings in order to move forward in its mission to be a sign and instrument of communion in the world. While there are many egregious failures of communion in the church's history (and the current sex abuse crisis is certainly among the most egregious), I prioritize the religious anti-Semitism and misogyny that have distorted Christianity since its beginning years and are even incorporated into the church's Sacred Scriptures. A real unity-in-diversity within and beyond the church requires that the church unlearn its early refusals to value the differences of women and of Jews. Embracing gender and religious diversity is integral to the church's witness as a community as well as to its work in the world, especially since the church still too often fails to respond appropriately to the oppression of women and to value Jews and members of other religions fully. A church unable to exemplify unity-in-diversity with its own primary others is not the sign and instrument of unity-in-diversity that the world needs in this global age—or that Jesus called the church to be.

Young people in the individualistic societies of the West often see little reason for the church. Belonging to the church just doesn't seem to make enough difference to be worth putting up with the annoyances, limitations, and inevitable failures of institutional (or frankly any) community life. At the same time, other young Christians yearn to live their faith heroically, as have past Christians. They too are inpatient with the rather pedestrian compromises of ecclesial Christianity. Yet to live the church's mission in the world today does indeed require that Christians and Christian communities live a radically different, even heroically countercultural, life. This mission does not pit the church against anyone but rather calls for heroic commitment to the call the church has always had: to live and to work for greater communion among God's diverse creation, including the divided human family. Given the urgent need for the world to transform its economic and transportation structures, along with many of the habits of daily life, Christians living sustainable, just lifestyles in joyful harmony with creation and with genuine welcome and care for the poor and vulnerable would be countercultural and truly, if quietly, heroic.

I would like to end with the message written on the plaque placed in memory of the Ok glacier in Iceland. Amid the many injustices and dysfunctions of the global economy, the ecological crisis poses the most immediate and demanding challenges. Yet the sentiment inscribed on this plaque applies to the entire complex of divisions and distortions that must be overcome to achieve the communion that is God's promise and our deepest hope:

> A letter to the future
> Ok is the first Icelandic glacier to lose its status as a glacier.
> In the next 200 years all our glaciers are expected to follow the same path.
> This monument is to acknowledge that we know
> what is happening and what needs to be done.
> Only you know if we did it.
>
> Ágúst 2019
> 415ppm CO_2[3]

---

3. This is the message as written in English; the plaque displays the message written in Icelandic above the English translation. See Jason Daley, "Plaque Memorializes First Icelandic Glacier Lost to Climate Change," Smithsonian *SmartNews*, July 23, 2019, https://www.smithsonianmag.com/smart-news/plaque-memorializes-first-icelandic-glacier-lost-climate-change-180972710/.

Index

abbess, 89
Abel, 161
Abraham, 53, 193
activism, 29, 164
Adam, 86, 161
Adversus Judaeos texts, 54, 56, 57
Africa, 31–33, 34, 167
aggiornamento, 8–9
Allen, Prudence, 101, 106
Ambrose, St., 58, 93
Amos, prophet, 125
androcentrism, 120, 132, 144, 169, 193, 203, 215, 220
Anselm, St., 91
anthropocentrism, 156–65, 181
anthropology, 111
    complementarian, 80, 100, 103–4
    theological, xix, 80, 109
anti-Semitism, xix–xx, 36, 39–74, 81, 114, 225
anxiety, xi, 96, 128, 224
Apollos, 84
Apostolic Constitutions, 88–89
Aquila, 84
Aquinas, Thomas, St., 91, 92
Armour, Ellen, 98, 170
Asia, 30–31, 34

asylum, 186, 188, 190, 191, 193, 194, 199–200, 212, 224
Augustine of Hippo, St., 58, 60, 91–92

von Balthasar, Hans Urs, 100–101, 108
baptism, 16, 53, 62, 107, 110–11
Bartholomew of Constantinople, Patriarch, 131, 154, 158
Beattie, Tina, 108
de Beauvoir, Simone, 96
Beguines, 90
Benedict XVI, Pope, xxi, 12n24, 13, 69, 124, 126, 144n50, 147
Bible, xiv, xx, 1, 8, 41, 52, 68, 112, 123, 194
bishops, xxi, 2, 7, 15, 32, 33, 87–89, 108, 131, 145, 158, 170, 193–203, 204, 211–15
Black Death, 60–61
Boff, Leonardo, 29
Bolsonaro, Jair, 151
Bonaventure, St., 91
Brigid of Ireland, St., 89

Cain, 161
capitalism, xii–xiii, 24–25, 117–49, 151, 176, 222

227

Cardman, Francine, 89
care economy, 133–37, 138–39, 141, 170
Carmona, Victor, 202
Carroll, James, 50
Carter, Jimmy, 77, 109
Catholic social teachings, xvii, 18, 119–21, 122–32, 137, 140–41, 143, 145–46, 156–65, 192, 193–203, 214
Catholic Worker, 4, 199
celibacy, 93
childbirth, 94, 97, 99
Chrysostom, John, St., 54–56, 93
clergy, 2, 14, 19, 21, 102, 106, 108, 113, 114, 122–23
clergy sexual abuse scandal, 36, 225
Clifford, Catherine E., 15
climate change, xiii, xviii, xx, 2, 7, 99, 118, 138, 141, 151–83, 186n5, 187–89, 204–5, 208, 212, 217–18, 221–26
  denial, 154, 160, 181–82, 222–23
Code of Justinian, 58
college of bishops, 15, 33, 145
collegiality, 15, 33
Collier, Elizabeth W., 198
Collier, Paul, 140
colonialism, 78–79, 98, 113, 172
common good, xiii, 19, 26–27, 123, 130, 145, 159, 161, 198–99, 202–3, 217
communalism, 6
communidades de base (Christian base communities), 4, 29
communion, xv, xvii–xviii, xix, 2, 4, 7, 11–12, 15, 16, 18, 20, 22, 24–27, 36, 120, 123, 141, 142, 158, 161–63, 176, 180, 182–83, 192, 202, 212, 217, 220, 223, 225
Communism, 64, 147
community, xi, xiv, xv, xvii, xxi, 2, 4–6, 15, 18, 26, 27, 31, 35, 108, 118, 123, 149, 182, 195, 214, 217–18, 223, 225
complementarity, gender, 80, 100–108, 110, 114
Cone, James, 33
Conference of Latin American Bishops (CELAM), 29, 124
Congar, Yves, 11
Congregation for the Evangelization of Peoples, 32
covenant, 40–42, 51, 53, 54, 59, 64, 66–67, 69, 70–73
creation, xx, 12, 14, 19–20, 22, 71, 85, 92, 113, 120, 128, 151–83, 223, 225
Crossan, John Dominic, 46
Crusades, 60
culture, 14–15, 22, 24, 30, 32, 33–34, 79, 111, 118, 195, 197–99, 202, 213–14
Curran, Charles, 2, 122

Dalit theology, 31
Dallavalle, Nancy, 111
Daly, Mary, 111
Damian, Peter, St., 93–94
deacons, 84, 87–89, 110
dialogue, xx, 15–17, 20–21, 26–27, 72, 113, 148, 181–82
Didascalia Apostolorum, 88
Dignitatis Humanae, 6, 17, 19, 21, 26–27
dignity, xv, 6, 14, 17–18, 19–20, 23–26, 113, 132, 146, 194, 195, 198, 200–201, 217, 219

disciples, xviii, 41, 45, 50–51, 68, 82–84, 110, 120, 122, 125, 210, 212
discipleship, 4, 29, 82, 84, 120, 123–24, 140, 142, 147, 156, 165, 177, 212
diversity, 14–15, 32, 96, 111, 113, 121
doctrine, 9, 34, 52, 56–57, 68–70, 91, 160, 194

early church, 8, 51–59, 60, 103, 123, 194, 210
Eastern Christianity, 88
Eastern religions, 181
ecclesiology, xvi–xviii, xx, 5, 6, 28–35, 44, 81, 114, 142–48, 176–82, 211–19
ecofeminism, 98–99, 158, 169–70, 179
economy, xii–xiv, xx, 19, 22, 25–26, 117–49, 151, 156, 164, 165–72, 179–80, 182, 185, 187–89, 195–97, 199, 205, 206–8, 212–13, 217, 221–23, 225
ecumenism, 2, 3, 8, 11, 16, 213
Elizondo, Virgilio, 34
embodiment, 94, 103, 105, 110, 111, 133
English Ladies, 90
Enlightenment, 63
environment, xiii, xiv, xxi, 22, 79, 98, 113, 118, 125, 128, 137–39, 141, 143, 151–83, 186–87, 204, 208, 213, 224
eschatology, 12–14, 35, 149, 155, 158, 223
Espín, Orlando, 34, 127
Eucharist, 58, 99, 108, 149

Evangelii Gaudium, 122, 124–28, 131, 140, 142, 146, 148, 159, 162, 202, 215
Eve, 87, 93, 161
Exodus event, 46, 193

Faith and Order Commission, xviii, 3
family, 22, 23, 31, 33, 75, 76, 79, 106, 119, 120, 132–37, 168–69, 189–90, 196, 199, 205, 213, 215–16, 218, 225
feminism, 35, 44, 78–79, 97, 112, 169–70
food, xx, 76, 128, 132, 134, 142, 144n50, 159, 168, 174–75, 186–87, 192, 196, 205, 222, 223
fossil fuels, xiii, xx, 152–54, 173, 175, 176–77, 180, 222, 223
Fourth Lateran Council, 59–60
Francis, Pope, xx, xxi, 2, 119–20, 122–32, 138, 140, 142, 144, 145–48, 152, 154, 156–65, 166–71, 176, 178–79, 182, 185, 189–90, 202, 203–4, 213, 215, 221–22
Francis of Assisi, St., 163, 178
Friedman, Thomas, 117, 127, 139

Gaillardetz, Richard, 15
Gaudium et Spes, xi, xiv, 6, 8, 11, 13, 14–15, 17–18, 19–20, 21–28, 123, 157–58
Gelasius, Pope, 88
gender, xii, 36, 44, 78, 80, 95, 100–108, 110–12, 114, 132, 136, 146, 165–72, 203–4, 211, 215–16, 225
Genesis, book of, 156–57

Giammarinaro, Maria Grazia, 207
Girard, René, 56, 96
globalization, xii–xiii, xvii, xviii, xx, 2, 21, 117–49, 189, 195, 216
global warming, xx, 151–53, 160, 164, 166, 172–75, 180, 187–88, 224
González, Michelle, 29
grace, xvi, 11, 12, 17, 22, 36, 44, 67, 92, 107, 178
Gregory Nazianzen, St., 107
Groody, Daniel, 215

Hebrew Bible, xiv, 1, 45–47, 50, 52–53, 67, 69–73, 110, 119, 148, 157, 178, 193
hierarchical dualism, 96–99, 104, 105, 107, 109, 111–13, 170–72, 179
Hinze, Christine Firer, 131, 133, 136
Hitler, Adolf, 64–65
Holocaust, 40, 64–66, 95
Holy Spirit, 14, 16, 31, 68, 69, 114
human rights, 32, 76–77, 194, 200

immigrants, 140, 185–220
Imperatori-Lee, Natalia, 34
inculturation, 28, 30, 32
indigenous peoples, 30, 121, 167, 181
individualism, xi–xii, 6, 18, 20, 31, 32, 54, 124, 165, 179, 218, 225
inequality, xviii, 7, 21, 25, 27, 85, 119, 123, 128–31, 132, 142, 146, 164, 171, 189, 212, 218
injustice, xiv, xvii, 4, 22, 25, 27, 29, 33, 124, 130–31, 146, 183

Inquisition, 61–62
instrument, xiv, xv, xvii–xviii, xix–xx, 2–5, 7, 11–12, 16, 21, 23–24, 29, 36, 72, 79–81, 99, 120, 131, 142, 148, 155–56, 158, 165, 171, 182, 192, 212, 218, 219–20, 223–25
Intergovernmental Panel on Climate Change (IPCC), 153, 172–75, 176
International Organization for Migration, 187
interreligious dialogue, 30–31, 181
Isaac, Jules, 41, 48, 59, 66
Isaiah, 125, 157
Islam, 215, 220

James, disciple, 83
Jesus Christ, xviii, 1, 14, 17, 34, 35, 41, 43, 44, 45–51, 53–55, 61, 66–71, 82–83, 101–3, 106–7, 110, 125, 149, 162, 165, 178, 193, 194, 210, 216, 220, 225
Jesus movement, 47, 50, 82, 84
John XXIII, Pope St., 8, 26, 66
John, disciple, 83
John, Gospel of, 46, 48–49, 54, 68, 82–83
John Paul II, Pope St., xxi, 73, 92n46, 101–2, 112, 124, 147, 160, 197
Johnson, Elizabeth, 97, 111, 163, 171
Judaism, xix–xx, 8, 10, 36–37, 39–74, 81, 95–96, 114–15, 121, 148, 149, 178, 181, 193, 220, 225
Junia, 84

justice, xiv–xv, xvii, 1, 4, 25, 29–30, 123, 145, 149, 195, 201–3, 217–18

Kara, Siddharth, 206
Keller, Catherine, 99
Kristof, Nicholas, 76–77, 109, 132, 206

labor. *See* work
laity, 2, 8, 11, 14–15, 19, 29, 102, 105–6, 113, 114, 122–23, 181
language, 9, 14, 97, 100, 104, 107, 109, 112, 185, 214, 216, 219, 223
Latin America, 29–30, 34, 147
Latinx theology, 33–34
Laudato Sí, 129, 152, 154, 156–65, 178, 182
Lazarus, 83
Leo XIII, Pope, 122
liberation theology, 124, 212
  black, 33
  Latin American, 29–30
liturgy, 8, 12, 80, 100, 112
Luke, Gospel of, 48, 82, 125, 194
Lumen Gentium, 5–6, 8, 10–19, 33

Macy, Gary, 95
Madigan, Kevin, 94
Malone, Mary, 83–84, 91, 92–93, 100
Marcion, 46, 52
Mark, Gospel of, 48, 82–83
Markey, John, 9
marriage, 22, 23–24, 86, 108
Martha, 83
Mary, 83, 210
Mary of Egypt, 210

Mary of Magdala, 83, 210, 211
Massingale, Bryan, 33
Matthew, Gospel of, 48–49, 68, 82–83, 110, 125, 193–94
McBrien, Richard, 12
Melito of Sardis, 49, 54
menstruation, 94, 99
Metz, Johann Baptist, 13
migration, xviii, xx, xxi, 7, 185–220, 221, 224
Milbank, John, 3
minjung theology, 30–30
misogyny, xix, 36, 75–115, 225
mission, xiv, xvi–xviii, xix, xxi, 2–4, 6, 8, 10–12, 14, 16, 21, 23, 27, 28, 29, 35–36, 42–44, 54, 57, 72–73, 81, 96, 112, 114, 122–23, 155, 158, 165, 171, 176, 183, 192, 217, 219, 223–25
Mitchell, Kathleen, 209
modernity, 8, 42, 63
Moses, 53
Murad, Nadia, 192
Muslims, 60, 193

natural disasters, 138, 167–68, 175, 186–89, 195–96, 204, 208, 211
Nazism, 64–66
New Testament, xix, 36, 41, 45–51, 52–53, 54, 57, 60, 61, 68, 70, 73, 82–87, 110, 194
Niebuhr, Reinhold, 127
Nirenberg, David, 53, 55–56, 61–62, 65
Nostra Aetate, 6, 17, 48, 66

Oduyoye, Mercy Amba, 33, 149
Oesterreicher, John, Msgr., 66

Ok Glacier, 151, 225–26
oppression, 21, 40, 58, 78, 79, 81, 86, 95, 96–99, 109, 113, 119, 143, 156, 170–71, 225
ordination, 80, 83n22, 90–91, 102–3, 112
  women's, 102–3, 113, 144
Orthodox Church, xiv, 3, 80, 100
Ortner, Sherry, 97–98, 169
Osiek, Carolyn, 94

Paul, St., 47–49, 66, 84–87, 91, 194
Pawlikowski, John, 71, 74
peace, xiv, 22, 27–28, 70, 154, 178
Pentecostalism, 34–35
people of color, 97–98, 165–66, 170–71, 179
personhood, 6, 18
persons-in-community, xvi, xix, 6, 20, 23, 25, 32
Peter, St., 68, 83
Phan, Peter, 31
Phoebe, 84
Pius XII, Pope, 64
polarization, xii, 5, 15, 113, 147, 154–55
politics, xiv–xv, xvii, 4, 12, 19, 21, 22, 26–27, 130, 141–42, 145–47, 154–55, 169, 180–81, 189, 196–98, 201–2, 208, 217–20, 222, 224
Pontifical Biblical Commission, 103
poor, the, 29, 30, 33, 90, 99, 119, 123–26, 128–30, 132, 134, 137, 143–44, 146, 148, 159, 161, 165–69, 174, 176, 178–81, 187, 192, 208, 220, 224, 225

pope, 15, 108
poverty, xxi, 21–22, 27, 28, 29, 30–31, 118, 120, 125–27, 132–33, 144n50, 146, 173, 182, 186, 187–89, 195, 204
prayer, 29, 100, 112, 118, 143
preferential option for the poor, 119, 123–24, 143–45, 146, 159, 162, 192, 220
priests, 89, 102, 108, 171
  women, 88
Prisca, 84
property, 40, 58, 59, 79, 119, 123, 138, 196, 220
prophet(s), xiv, 8, 46–50, 119, 123
prophetic witness, xiv, xv–xvi, xix, 4–5, 11, 16, 22, 28, 72–73, 97, 113, 120–21, 142–45, 156, 176–79, 211–17, 223–24
prostitution, 203–11
public agent, xiv, xv–xvi, 5, 22, 28, 72–73, 97, 120–21, 145–48, 156, 179–82, 217–19, 223–24
Putnam, Robert, xi

race, 33–34, 61–62, 79, 111, 167, 215
racism, 33n61, 98, 113, 121, 129, 164
Rahner, Karl, 28
Rauschenbusch, Walter, 129–30
reason, 18–20, 159–60, 181
redemption, 2–3, 22, 35, 44, 52, 67, 70, 72, 92–93, 126, 165
refugees, 2, 128–29, 167, 176, 185–220, 221–22
reign of God, xii, xiv, 1, 4, 12, 13, 70, 74, 119–21, 124, 147, 149, 158

religious freedom, 8, 10–11, 21, 26–27, 156
Rerum Novarum, 122
ressourcement, 8–9
revelation, 18–21, 68, 71, 73
Roman Empire, 50–51, 52, 57–59, 84
Romero, Óscar, St., 30
Rosenzweig, Cynthia, 174
Ross, Susan, 108
Ruether, Rosemary Radford, 43, 50, 54, 58–59, 60, 64, 69, 79, 93, 96, 98
Rush, Ormond, 10
Ruth, 110

sacrament(s), xiv, xvi n10, 1, 2, 5, 11, 121, 164
salvation, xvi, 3, 16, 56, 59, 68, 87, 102, 106–7, 110, 149, 155, 157, 162, 179, 212
salvation history, 52–54
Sasvin Dominguez, Romeo de Jesus, 191
scapegoating, 56–57, 60, 72, 96
Schachter-Shalomi, Zalman, Rabbi, 74
Schüssler Fiorenza, Elisabeth, 82
Scripture, 8, 12, 41, 43, 52, 68–69, 72, 79, 225
Second Vatican Council, xiv, xviii–xix, xxi, 1–37, 66, 122, 124, 158
secularism, 18–21, 63
secularity, 18–21
Sen, Amartya, 76, 133
sensus fidelium, 3, 34
sexism, 79–81, 97–98
sex tourism, 77, 78n13, 206
Shoah. *See* Holocaust

sign, xiv, xv, xvii–xviii, xix–xx, 2–5, 7, 11–12, 16, 23–24, 29, 36, 72, 79–81, 99, 120, 131, 142, 148, 155–56, 158, 165, 171, 182, 192, 212, 217, 218, 219–20, 223–25
Simeon Stylites, St., 58
sin, 22, 26, 27, 36, 43–44, 67, 71, 72–73, 86–87, 93
Sisters of the Visitation, 90
Sobrino, Jon, 30
social media, xii, 175, 179
society, xiv, xv, xvii, 2, 4, 11, 16, 18, 19–21, 25, 106, 131, 136, 145, 178
solidarity, 33–34, 140, 145, 159, 161, 213, 215
Sollicitudo Rei Socialis, 124
Soulen, R. Kendall, 52–54, 70–71
Strain, Charles R., 198
Strangers No Longer, 193–203, 211
subsidiarity, 27–28, 137, 141–42, 145
Summers, Lawrence, 166
supersessionism, 42, 47, 51n24, 52–54, 59, 67, 69–71, 73, 114, 148

Tamar, 110
Teresa of Ávila, 90
Tertullian, 93
Theodosian Code, 58
trafficking, xx, 77–78, 109, 169, 189, 191–92, 203–11, 216–17, 218–19
tribalization, 5, 145
Trinity, 12–14, 18, 101–2
Trump, Donald, 219

uniformity, 14, 18, 24, 32, 36, 88, 89, 218

United States Conference of Catholic Bishops (USCCB), 158, 160–61, 219
unity, 11–12, 14–19, 22, 23, 27, 33, 72, 79, 119, 131, 158, 165, 182, 219, 224
unity-in-diversity, xix–xx, 6–7, 14–18, 21, 28, 30–31, 34, 36–37, 42–44, 57, 70–72, 81–82, 99, 101, 111–15, 120–21, 123, 132, 147, 148–49, 172, 202, 211, 213–15, 218, 219, 224–25
Universal Declaration of Human Rights, 109
Urban II, Pope, 60
Ursulines, 90
Uzukwu, Elochukwu, 32–33

violence, 130, 140, 176, 186–89, 190, 195–96
  against women, 76–77, 97, 109, 168–69, 190–92, 203–11
Volf, Miroslav, 3

wages, 75, 123, 129, 134–37, 143, 166, 169, 186–87, 197, 204, 222, 223
war, 175, 176, 186–89, 192, 196, 211, 217
Ward, Mary, 90
Welcoming the Stranger among Us, 203
Western Christianity, 58, 87–88
White, Lynn, Jr., 156–57
Whitehead, Alfred North, xii
widows, order of, 88–90
witness, xv, xxi, 4, 5, 12, 16, 97, 147, 224
women, xix–xx, 23–24, 34–37, 44, 75–115, 120–22, 132–37, 144–45, 149, 156, 165–72, 179, 181, 182, 190–93, 203–11, 215–16, 218, 220, 225
  religious, 170–71, 216
work, 25, 118, 123, 128, 133–37, 139–40, 144, 146, 164, 168–69, 187, 189, 190, 197, 204, 223
World Council of Churches, xviii, 3
worship, 12, 30, 41, 100, 102, 104, 108, 143–44, 214, 215
WuDunn, Sheryl, 76–77, 109, 132, 206

Yan, Wudan, 205
Yousafazi, Malala, 76

Zachary, Pope, 88

www.ingramcontent.com/pod-product-compliance
Lightning Source LLC
Chambersburg PA
CBHW051940290426
44110CB00015B/2045